D1199157

Flags of the World

FLAGS OF THE WORLD

A PICTORIAL HISTORY

WILLIAM CRAMPTON

DIRECTOR, THE FLAG INSTITUTE

DORSET PRESS
NEW YORK

Flags of the World: A Pictorial History

This edition published 1990 by Dorset Press, a division of
Marboro Books Corporation,
120 Fifth Avenue, New York, NY 10011, USA

Edited and designed by
Anness Law Limited
4a The Old Forge,
7 Caledonian Road,
London N1 9DX

ISBN 0 88029 561 9

Printed and bound in Hong Kong

Publishers' Note

The vast majority of the pictures in this book are from the archives of the Flag Institute, the largest collection of flag material in Europe, which has been assembled over many years from a variety of sources. We gratefully acknowledge the generosity of the Institute and its sponsors in allowing us to use this material.

Every attempt has been made to trace the copyright holders of the photographs featured in this book and a list of acknowledgements is given below. In the event of any omission, please contact the publisher.

a = above, b = below, m = middle, r = right, t = top

British Library Board, 115tr; Copernic/Rigo 122bl; Imperial War Museum, 11tl, 127tr; Alfred A. Knopf Inc./Mr Mastai/Robert Brandau Associates 132b; J. L. Loughran, 151b; Macdonald & Janes 144, 145t; Leonard von Matt, Buochs, 156b; McGraw-Hill Book Company 153tr, 156tr; National Library of Scotland, 130bl; National Maritime Museum, 117b; University of Pennsylvania Press, 120r; Zefa, 127br.

CONTENTS

INTRODUCTION

THE ART OF FLAG STUDY

Vexillology is the study of flags (from Latin *vexillum*, see 'The Ancient World'). It is only in very recent times that it has become systematic and organized, although that is not to say that there were no serious students in former times. The 'Flag Circle' that used to exist in Great Britain linked several well-known writers on the subject, and many of the reference books used today were put together by these and scholars in other countries.

Flag information is derived from books, manuals, charts, and printed material of all kinds, from news items in the mass media, from direct observation, from indirect sources such as postage stamps, cigarette cards, posters, and glancing references in books on quite different subjects. As with most academic research, sources can be primary as well as secondary. Primary sources would include government gazettes, official flag models, specifications, regulations, clauses in the national constitution, heraldic blazons, and official manuals. It is possible for flag enthusiasts to sink themselves into the subject deeply or superficially and to concentrate on data or on theory.

Today the pursuit is aided considerably by the establishment of an international network, and a series of journals published by groups in various countries, as well as by meetings and conferences. Journals are published in English and in other lanuages, and meetings are held on a national and an international basis. In Great Britain the Flag Institute brings enthusiasts together and also maintains the largest archives and library in the country. The North American Vexillological Association concentrates on meetings rather than documentation, and the Canadian Flag Association communicates by means of its magazine. The Flag Research Centre in the USA is primarily a documentation centre, but also publishes the international journal, *The Flag Bulletin*.

In addition, a number of bulletins are produced by individual researchers, such as the *Info-Bulletin* from the Flag Docuemtation Centre in the Netherlands and the *Flaggenmitteilungen*, issued by Dr Mattern. It will be seen that a command of languages is a useful attribute for a flag researcher.

International meetings are held every two years and are in the form of conferences at which papers are given and interesting places visited. The most recent Congress (1989) was in Melbourne. The next ones are scheduled for Barcelona (1991) and Switzerland (1993). These conferences take place under the aegis of the *Fédération Internationale des Associations Vexillologiques*, founded in 1967.

So far there is not specific library or public documentation centre on the subject of flags alone that is open to the public. Some existing libraries have good collections of material on flags, of which the best in Great Britain is the Caird Library of the National Maritime Museum Greenwich. Maritime museums in other countries are also good sources, as are large national libraries such as the British Library in London and the Library of congress in Washington, D.C., which routinely collect all published titles. However, sometimes valuable documents are in special collections to which access is difficult, including the College of Arms and the Ministry of Defence.

Research can be done entirely by correspondence, and a good example of that is the excellent work done in the last two decades by researchers into the flags of the former princely states of India. This is an example of a job where great patience is needed but where it does eventually bear fruit.

Title	Responsible Body	Language
The Flag Bulletin	Flag Research Center	English
Flagmaster	The Flag Institute	English
Crux Australis	Flag Society of Australia	English
Flagscan	Flag Society of Canada	English
Vexillinfo	Societas Vexillologica Belgica	French
Vexilla Belgica (year book)	Societas Vexillologica Belgica	French
Vexilla Nostra	Nederlandse Verenigning voor Vlaggenkunde	Dutch
Vexilologie	Czech Vexillological Club	Czech
Banderas	Sociedad Española de Vexilologia	Spanish
Vexilla Italica	Centro Italiano di Studi Vessillologici	Italian
Emblèmes et Pavillons	Société Française de Vexillologie	French
NAVA News	NAVA	English
Nordisk Flagkontakt	Nordisk Flag Selskab	Danish

Opposite page: *This early 19th-century engraving shows Washington with 19 state shields (each signifying state membership of the Union in 1819) above him, and French and American flags to his left and right respectively.*

SIC TRANSIT
In MEMORY OF WASHINGTON
This Most Illustrious and Much Lamented Patriot, Died on the of Dec. 1799, in the 68 Year of his Age, after a short Illness of 30 hours, in the full Possession of all his Fame, like a Christian and a Hero, Calm and Collected, without a Groan or a Sigh.
GLORIA MUNDI!
He united and adorned many excellent Characters, at once the Patriot and the Politician; the Soldier and the Citizen; the Husbandman and the Hero; the Favourite of the Genius of Liberty; the Father of American Independence; the Promoter of her extensive and Brotherly Union; the Pillar of her Constitution; the President of her Senate and the Generalissimo of her Armies. He possessed and displayed extraordinary Abilities, exalted Virtues, and unexampled Self-Command and Self-Denial; moderate in Prosperity, undaunted amid Dangers, unbroken by Adversity, firm and unmoved amidst the Violence and Reproach of Faction, unperverted by great and general Applause— He was great in Arts and in Arms— He was great in the Council and in the Field.!
He was First in Peace, First in the Hearts of the AMERICANS, First in the Eyes of the World; He was unrivalled as a Statesman, as a Senator, And he is embalmed by the Tears of AMERICA; Entombed in the Hearts of his Countrymen; Admired by the Enlightened of all Lands; Immortalised by his own great Actions and the Regrets of Mankind— Why doth America weep? Why are her Courts and her Churches covered with funeral Black? Why are her Sons Clad in Sable and appointed to a long Mourning? —Senator! It is because He, who gave Stability to our Constitution, and Energy to our Councils, He, who was the Guardian of our Rights and our Liberties, is now Withdrawn.
This PLATE is with due RESPECT Inscribed to the CONGRESS of the UNITED STATES
SOLDIER
SAILOR
SACRED TO PATRIOTISM
LIBERTY
INDEPENDENCE
BUT ALL IS NOT LOST FOR PROVIDENCE SURVIVES

Construction and Display

As can be deduced from the following technical terms, much of the terminology of flags is derived from maritime usage.

When describing flags it is assumed that they are rectangular and displayed with the staff or pole on the observer's left. This view of the flag is the *obverse*. Flags usually have a *sleeve*, or *heading*, of heavier fabric along the hoist side. This is used for securing the flag to the staff or the pole.

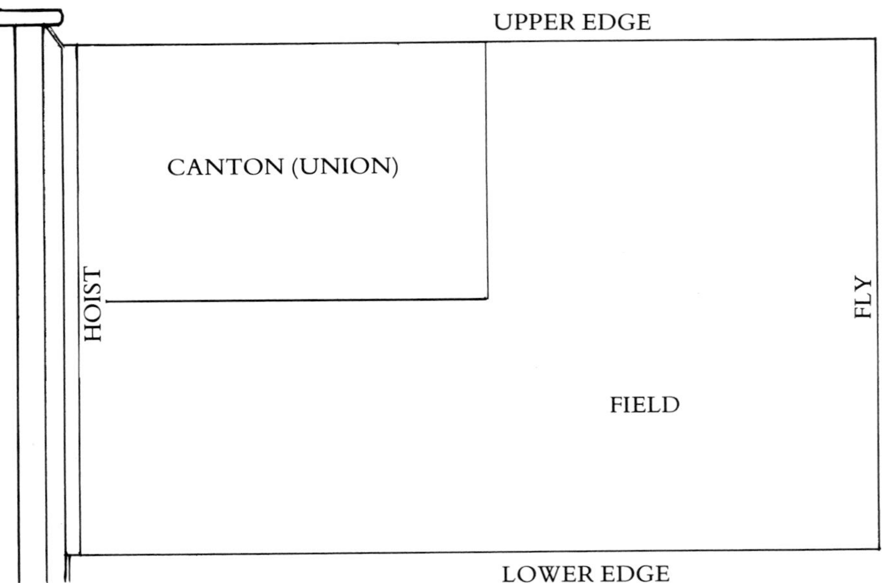

Flags carried by hand usually have a hollow sleeve, which the staff passes through. Flags for flying can have a *hoist-rope* sewn into the sleeve. This rope has two ends that can be fastened to the *halyards*. The hoist rope may carry a *toggle* at its upper end, and end in a *becket*, or loop, at its lower end, or else both ends may be fitted with *Inglefield Clips*, which attach to similar devices on the halyards. Another system is to place an *eyelet*, or grommet, at each end of the sleeve, to which swivel clips on the halyards can be attached.

Flags for use in parades and not intended to be flown from poles often have optional extras in the way of decorative rings and finials on the carrying stave, and perhaps also *cravats* (streamers) attached above the flag. They may also have cords and tassels, and on some kinds of parade flags, such as military colours, the cord may pass through an eyelet in the upper hoist part of the flag. Parade flags usually also have fringes on the three free edges.

Flags are flown by fastening the upper and lower ends of the hoist rope to the upper and lower ends of the halyards, which is the name given to the long rope that passes through a block at the top of the flag pole. After hoisting the surplus halyard is attached to a cleat near the bottom of the pole. Poles can be simple or sophisticated. A simple pole will carry only one flag at a time, although it can be improved by having, for example, internal halyards, or spring-loaded and swivelling halyards that respond to the force and direction of the wind. The block at the top of the staff can be built into the pole or attached to it by an eye. It is also possible to mount a short horizontal bar to the top of the pole. A tall, narrow flag can be hung from this, and attached to the pole by rings. The flag, bar, and rings can all revolve around the pole.

A multiple flagstaff has a yardarm at right angles to the vertical pole, to which blocks for further halyards can be attached, usually by eyes.

Parts of a Flag

For purposes of description a flag is assumed to be divided into four quarters, known as *cantons*. The two quarters nearest the flagpole are called the *hoist* and the other two the *fly*, or *flying end*. The upper hoist quarter is usually just known as the *canton*, or in the USA as the *union*.

The vertical dimension of a flag is known as the *width* (formerly the *breadth*) and the horizontal dimension as the *length*. The proportions of a flag's width to its length are stated as a ratio (width first) as, for example 2:3, 1:2.

A flag divided into two parts either horizontally or vertically is known as a *bicolour*, and into three parts is a *tricolour*, if three colours are involved, or as a *triband* if there are three stripes but only two colours. Normally in describing a simple flag the colours of the stripes are given in the order top to bottom, or hoist to fly. Simple stripes or patterns make up the field of a flag.

Extra Emblems

Flags often have badges, arms, or other devices on top of the basic field. If the device is laid over two or more parts of the field, it is said to be *over all*. When a cross appears on a flag and its arms reach from one edge to another it is described as a cross *throughout*, as in the flag of

Below: *The two basic arrangements for the* bicolour *flag, in which the flag is divided into two parts, either horizontally or vertically. The lower* bicolour *has an emblem in the canton.*

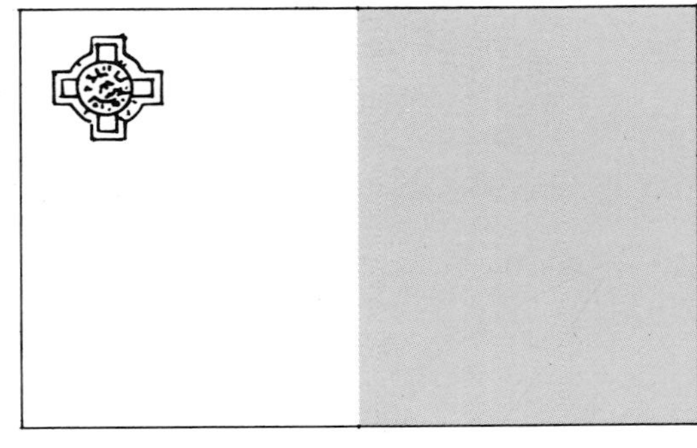

Above: A triband *in which the flag is divided into three stripes with only two colours, and two* tricolours *each with three colours arranged vertically and horizontally.*

Left: *An example of a flag with a* Scandinavian *cross in which the cross is positioned away from the middle near the hoist.*

Types of Flag

In modern parlance, *flag* is a general term for all kinds of flying fabrics. *National flag* is also a general term, referring to the flag normally and habitually used to denote nationality. It has to be noted, however, that some countries have different flags fulfilling this function in different circumstances, of which Great Britain is the outstanding example. On land the national flag is the Union Jack, but at sea it is the Red Ensign for civil vessels, the White Ensign for naval vessels, and the Blue Ensign for government vessels. There are even national flags for the air, the Civil Air Ensign and the Royal Air Force Ensign. Not many countries go so far as this, but several do have distinct naval and/or civil ensigns (*ensign* is the term applied to national flag at sea). A common distinction is between the *state* flag/ensign and the *civil* flag/ensign. Many countries have a simple, unadorned flag for general use by their citizens, and an embellished form, usually with the national emblem added, for use by the government. The flags flown outside the United Nations building are *state* flags, and hence, where appropriate, they are augmented with the national emblem.

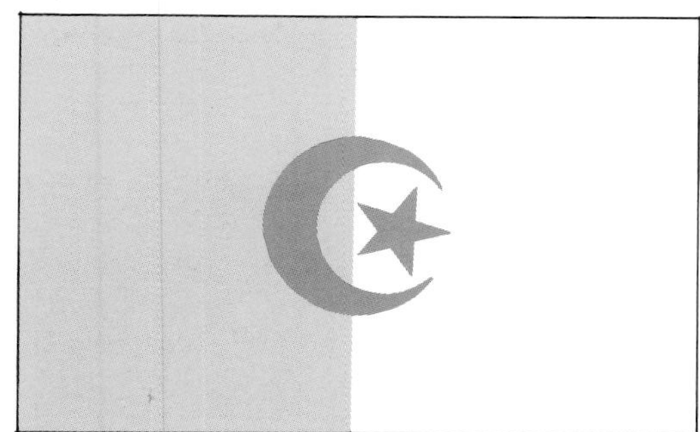

England. A *Scandinavian* cross has unequal arms, ie, it is centred on a point near the hoist of the flag, not on its exact centre. A point one-third of the horizontal distance from the hoist is a favourite one for centring flag emblems, as the badge or device can still be seen when the flag is not flying out fully.

Far left: *A flag with a device placed on two parts (or more) of the field is said to have an* over all *device.*

Far left below: *The arms of the cross on this flag reach from one edge to another – an example of a cross* throughout.

Left, above left and below left: *The Union Jack evolved from three flags each with crosses* throughout; *the White Ensign retains one cross* throughout *and has the Union Jack in the* canton, *while the Red Ensign has only a Union Jack in the* canton *on a plain field.*

AFGHANISTAN, REPUBLIC OF

JAMHURIA AFGHANISTAN

Afghanistan was formed as a separate kingdom in 1747 and since then has managed to secure its independence against Persia, Great Britain, and Russia. However, the monarchy was overthrown in 1973 and in 1979 Soviet troops moved in. Although the Russians evacuated the country in 1989, a civil war has continued between the Communist central government and *mujaheddin* guerrillas.

The present flag of Afghanistan is the eighth since 1919, when Great Britain finally recognized the country's independence. However, most of these flags have been vertical or horizontal tricolours of black, red, and green. These colours were introduced in 1928 as part of the modernization programme of Amanullah Khan. The arms during the kingdom were based on the representation of a mosque with a prayer niche and pulpit. These elements are now combined in the modern arms, but the rising sun and wreath of wheat are also traditional.

The colours were laid horizontally when the republic was formed in 1973, but were replaced by a red flag during the period 1978–80. The tricolour version was restored on 21 April 1980, but the arms were altered to the present form on 30 November 1987.

The flag of the People's Democratic Party of Afghanistan is red with the emblem of a cogwheel and wheat in gold near the hoist.

Above and above left: *The new emblem and the national flag with the old emblem, with the red star and open book.*

ALBANIA, PEOPLE'S REPUBLIC OF

REPUBLIKA POPULLORE SOCIALISTE E SHQIPËRISË

Established 14 March 1946

Right and below: *The national flag and arms of Albania with the red star added in 1946. The black eagle is the traditional national emblem.*

In the fifteenth century, Albania was incorporated into the empire of the Ottoman Turks, despite the efforts of the national hero, George Kastriota, or 'Skanderbeg'. Independence was regained in 1912, but there was no settled government until about 1920. The country became a kingdom in 1928, but was occupied by Italy in 1939. The Communists led the struggle for independence and took over in 1944, forming the people's republic in 1946.

The black, eagle emblem of Albania reflects the citizens' name for themselves ('People of the Eagle') and also recalls the Byzantine Empire to which they once belonged. The flag was plain red with the eagle from 1912 onward, except for an interregnum from 1914 to 1920. After the Italian invasion the eagle was surrounded by parts of the Italian arms (crown, fasces, scroll), but these were dropped in 1942. The red, yellow-edged star was added in the constitution of 1946. There is also a civil ensign, introduced in 1912, which also now has a red, yellow-edged star in the centre. The black eagle remains the national emblem, but is now accompanied by Communist additions. The date refers to the Anti-Fascist Congress held at that time.

Above: *The flag of Albania prior to 1928, as shown on a cigarette card of the period.*

Algeria, People's Democratic Republic of

AL-JUMHURIYA AL-JAZAIRIYA AD-DIMUKRATIYA ASH-SHABIYA

Established 3 July 1963

***Above:** Algerian troops in the French service with a flag displaying the Hand of Fatima.*

Algeria was taken over by the French in the nineteenth century, but they met with severe resistance from the indigenous population, which continued until the civil war of 1954 to 1963. The independence movement was led by the *Front de Libération National*, which has been the dominant party in the republic ever since.

The flag of the FLN was designed by the nationalist leader Messali Haj in 1928 and was adopted as the flag of the Provisional Government in 1954. The colours are said to represent Islam (green), purity (white), and liberty (red). A new national emblem was adopted in 1976, which features the Hand of Fatima above a scene denoting prosperity.

***Above left and above:** The national flag of Algeria today, and a pirate flag of the Barbary Coast as shown on an eighteenth-century flag chart.*

Andorra, Principality of

PRINCIPAT D'ANDORRA

Established 1278

The settlement of 1278 placed Andorra under the tutelage of the Counts of Foix and the Bishops of Urgel. The role of the Count of Foix is now exercised by the President of France, but in effect the valleys are an independent republic.

***Above and above right:** The national coat of arms and the national flag of Andorra.*

The arms depict the areas on which Andorra has been dependent: Urgel (crozier and mitre), Foix (three vertical red strips), Catalonia (four red stripes), and Béarn (two cows). The motto means 'United Strength is Greater'. The flag is in the traditional colours, and dates from about 1866.

ANGOLA, PEOPLE'S REPUBLIC OF

REPÚBLICA POPULAR DE ANGOLA

Established 11 November 1975

Above and above right: *The arms and flag of Angola with the machete and half cog-wheel that correspond to the hammer and sickle.*

Angola was settled by the Portuguese in 1491 and controlled by them until 1975. It includes the enclave of Cabinda, north of the Zaïre River. From 1961 Angola was subject to uprisings from nationalist groups. One of these, the *Movimiento Popular de Libertação de Angola* (MPLA), seized power in 1975, while another, UNITA (*União Nacional para e Independencia Total de Angola*), took over in the south, where it has held out ever since. The third group, the *Frente National de Libertação de Angola*, still has a presence in the north.

The flag of the MPLA, dating from about 1964, is red over black with a central yellow star. The government formed in Luanda in 1975 adopted a variation of this as the national flag, with a smaller star and a section of cogwheel crossed with a machete, clearly representing agriculture and industry. The red stands for blood shed in the struggle for freedom and the black for Africa. The national emblem contains the same elements, and the rising sun appeared on an earlier MPLA flag.

ANTIGUA AND BARBUDA

Established as a Queen's Realm of the Commonwealth 1 November 1981

Above and right: *The arms of Antigua showing the rising sun also used on the flag, this flag dating from 27 February 1967.*

Antigua and Barbuda are islands in the West Indies, colonized by the English from 1632 onward. They became a crown colony on 30 June 1956 and an Associated State on 27 February 1967, a status that allowed it to set its own date for independence.

The flag was adopted when Antigua became an Associated State. It was designed by Reginald Samuel and uses the same rising sun on black as in the arms, which stand for a new era for the islands. The V-shape is for victory, red for the dynamism of the people, blue for hope, and white for the sea.

ARGENTINA, REPUBLIC OF

REPÚBLICA ARGENTINA

Established 9 July 1816

Above and right: *The arms and state flag both feature the "Sun of May" emblem; the civil flag is plain.*

Argentina was originally part of the Spanish Viceroyalty of the River Plate and was divided into provinces. The independence movement broke out in Buenos Aires in 1810.

The blue and white colours date from 25 May 1810, the day on which the insurrection began in Buenos Aires. The flag was designed by General Belgrano and adopted on the day of the declaration of independence. The form with the sun (known as 'The Sun of May') was added on 25 February 1818, and is principally the flag for use by the government, although it may be used by the civil population as well. Some provinces of Argentina have their own flags as well as coats of arms, and the Red Dragon flag is in use by the Welsh population of Patagonia.

AUSTRALIA, COMMONWEALTH OF

A QUEEN'S REALM OF THE COMMONWEALTH

Established 1 January 1901

Australia was originally six separate colonies established at various dates over the continent. The movement for federation obtained momentum in the last quarter of the nineteenth century and resulted in the formation of a federal government. The colonies are now the six states, and the Federal Government administers the Northern Territory and seven external territories.

The federation movement had a flag of its own, but the new state had no flag when it came into existence. A semiofficial competition was held to find a new design, which was won by the creator, of the forerunner of the present flag. In this the large star represents the Federation, and is known as the 'Commonwealth Star'. The Southern Cross, similar to the one on the flag of Victoria, stands for Australia itself and the Union Jack for the British connection. The flag was revised in 1903 and 1909. The version with the red field was for civil vessels, although the blue version, now known as the National Flag of Australia, can also be used for this purpose.

The arms now in use were introduced on 19 September 1912 and contain quarters for each of the states, the same emblems that are on their distinctive ensign-badges. The arms form the basis of the banner of the Queen of Australia.

***Top and left:** The national flag, and the arms introduced on 19 September 1912. Both contain the large "Commonwealth Star".*

***Above:** The flag used by the Federation movement prior to 1901.*

***Above:** The flag of the Governor-General of Australia.*

***Above:** The banner of HM the Queen of Australia combines all the state badges.*

The Governor-General has a flag of the pattern introduced in the 1930s, with the royal crest and the name on a scroll, all on a field of royal blue.

All the states have flags based on the British Blue Ensign, which were adopted during the colonial period. Their governors now have flags that are in general the same designs, but with crowns above the badges (except in the case of Victoria, where the governor's flag is the same as the state flag but with red stars on a yellow field). Queensland's governor still uses the old model, consisting of the Union Jack with the badge within a garland in the centre.

New South Wales

Queensland

South Australia

Tasmania

Victoria

Western Australia

The flags of the states, based on the Blue Ensigns used when they were separate colonies. The badges on the flags are those used in the national arms. The state Governors add a crown above the badge for their own flags, except in the cases of Queensland and Victoria.

The following are the dates of the introduction of the state flags:

New South Wales: 11 July 1876
Governor: 19 January 1981
Queensland: 29 November 1876
South Australia: 13 January 1904
Governor: 20 November 1976
Tasmania: 25 September 1876
Governor: February 1977
Victoria: 1877
Governor: 18 April 1984
Western Australia: November 1875 (the swan faced the fly prior to 1953)
Governor: 12 April 1988

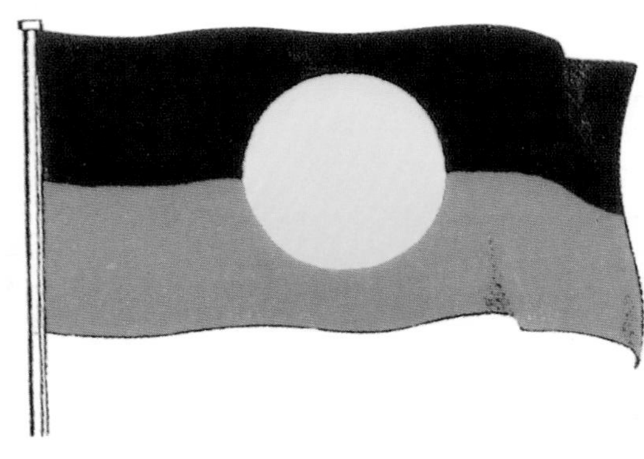

Above: *The flag of the Australian Aboriginals.*

The only three territories to have their own flags are the Northern Territory, Norfolk Island and Christmas Island.

Northern Territory The Territory has a flag adopted on 1 July 1978. The device in the centre is a Sturt's Desert Rose, the Territory's plant-badge. Black, white, and ochre are the official colours of the Territory.

Norfolk Island The flag was adopted on 11 January 1980. The device in the centre is a Norfolk Island pine.

Christmas Island The flag was adopted in April 1986 but is so far unofficial. The Southern Cross represents Australia; in the centre is a map of the island, and in the fly triangle is a stylized frigate bird, symbolizing the source of the phosphate wealth of the island. The flag was the winning design in a local competition, and was created by Tony Couch.

Other Flags

Aboriginals The flag was designed by the Aboriginal artist Harold Thomas and first hoisted in 1971. The black stands for the people, the red for the land, and the yellow disc for the sun.

Ausflag At the time of the Bicentenary celebrations there was a move to create a new national flag. A new competition was run by the Ausflag organization and a final design was arrived at, which keeps the same colours as the present flag, but emphasizes the particularly Australian Southern Cross.

Above: *The flag of the Northern Territory.*

Above: *The flag of Norfolk Island.*

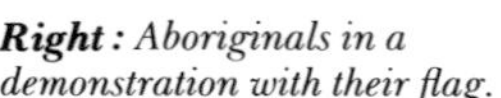

Right: *Aboriginals in a demonstration with their flag.*

AUSTRIA, REPUBLIC OF

REPUBLIK OESTERREICH
Established 12 November 1918

Present-day Austria is the German-speaking heartland of what was once the extensive Austro-Hungarian Empire, which collapsed in 1918. The republic was incorporated into Germany from 1938 to 1945 and occupied by the Allies from 1945 to 1955. The constitution is a federation of nine states.

The traditional red-white-red flag of Austria was readopted in 1918 as the flag of the new republic, and the black eagle of the Holy Roman Empire was retained as the arms. The flag dates from the early thirteenth century and is one of the oldest in continuous use, although it played only a minor role during the Hapsburg period. In 1918 the eagle was redrawn with only one head and grasping a hammer and sickle in place of the traditional orb and sceptre. In 1945 broken shackles were added to its legs to symbolize Austria's liberation. The state flag has the arms over all in the centre.

Each of the states has its own arms and flag.

Above and right: *The state flag has the national arms over all in the middle.*

Above: *The flag of Austria.* ***Right:*** *The arms of the Länder of Austria from which the colours of their flags are derived.* ***From top row, left to right:*** *Salzburg, Styria, Lower Austria, Upper Austria, Vorarlberg, Vienna, Tirol, Carinthia and Burgenland.*

BAHAMAS, COMMONWEALTH OF THE

A QUEEN'S REALM OF THE COMMONWEALTH
Established 10 July 1973

Christopher Columbus made his first landfall in North America on one of the islands of the Bahamas on 12 October 1492, but it was only in the seventeenth century that the islands began to be permanently settled. At one period the islands formed a refuge for pirates, until they became a crown colony in 1717. A legislative assembly was formed in 1841 and internal self-government was achieved in 1964. Today over 80 per cent of the population are of African or mixed descent.

The flag of the Bahamas emerged from designs sent in by the public in a competition held prior to independence. The blue and gold are intended to represent the golden beaches and aquamarine seas of the archipelago, while the black triangle represents the vigour of the population. The flag for civil vessels is red with a white cross throughout and the national flag in the canton.

The coat of arms was adopted in 1971 and shows Columbus's ship, the *Santa Maria*, beneath a blue chief with a rising sun. This replaced a previous coat of arms dating from 1959, which used the motto of the first royal governor: *Expulsis piratis restituta commercia.*

See: Flag Competitions

BAHRAIN, STATE OF

DAWLAT AL BAḪRAYN

Established 1783; fully independent 15 August 1971

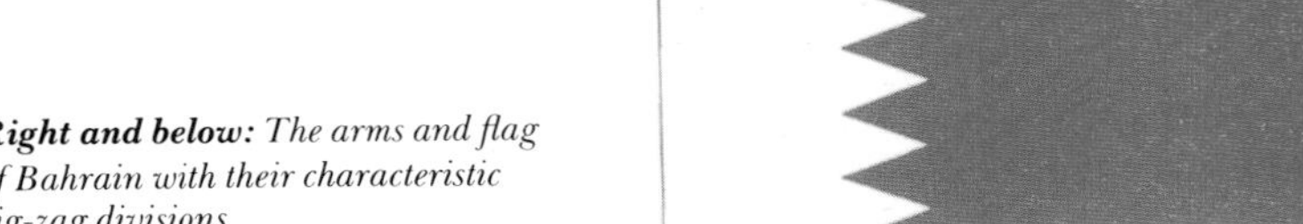

Right and below: *The arms and flag of Bahrain with their characteristic zig-zag divisions.*

Bahrain is an archipelago of about thirty islands in the Persian Gulf near the coast of Saudi Arabia. Despite Iran's claims of sovereignty over the state, Bahrain has retained its independence into modern times, although in treaty relations with Great Britain between 1820 and 1971. The General Maritime Treaty of 1820 was aimed at the suppression of piracy, and applied to Bahrain as well as to other states in the area. From 30 March 1968 until independence, Bahrain was part of the Federation of Arab Emirates, the predecessor of the United Arab Emirates.

By the terms of the General Treaty all the signatory states, which included what are now the United Arab Emirates (q.v.), undertook to add white borders to their red flags. In the case of Bahrain this meant adding a white strip in the hoist. In 1932 the flag achieved its modern serrated form, which was created to distinguish the flag from that of Dubai. The coat of arms dates from the same time, and was designed by the British Resident. The flag of the Amir is like the national flag, with two additional white stripes along the top and bottom edges.

Right: *Postage stamps showing the flag of Bahrain with those of other Persian Gulf states.*

BANGLADESH, PEOPLE'S REPUBLIC OF

GHANA PRAJA TANTRI BANGLADESH

Established 23 March 1971

Right: *The arms of Bangladesh.*

What was formerly East Bengal (the Islamic part of the old province of Bengal in the Indian Empire) became East Pakistan when the new state was formed on 14 August 1947. A movement for secession began in 1970, culminating in a civil war from which Bangladesh ('Land of the Bengalis') emerged as an independent republic.

The first flag of Bangladesh appeared at the outbreak of the civil war in February 1971, and consisted of a yellow map of Bengal on a red disc on a green field. The gold outline reflected the words of the national anthem (a poem by Rabindranath Tagore): *Amar sona Bangla, ami tomay bhalobashi* ('My golden Bengal, I love you'). On 13 January 1972 the map was dropped from the flag, leaving only the red disc, which symbolizes the struggle for independence.

The coat of arms is a stylized water lily within a wreath of rice ears, and beneath are a sprig of jute and four stars representing nationalism, socialism, democracy, and secularism (the motives for independence, as expressed by Sheik Mujibur Rahman).

The flag for civil vessels is red with the national flag in the canton.

Above: *The emblem of Bangladesh.*

BARBADOS

A QUEEN'S REALM OF THE COMMONWEALTH

Established 30 November 1966

Barbados was a British colony from 1627 until 1966. Its name is derived from the bearded fig tree, which was a prominent feature of its vegetation. During the colonial period Barbados was a major source of sugar. Full internal self-government was achieved in 1966.

The flag of Barbados was the winning entry in a design competition held prior to independence; it is the work of Grantley W. Prescod. He explained that the blue and yellow represent the seas and beaches around Barbados (see also Bahamas), and the trident represents a break with the colonial past – the colonial badge portrayed Britannia with her trident.

The arms were adopted on 21 December 1965 and portray the bearded fig tree and two Pride of Barbados orchids. The crest is a hand holding two sugar canes.

See: Flag Competitions

Above and left: *The arms and flag of Barbados. The word "pride" also refers to the orchids in the shield.*

BELGIUM, KINGDOM OF

ROYAUME DE BELGIQUE/KONINKRIJK BELGIË

Established 4 October 1830

Originally part of the Spanish Netherlands, being the area left to Spain after the secession of the Dutch provinces, Belgium passed to Austria in 1713, to France in 1795, and to the Kingdom of the Netherlands in 1815. It declared its independence from Dutch rule in 1830, and secured part of the Duchy of Luxembourg in 1839. The country is divided into Dutch-, French-, and German-speaking communities, as well as the Region of Brussels.

The Belgian colours are said to date from the rising of 1789, which began the end of Austrian rule, and according to a contemporary print were arranged as a horizontal tricolour of red, black, and yellow. These colours are thought to be derived from the arms of Brabant, although several other provinces, including Flanders and Hainault, also use the same combination in their arms.

The colours were revived on 26 August 1830, when the revolt against the Dutch began. Two patriots had a horizontal tricolour of red, yellow, and black made up and flown from the Hôtel de Ville, and the flag soon became widespread. However, on 23 January 1831 the provisional government decreed that the colours would be arranged vertically.

The flag for use on land has the unusual proportions of 13:15, although for use at sea it is the more usual 2:3. Its unusual proportions derive from the fact that it was principally used as a military colour during the 1830 revolt.

The Flemish, Walloon (French-speaking), and German communities have distinctive flags. The Flemish flag is a version of the black lion of Flanders and was adopted on 2 July 1973. The Walloon flag is also yellow, with a red rampant cockerel; it was adopted on 24 June 1975, although it is of much older origin.

See: Revolutionary Tricolours

The Germanophone flag is white with a red rampant lion within a ring of nine blue cinquefoils. The flags of the nine provinces are widely seen, and are heraldic banners of their arms.

The royal standard of Belgium is crimson-purple, with the crowned shield in the centre and the royal cipher in each canton (a crowned 'B', for Beaudoin, or 'F', for Fabiola).

The flag of the city of Brussels is divided green over red with the device from the arms in the centre: St Michael overcoming Satan. There is no flag for the Region of Brussels.

Above and left: *National flag for use on land and the armorial banners of the provinces.* ***From top row, left to right:*** *Brabant, Limburg, Hainault, Namur, Luxembourg and Liège.*

Left: *The emblems of the Flemish and Walloon communities; the latter is frequently seen as a car-sticker.*

BELIZE

A QUEEN'S REALM OF THE COMMONWEALTH

Established 21 September 1981

***Right and below:** The flag and arms of Belize. The motto means "I flourish in the shade", a reference to the country's abundant forests.*

British Honduras, as the territory was originally known, was settled by British woodcutters from about 1638, and was recognized as a colony in 1862. Self-government was achieved in 1964, but objections from Guatemala (which claims the territory for itself) delayed independence until 1981.

As a colony, British Honduras had both a coat of arms, granted 28 January 1907, and an ensign-badge based on the arms. An unofficial flag was introduced in 1950, consisting of the arms within a garland of fifty leaves on a white disc in a blue field. This flag was particularly associated with the People's United Party, which led the country to independence. The opposition United Democratic Party has a flag of red, black, and blue, and it was decided to add red from their flag to the national flag hoisted at midnight on independence day (which was otherwise the 1950 flag). In December 1981 the arms were amended and now include the fifty-leaved garland.

BENIN, PEOPLE'S REPUBLIC OF

REPUBLIQUE POPULAIRE DU BENIN

Established as Republic of Dahomey 1 August 1960

See: The Red Flag

Dahomey was an African kingdom founded in 1625, but was subject to the establishment of forts by the Europeans along the coast. French influence eventually predominated, and France conquered the territory in 1892–4, deposing the last king, Behanzin. In 1958 the territory became an autonomous republic within the French Community, and in 1960 an independent republic. The Marxist government changed the name of the state to Bénin in 1975.

A flag in the Pan-African colours was adopted for the autonomous republic on 16 November 1959, consisting of two stripes of yellow over red with a green vertical strip in the hoist; this was in use until 1 December 1975, when the name, arms, and flag were all changed. The flag is now green with a red star in the canton, the reverse of the flag of the single party, the *Parti de la Révolution Populaire du Bénin.*

***Above and right:** The arms and flag of Benin: "R.P.B." stands for its title in French. These arms are very similar to those of other Marxist states.*

***Above:** The first flag of independent Dahomey, 1960–75. See: Pan-African Colours.*

Bhutan, Kingdom of

DRUK-YUL/DRUK GAYKHAB
Established *c*900

Bhutan is a Tibetan kingdom on the southern slopes of the Himalayas. It came under British protection in 1910 and made a similar arrangement with India in 1949. Until 1885 Bhutan had two rulers, the spiritual and the temporal, reflecting the strong influence of the Dukpa lamas. A hereditary ruler, the Druk Gyalpo, was established in 1907 and is now known as the King of Bhutan.

The flag of Bhutan represents the temporal and spiritual rulers, with yellow for the Druk Gyalpo. The dragon represents the name of the country, *Druk Yul*, or 'Land of the Thunder Dragon', which was given to it by the first lamas to establish themselves there. The present design of the flag dates from about 1965. A new national emblem was introduced in 1980, in which two dragons support a *khorlo*, the Bhuddist wheel of law.

Above: *The national flag of Bhutan with the "Thunder-Dragon" grasping four white gems.*

Bolivia, Republic of

REPÚBLICA DE BOLIVIA
Established 6 August 1825

Bolivia is named after Simón Bolívar, who played a major role in the liberation of South America and who established the republic, previously part of Peru, in 1825.

The first flag of Bolivia was of three stripes of green-red-green, with five stars within laurel wreaths, representing the five original provinces, in the green part, which was of double width. In 1826 the upper stripe was changed to yellow, and the stars were replaced by the arms. On 30 November 1851 the present design was adopted. The present arms, which are placed in the centre of the state flag, depict an allegorical landscape with typical Bolivian flora and fauna. The nine stars on the band represent the nine modern departments.

The ensign contains a tenth star that represents the province of Arica, lost to Chile in 1884. The ocean-going ships are based in Argentina and Uruguay, since Bolivia no longer has a coast.

See: Central and South America

Above and top: *The arms and flag of Bolivia. The arms are normally depicted on a blue disc but do not appear on the flag for everyday use.*

BOTSWANA, REPUBLIC OF

Established 30 September 1966

Above and above right: *The arms and flag of Botswana. The word "pula" is symbolized on the flag by the light blue field.*

Formerly known as Bechuanaland, the territory came under British protection in 1890. The name is taken from that of the dominant Tswana people, who are related to those of the Bophuthatswana Bantustan in South Africa and also to the people of Lesotho.

The arms were introduced on 25 January 1966; they represent industry and stock-raising linked by waves of water, which stand for the lifeblood of the country. This is also referred to in the motto *Pula*, which means rain, water, welfare. The light blue of the flag also symbolizes water, and the black and white stripes, similar to those of the zebras in the arms, stand for racial harmony.

Above: *The Presidential Standard containing the whole arms.*

BRAZIL, FEDERAL REPUBLIC OF

REPÚBLICA FEDERATIVA DO BRASIL

Established as an Independent Kingdom 7 September 1822

Below and right: *The modern national flag of Brazil, and the flag of the Emperor prior to 1889 as shown on a German cigarette card.*

See: Portugal and Brazil, Stars and Stripes.

Brazil was a Portuguese colony from 1500 to 1815, when it was made a separate kingdom dynastically linked with Portugal. In 1822 the Crown Prince, Dom Pedro, threw off his allegiance to Portugal and declared Brazil to be independent. He made himself Emperor soon afterward, and his dynasty ruled until 15 September 1889, when the country became a republic. The former provinces became states, of which there are now 23.

The flag of Brazil is based on that adopted in 1822, although there was a move in 1889 to substitute a new design based on the Stars and Stripes. Green and yellow were the colours adopted by Dom Pedro (in contrast to the blue and white of Portugal). His flag had the royal arms in the centre, but in 1889 these were replaced by a disc bearing the stars as they appeared over Rio de Janeiro on the night of the 15 November, with the Southern Cross as a prominent feature. The band, or zodiac, across the disc bears the motto *Ordem e Progresso* ('Order and Progress'). There are supposed to be as many stars as there are states, but each star does not necessarily represent a specific state. The celestial map also recalls the armillary sphere used in the Imperial arms, and before that in the flags of Portugal.

Each state has a flag and a coat of arms. Many of these flags date back to revolts in the nineteenth century (eg, Minas Gerais, Pernambuco, São Paulo), and others are derived from the first republican flag (Goiás, Piauí, Sergipe).

Above: *The arms of the Republic, with its title and date of foundation.*

The flag of the President is like that of the Emperor, but in place of the Imperial arms has the emblem of Brazil, a large prismatic star with a disc containing the stars of the Southern Cross. Around the disc is a band with stars for the 23 states and behind it is a sword. It is surrounded by a wreath of coffee and tobacco (also on the Imperial flag) and has a scroll with the title of the country and the date '15 November 1889'.

BRUNEI, SULTANATE OF

NEGARA BRUNEI DARUSSALAM

Independent 31 December 1983

Brunei was originally much larger than it is today, since Sarawak, Labuan, and part of Sabah have been detached from it. The Sultanate was founded in the fifteenth century after the destruction of the Hindu Empire of Majapahit, to which it was once tributary. Brunei today is really just a city-state based on Bandar Seri Begawan, the capital.

The flag of Brunei dates from 1906 and is akin to the state flags of peninsular Malaysia. Its three colours represent the Sultan (yellow) and his two chief ministers (white and black). The emblem in the centre has been built up over the years, and was added to the flag on 29 September 1959. On the crescent is the motto 'Always render Service by God's Guidance' and on the scroll beneath the title are the words *Brunei Darussalam* ('Brunei City of Peace').

The Sultan's standard is yellow, with the arms in red supported by two seated cats.

Above and left: *The arms and flag of Brunei. In the Far East, yellow is the colour of royalty.*

BULGARIA, PEOPLE'S REPUBLIC OF

NARODNA REPUBLIKA BULGARIA

Established as a Kingdom 5 October 1908

The first Bulgar state was established in 681, but eventually became part of the Ottoman Empire. In 1878 Bulgaria and Rumelia achieved home rule, being united in 1885. In 1887 Ferdinand of Saxe-Coburg-Gotha became Prince. In 1908 he declared himself Tsar of an independent Bulgaria. On 28 October 1944 a Communist government took over, and the People's Republic was declared on 15 September 1946.

The Pan-Slav colours took a new turn in Bulgaria, where they were adopted during 1878, a time when Russian influence was predominant. The blue of the Russian flag was changed to green as a method of differentiation, but most of the country's flags were based on those of Imperial Russia.

See: The Pan-Slav Colours

The present arms date from 1947 but have preserved the lion rampant, which is the ancient emblem of the country. It has changed its form somewhat over the years, most recently in 1971. The scroll now bears the dates '681' (foundation of Bulgaria) and '1944' (formation of the Fatherland Front government). Since 6 December 1947 the state emblem has been placed in the canton of the national flag, although changing its size and location slightly over the years. The flag's proportions have also changed, from 2:3 to 3:5.

Subsidiary flags are still based on Russian models, or, rather, those of the Soviet Union. The ensign is white with a large red star and green and red strips along the bottom. The jack is red with a large white-bordered red star in the centre, the same as that of Albania.

Above and above right: *The arms and flag of Bulgaria, in which the traditional lion is surrounded by typically Communist features.*

BURKINA FASO, REPUBLIC OF

Established as Upper Volta 5 August 1960

See: The Pan-African Colours

Above and above right: The flag of Upper Volta (above) and the modern arms and flag. The star on the modern flag can vary considerably in size.

The territory of Upper Volta was established by the French in 1919 from other parts of French West Africa in an area taken over in 1904. From 1932 to 1947 it was redistributed to neighbouring provinces. On 11 December 1958 it became an autonomous republic within the French community, and independent in 1960. Following a coup in 1983 the name of the country was altered on 4 August 1984.

The flag of Upper Volta was adopted on 9 December 1959 and was a tricolour of black, white, and red. The colours were intended to represent the three branches of the Volta River. This flag and the coat of arms were castigated as neo-colonial by the regime that took over in 1983 and introduced the present emblems on 4 August 1984. The new flag is in the Pan-African colours used by most of Burkina Faso's neighbours. The emblem contains a hoe and a Kalashnikov rifle under the guiding star of Marxism (see also Bénin). The motto is 'Our country or death: we shall conquer'.

BURMA (MYANMA), UNION OF

PYIDAUNGSU MYANMA NAINGNGANDAW

Established as Union of Burma 4 January 1948

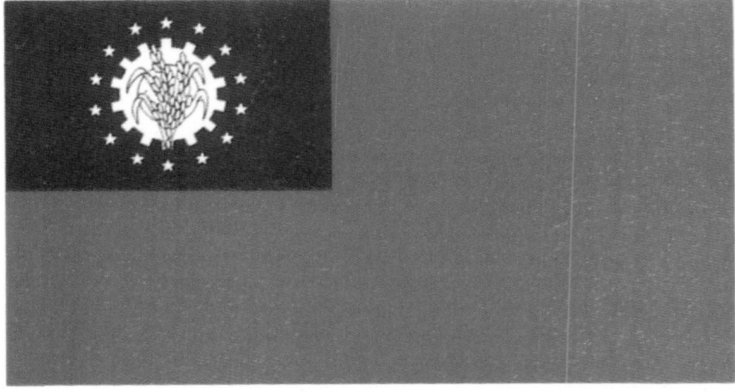

Burma was taken over by the British in various stages throughout the nineteenth century, culminating in the annexation of Burma proper and the Shan States in 1885, which were added to the Indian Empire. In 1937 Burma became a separate colony with internal self-government. From 1942 to 1945 the country was occupied by the Japanese, who set up a puppet state in August 1943. The Anti-Fascist People's League won the elections of 1947, which led to independence outside the Commonwealth. From 1974 to 1988 Burma was a Socialist Republic, and the Burmese name for the country was adopted for international use in 1989.

The peacock was the emblem of the old kingdom of Burma, and was readopted for the flag-badge in 1939. It was used on the flag of the puppet state (1943-5). The flag of the President (1948-62) was orange with a peacock in the centre. However, the national flag is derived from that of the Anti-Fascist People's League, which was red with a white star in the canton. The flag of 1948 had a blue canton with a large star and five smaller ones, intended to represent the five main ethnic groups. The present design dates from 4 January 1974 and has fourteen stars, one for each state and division, surrounding a cogwheel with an ear of rice. The cogwheel now appears in the centre of the coat of arms, with an outline map of the country superimposed. The circular band, which used to carry the motto 'The pursuit of unity is happiness and prosperity', has been replaced by a wreath of rice. The scroll carries the name of the country.

Above: The arms of Burma (Myanma). The 14 teeth of the cogwheel represent the states and divisions of the country.

Above right: The modern national flag. The ear of rice sits in the middle of the cogwheel.

Left and above: The flag of the President of the Republic of Burma and the first national flag (1948–74).

BURUNDI, REPUBLIC OF

REPUBLIKA Y'UBURUNDI

Established as an Independent Kingdom 1 July 1962

The Tutsi kingdom dated back to the early sixteenth century. It was occupied by the Germans in 1890 and transferred to Belgium as a mandated territory in 1919. It became independent in 1962, but on 28 November 1966 the kingdom was abolished. In the civil war of 1972 the Tutsi supremacy was destroyed.

The basic design of the flag of Burundi has remained the same since it was first hoisted on

***Above:** The first flag of Burundi (1962–66).*

the day of independence, but the emblems in the circle have been altered. Originally the device was a drum (emblem of the Tutsi monarchy) and a sorghum plant. On the formation of the republic the drum was deleted, and in 1967 the present three stars were substituted. These are said to represent the three main ethnic groups.

***Above and above left:** The arms and flag of Burundi. The motto is "Unity, Work, Progress".*

CAMBODIA, STATE OF

ROT KAMPUCHEA

Established as an Independent Kingdom 25 September 1955

The Khmer state emerged in the sixth century and maintained itself in existence until 1863, when it became a French Protectorate. Between the ninth and thirteenth centuries the famous buildings of Angkor were erected, including Angkor Wat (built AD 1113-50). The state resumed its independence in 1955, but on 18 March 1970 was replaced by a republic (the Khmer Republic). 'Democratic Kampuchea' was instituted in April 1975, but was in turn replaced by the People's Republic in January 1979. Democratic Kampuchea continued in exile and kept the Cambodian seat at the United Nations. On 1 May 1989 the present name was instituted.

The flag of Cambodia has always contained a depiction of the temple of Angkor Wat in some form or other. In 1893 it was in white on a red field with a blue border. In 1948 the temple in simplified form appeared in the centre of a red flag with blue borders at the top and bottom. The flag of the Khmer Republic was blue with the temple in a red canton and three white stars in the upper fly. The flag of

See: The Red Flag

***Above left:** The modern flag of Cambodia as from 1 May 1989, showing five towers of the Temple of Angkor Wat.*

Democratic Kampuchea is red with a highly stylized and simplified version of the temple in yellow in the centre. The flag of the People's Republic was the same, but with a temple of five towers. The present flag was introduced on 1 May 1989 and reverts to the red and blue of previous flags, but retains yellow for the temple, which is more elaborate and representational than before. It is intended to be a flag of unity between the rival factions.

***Left and far left:** The flags of the People's Republic and Democratic Kampuchea.*

Cameroon, Republic of

REPUBLIQUE DU CAMEROUN

Established 1 January 1960

*Flags of Cameroon: (**above, top**) 1957–61; (**above**) 1961–75; (**above right**) modern.*
***Far right:** arms. Motto is "Peace, Work, Fatherland"; shield now has only one star.*

See: The Pan-African Colours

The territory of the republic was occupied by the Germans in 1884, but lost to the British and French in 1916. It then became mandated to these two powers, with the larger section by far going to France. The French part became autonomous on 1 January 1959 and independent in 1960. The British part divided into two in 1961, with the southern area electing to join the Cameroon Republic and the northern to join Nigeria. The Federal Republic was formed on 1 October 1961, which became a unitary republic on 2 June 1972.

The Cameroon flag was adopted on 29 October 1957. It was the first flag after that of Ghana to employ the Pan-African colours, and was at that time a plain tricolour. When the southern British Cameroons was federated in 1961, two yellow stars were placed in the upper hoist to represent the two units in the federation. On 20 May 1975 these were replaced by a single star in the centre of the red strip. Like the flags of most Francophone countries, the tricolour is in vertical form.

Canada

A QUEEN'S REALM OF THE COMMONWEALTH

Established 1 July 1867

Canada originally consisted of the four provinces of Ontario, Québec, Nova Scotia, and New Brunswick, which were federated to form the new Dominion in 1867. Québec had originally belonged to France, from which it was taken by the British in 1763. Other provinces were added after federation. The Northwest Territories were bought from the Hudson's Bay Company in 1869. Yukon was formed as a separate territory in 1898, and plans are under consideration for the further division of the Northwest Territories.

Canada had no distinctive flag until 1965, although on 5 September 1945 it was laid down that the Red Ensign with the Canadian shield in the fly could be used on land as a national flag. The shield was from the arms, which were first granted in 1868 and revised in 1921. The 1868 arms quartered the then arms of the four provinces, but the present ones quarter those of the countries from which Canada's European population originated, with the maple leaf emblem in the base. In 1957 the maple leaves were changed from green to red.

Red and white were the heraldic colours of Canada, and many of the new flags suggested

***Above left:** The modern national flag with the stylized maple leaf, adopted 15 February 1965.*

***Above:** The Red Ensign, Canada's only national flag, prior to 1965.*

***Far left:** The modern arms of 1921.*
The motto is "From Sea to Sea".

after the Second World War were in these colours. A long debate went on in the country in the 1960s over the new flag, which culminated in a choice made in December 1964. The new flag was officially hoisted on 15 February 1965. It contains a large red maple leaf in the central white square (known as a 'Canadian pale'), between two vertical red strips.

The banner of the Queen of Canada was introduced on 15 August 1962, and is of the same pattern as those for other Queen's Realms. It is a heraldic banner of the arms with the Queen's crowned initial on a blue disc within a ring of golden roses. The flag of the Governor-General is blue with the royal crest of Canada in the centre.

All the provinces and territories have arms and flags, and also flags for their lieutenant-governors; the latter flags are in general blue with the crowned shield of arms of the province in the centre with a wreath of ten golden maple leaves. Those of Nova Scotia and Québec do not follow this pattern. In the following, the first date is that of the incorporation of the province, the second that of the introduction of the present flag, and the third that of the introduction of the lieutenant-governor's flag.

***Above:** The flag of the Governor-General. The crest is from the arms.*

Flags of the Provinces and Territories

Alberta: 1905; 1 June 1968.
Lieutenant-governor: 26 September 1981

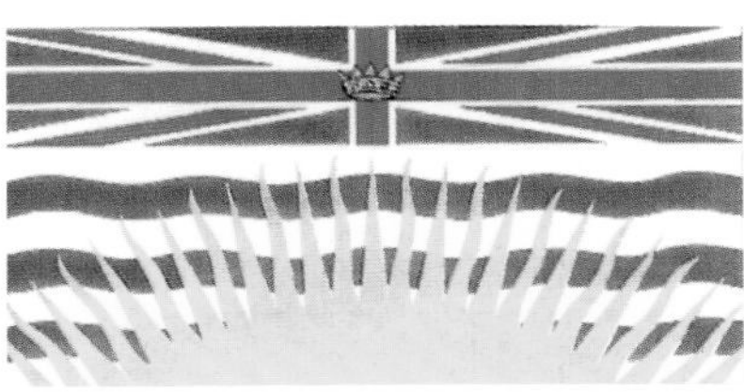

British Columbia: 1871; 27 June 1960.
Lieutenant-governor: 1 February 1981

Manitoba: 15 July 1870; 12 May 1966.
Lieutenant-governor: 11 May 1984

New Brunswick: 1867; 24 February 1965.
Lieutenant-governor: 22 September 1981

Newfoundland: 1949; 28 May 1980.
Lieutenant-governor: January 1987

Nova Scotia: 1867; 28 May 1625.

Ontario: 1867; 21 May 1965.
Lieutenant-governor: 27 June 1981

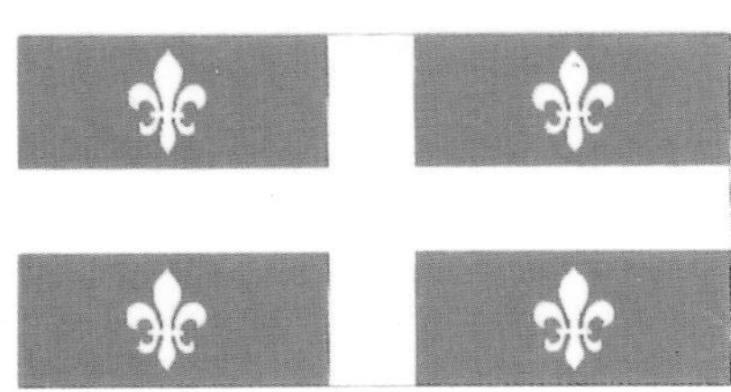

Prince Edward Island: 1873; 24 March 1964.
Lieutenant-governor: 18 November 1981

Quebec: 1867; 21 January 1948.
Lieutenant-governor: 1950

Saskatchewan: 1 September 1905; 22 September 1969.
Lieutenant-governor: 26 September 1981

North West Territories: 1870; 1 January 1969; (no flag for Commissioner)

Yukon: 1898; 1 December 1967; (no flag for Commissioner)

Cape Verde, Republic of

REPÚBLICA DE CABO VERDE

Established 5 July 1975

See: The Pan-African Colours

Above and left: *The flag and arms of Cape Verde. The motto is "Unity, Work, Peace").* ***Below:*** *The flag of Cape Verde as a Portuguese dependency.*

The Cape Verde Islands were first colonized by the Portuguese in the fifteenth century and annexed by them in 1587. On 11 June 1951 the colony became an overseas province of Portugal. During the 1970s the *Partidò Africano da Independencia de Guiné a Cabo Verde* was active, and on 30 December 1974 the Portuguese recognized their government. Full independence followed in 1975.

The flag of Cape Verde is based on that of the PAIGCV, which was created in 1961, and is clearly influenced by that of Ghana, with the black star of African freedom. The present flag, adopted in 1974, is distinguished from that of Guinea Bissau by its proportions (2:3 not 1:2) and by the wreath and scallop shell.

Central African Republic

REPUBLIQUE CENTRAFRICAINE

Established 13 August 1960

See: The Pan-African Colours

The territory of Ubangui-Shari was taken over by the French in 1894 and became part of the vast province of Equatorial Africa in 1910. On 1 December 1958 it became the autonomous republic of Central Africa within the French Community, and independent in 1960. On 4 December 1976 it became the Central African Empire under Bokassa I; he was deposed on 21 September 1979, when the republic was restored.

The flag is a combination of the Pan-African red, yellow, and green with the French Tricolour, expressing the current desire to remain in contact with France. The gold star represents the aim of union with neighbouring states.

The flag of the Emperor Bokassa was green with a large yellow sun in the centre containing a gold eagle. No change was made to the national flag during his reign.

Above and above left: *The arms and flag of Central Africa. The motto is "Unity, Dignity, Work" and the gold star represents African unity.*

CHAD, REPUBLIC OF

REPUBLIQUE DU TCHAD
Established 11 August 1960

See: The Pan-African Colours.

The Chad area became a French Protectorate on 5 September 1900 and later a province of Equatorial Africa. On 28 November 1958 it became an autonomous republic within the French Community and independent in 1960. Since 1965 the country has been in a state of intermittent civil war between the northern and southern ethnic groups.

The flag was adopted on 6 November 1959 on the basis of the French Tricolour, merely importing yellow from the Pan-African colours. The flag of the *Forces Armées du Nord*, which now control the country, has a crescent and star to symbolize its Moslem affiliation.

***Above and above left:** The arms and flag of Chad. The arms were designed by a Swiss heraldist. The motto is "Unity, Work, Progress". Chad also has an official seal.*

CHILE, REPUBLIC OF

REPÚBLICA DE CHILE
Established 12 February 1818

See: The Heritage of the Stars and Stripes

Chile began its struggle against Spain on 18 September 1810, but there were several years of civil war before the achievement of independence. The first republic was formed in 1812 but suppressed in 1814. Insurgence broke out again in 1817, and under the rule of Bernardo O'Higgins (a lieutenant of José de San Martín) a popular plebiscite decided for independence in 1818. The first republic is now known as the period of the *Patria Vieja*, as opposed to the second, the *Patria Nueva*.

The flag of the *Patria Vieja* was a horizontal tricolour in various forms, of which blue, white, and yellow were the most frequent (later blue, white, and red were predominant). When the independent regime was established, the modern flag was adopted. It is said to have been commissioned by the Minister of War, Zenteno, and to have been designed by Charles Wood, an English painter, although it is clearly inspired by the Stars and Stripes and the colours of the *Patria Vieja*.

The flag was officially adopted on 18 October 1817. The arms date from 1834, are based on the flag, and were designed by Zenteno himself. They appear in the centre of the national flag to form the President's standard.

***Above left:** The national flag of Chile.*

***Above:** The flag of the Communist Party displayed at the graves of murdered militants, 1988.*

***Above:** The arms of Chile. The motto is "By Reason or by Force". The whole arms appear in the middle of the national flag to make the Presidential Standard.*

China, People's Republic of

ZHONGHUA RENMIN GONGHE GUO

Established 1 October 1949

See: The Red Flag

China was an Empire until 12 February 1912, when the infant Emperor was obliged to abdicate. At this time Tibet and Mongolia asserted their independence, and the Kuomintang Party was formed. In 1921 the Communist Party was founded, and established Soviet states in some parts of the country. Chiang Kai-shek obtained control of most of the country in 1928, but civil war continued. In 1931 the Japanese seized Manchuria and set up the puppet state of Manchukuo. War between China and Japan broke out in 1937, and after Japan's defeat the civil war continued, until the Kuomintang were expelled from the mainland in 1949. Manchuria and Tibet were reclaimed for China in 1948 and 1951.

***Above right:** The national flag of China, adopted 1 October 1949.*

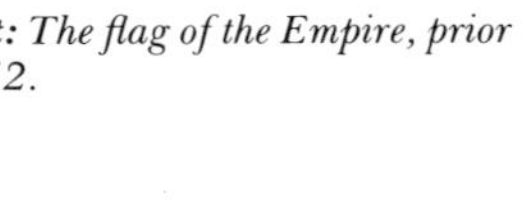

***Right:** The flag of the Empire, prior to 1912.*

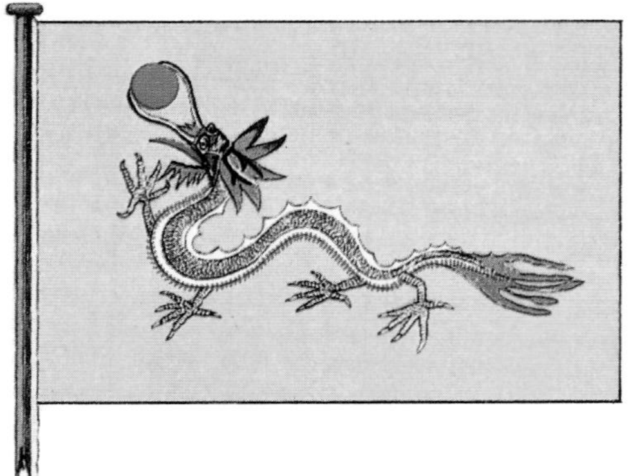

The flag of the Empire was yellow with a blue dragon, representing the East, but a flag in European form was not adopted until 1880. This gave way in 1912 to a flag of five horizontal stripes, intended to represent the five races of China, with red at the top for the Han Chinese. The flag adopted by the Kuomintang at the same time was red, with a blue canton containing a white sun. This part was the flag of the China Regeneration Society in 1895. In 1928 the KMT flag became the national flag. By contrast the flag of the People's Liberation Army was red with a gold star in the canton and the figures '1' and '8', standing for its foundation date, 1 August 1928. It is now the military and naval ensign of China.

***Above:** The arms of China depicting the Tiananmen.*

***Above:** The naval and military ensign.*

The flag of the People's Republic was not adopted until the day the republic was declared. It has the same gold star in the canton, together with four smaller stars. These are officially said to represent the four classes of society: workers, peasants, bourgeoisie and 'patriotic capitalists'. The arms were adopted on 20 September 1950 and portray the *Tiananmen*, or Temple of Heavenly Peace, with the five stars from the national flag above, and a cogwheel for industry and ears of wheat and rice for agriculture.

Tibet and the other autonomous regions have no arms or, flags, although the flag of Tibet is widely used in exile. It dates from 1912, and depicts the sun rising above a mountain with two lions holding magic jewels.

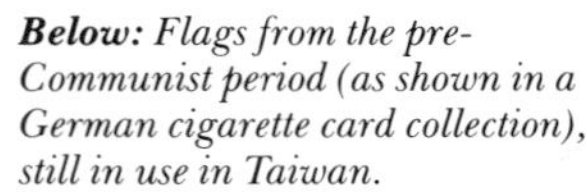

***Below:** Flags from the pre-Communist period (as shown in a German cigarette card collection), still in use in Taiwan.*

China, Republic of

TA CHUNGHUA MINKUO

Established in Taiwan 8 December 1949

Taiwan is the home of the 'Republic of China', the survivors of the regime expelled from mainland China in 1949. The island was in Japanese hands from 1895 to 1945 and became a convenient base for the exiled Kuomintang government of Chiang Kai-shek. Although the regime is not now recognized by any major power as that of the government of China, Taiwan has continued to have an independent existence.

The emblems and flags of Taiwan are the same as those established for the Republic of China by the Kuomintang government in 1928. The flag is known as 'White Sun in Blue Sky over Red Land': its canton is the old Kuomintang flag, which also forms the naval jack.

The red field signifies the land of China. Unlike the People's Republic, Nationalist China has a wide range of subsidiary flags.

***Left and below:** The flag and arms of Nationalist China, based on the emblem of the Kuomintang.*

Colombia, Republic of

RÉPUBLICA DE COLOMBIA

Established 17 December 1819

Colombia was originally known as New Granada, a Spanish territory that included what is now Ecuador, Panama, and Venezuela. Rebellion against Spanish rule began in 1811 and independence was achieved with the aid of Simón Bolívar. The name Greater Colombia was adopted in 1819, but in 1830 Ecuador and Venezuela broke away. In 1858 the country became a Confederation, and in 1863 the United States of Colombia. Since 1886 it has been a unitary republic. In 1903 Panama seceded.

***Above left and left:** The flag and arms of Colombia. The motto is "Liberty and Order".*

The flag of Colombia is based on that of Francisco Miranda, who had attempted to liberate New Granada in 1806. A flag of these colours was hoisted in Bogotá in 1813, and officially adopted for Greater Colombia in 1819. In order to make room for a large canton containing an allegorical depiction of the republic's self-image, the upper yellow stripe was enlarged to twice the width of the others. From 1822 to 1830 the canton contained three blue stars to stand for its three components (Colombia, Venezuela, Ecuador). In 1834 the flag consisted of three equal vertical strips, but on 26 November 1861 the 1819 pattern was resumed. The national flag has no arms in the centre, unlike that of Ecuador, and also has different proportions from that of Ecuador. Each of the modern departments (formerly the states) has a flag, and some of these recall the flags of the revolutionary period.

See: Ecuador and Venezuela, Central and South America.

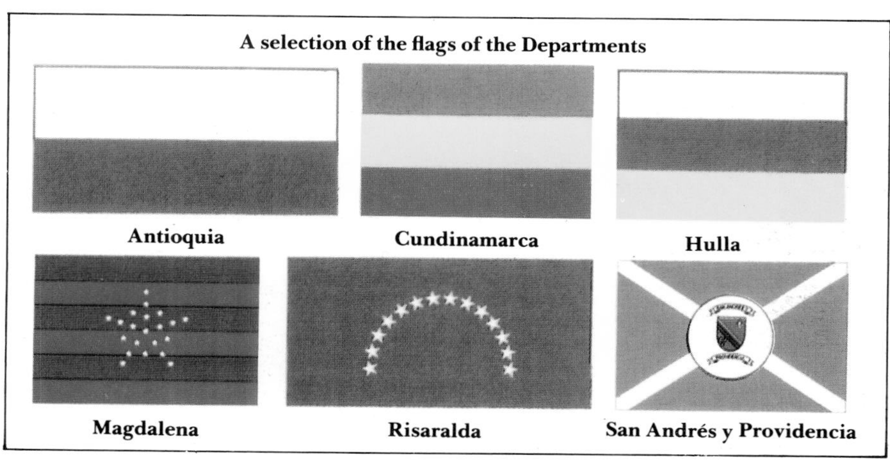

Comoros, Federal Islamic Republic of

REPUBLIQUE FEDERALE ISLAMIQUE DES COMORES/
JAMHOURI FEDERAL YA KISLAM YA COMORES

Established 6 July 1975

***Right:** The flag of Comoros, as from 1 October, 1978.*

The archipelago consists of four main islands north of Madagascar, which have been ruled for many centuries by people of Arab descent. An Arab sultan formerly ruled the islands from Anjouan, but he ceded his rights in 1843 to the French, who occupied Mayotte in that year. In 1886 they took over the whole group, which they ruled from Mayotte. A nationalist party (MOLINCO) began agitation in the 1960s, but Mayotte remained under French influence. In 1975 the other three islands threw off French rule. The federal constitution was adopted in 1978.

There have been several changes of flag in the Comoros. In 1963 a flag for local use was adopted of green with a crescent and four white stars. On independence a flag was adopted with a red stripe along the bottom edge, and a pattern of a crescent and four stars in the canton. The four stars represent the four main islands, although Mayotte still remains in French hands. Following the return to power of the late President, a plain green flag was re-established, also with a crescent and four stars.

***Above:** The arms with the motto "Unity, Justice, Progress".*

***Above:** A variant (unofficial) form of the national flag used on a postage stamp.*

Congo People's Republic

REPUBLIQUE POPULAIRE DU CONGO

Established as Republic of Congo 15 August 1960

***Right:** The flag of the Congo.*

The Middle Congo was occupied by France in 1882 and was a province of French Equatorial Africa until 28 November 1958. The republic became independent in 1960. The name was changed to the present one on 1 January 1970.

The flag adopted for the republic on 18 August 1959 was in the Pan-African colours

***Above:** The flag of the Congo 1959–70. See also Pan-African Colours.*

and was the fifth national flag to use these colours. They were arranged diagonally from upper hoist to lower fly in green, yellow, red, with the yellow stripe narrower than the other portions. The new constitution of 1970 introduced the present flag, which is more Soviet-inspired but still uses the same three colours. The hammer and hoe are a variation of the hammer and sickle, and the yellow star represents the leading role of the one legal party.

See: The Pan-African Colours

***Left:** The arms of the Congo with the motto "Travail, Democratie, Paix" ("Work, Democracy, Peace").*

Costa Rica, Republic of

REPÚBLICA DE COSTA RICA

Established 14 November 1838

Costa Rica was part of the Spanish Viceroyalty of New Spain until 15 September 1821, when along with the rest of what was then Guatemala it seceded from Spain. From 5 January 1822 to 1 July 1823 Guatemala was annexed to Mexico, but it then became the United Provinces of Central America, of which Costa Rica was one. The United Provinces broke up in 1838, but the full independence of Costa Rica was not achieved until 30 August 1848.

Costa Rica used the flag of the United Provinces from 21 August 1823 to 2 November 1824, when a seal representing Costa Rica was added to the centre of the lower blue stripe. This remained in use until 21 April 1840, when a flag with reversed colour, ie, of white-blue-white, was adopted, with the badge of Costa Rica in the centre. When Costa Rica's independence was confirmed in 1848 it was decided to imitate the colours of France, which was also in a revolutionary state at that time. The old blue and white stripes were retained, but with a wide red stripe across the centre. The arms were placed over all in the centre. Since 27 November 1906 the arms have been contained in an oval near the hoist, and the arms have been modified several times. They show an isthmus with three volcanoes and ships sailing on the Pacific Ocean and the Caribbean, with a setting sun and an arc of seven white stars, all within a baroque frame. This form dates from 21 October 1964: the stars stand for the seven departments of the country.

***Above:** The arms of Costa Rica. "America Central" on the arms refers back to the United Provinces of 1823.*

***Left:** The flag of Costa Rica.*

See: El Salvador, Guatemala, Honduras and Nicaragua.

***Above:** The state flag with the arms in their old position, shown on a German cigarette card.*

***Above left, left and below left:** The first flag of Costa Rica, 1823–24, with its red star, the flag of 1824–38 and the flag of 1842–48.*

CUBA, REPUBLIC OF

REPÚBLICA DE CUBA
Established 20 May 1902

The three blue stripes stood for the then three provinces and the triangle is an emblem of Masonic origin representing liberty, equality, and fraternity. The white star (*La Estrella Solitaria*) represented a new state to be added to the USA. The red, white, and blue also referred deliberately to the Stars and Stripes. After having been briefly used in the rising of 1850, the flag became the national flag in 1902.

See: The Heritage of the Stars and Stripes

Cuba belonged to Spain from 1492 to 1898, when it was surrendered to the United States of America, which had intervened in the struggle between Spain and the insurgents. The Americans occupied the island until 1909, although a Cuban government was established in 1902. This was reinaugurated on 28 January 1909, although Cuba still remained subject to limitations imposed by the USA until 1934.

Several flags were created in the nineteenth century by nationalists trying to free Cuba from Spanish rule. The present flag dates from 1848 and was designed in the United States.

***Above:** The flag of the President of Cuba.*

***Above and above left:** The arms and flag of Cuba featuring the "Lone Star".*

CYPRUS, REPUBLIC OF

KYPRIAKI DIMOKRATIA
Established 16 August 1960

See: Aspirant and Colonial States

Cyprus was taken by the Turks in 1571 but was occupied by the British in 1878. In 1914 it became a British colony. The Independence Constitution was intended to make joint government between the Greeks and Turks possible, but this broke down in 1974 when moves were made to unite the island with Greece. In 1975 the Turks occupied the north of the island and an autonomous government was set up (13 February 1975).

The flag of Cyprus was intended to be a common symbol for both ethnic communities, with a white field as well as two olive branches for peace. The map of the island is intended to be copper-coloured to recall the origin of the island's name. The arms include a dove – the symbol of Aphrodite but also an emblem of peace – with an olive branch in its beak. In practice the Greek flag is widely used.

***Above and above right:** The arms and flag of Cyprus, with the dove and olive branches.*

***Above:** Partisans of Turkish Cyprus manning a road-block in the 1960s.*

CZECHOSLOVAKIA, SOCIALIST REPUBLIC OF

CESKOSLOVENSKÁ SOCIALISTICKÁ REPUBLICA

Established as Czechoslovakia 14 November 1918

Bohemia, Moravia, and Slovakia were originally provinces of the Austro-Hungarian Empire, which became independent with the collapse of the Dual Monarchy in 1918. In 1938 the Sudetenland was annexed to Germany and in 1939 the country was partitioned. A German regime was set up in Bohemia-Moravia and a puppet state in Slovakia. Independence was regained in May 1945 and a Communist regime inaugurated in 1948. The 1960 Constitution provides for separate states in Bohemia-Moravia and Slovakia.

Slovak nationalists adopted the Pan-Slav colours in 1848, in a form identical with the flag of Russia. In the Czech lands the red and white of Bohemia were used as soon as independence was proclaimed, and a government commission was set up to design a new national flag. The present design was inaugurated on 30 March 1920 and combines the Czech and Slovak colours. The flag was abolished by the Germans in 1939 and restored on 9 May 1945. The arms, which appear on the President's flag, were altered in 1960, although they still retain the lion of Bohemia.

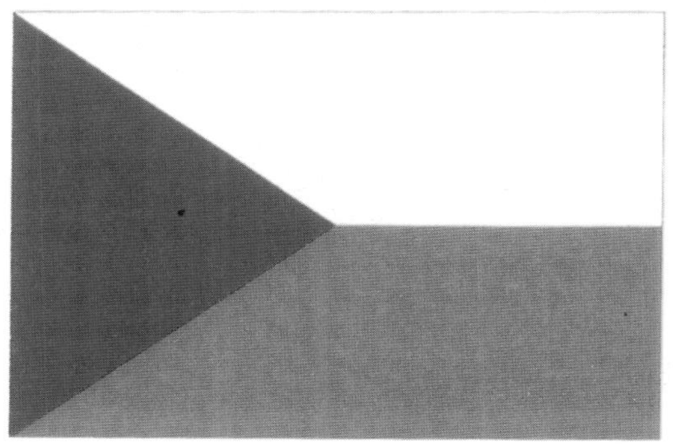

***Above:** The modern flag of Czechoslovakia.*

***Above:** Pre-War military ensign of Czechoslovakia with original shield of arms.*

***Above:** The arms of the Socialist Republic. The small inner shield represents Slovakia, placed on the white lion of Bohemia.*

DENMARK, KINGDOM OF

KONGERIGET DANMARK

Denmark has been a kingdom since at least the ninth century, and was ruled by the direct descendants of Gorm the Old until 1448. From then until 1863 the dynasty of Oldenburg provided the monarchs (alternately named Christian and Frederick). Christian IX was the first of the House of Schleswig-Holstein-Sønderburg-Glücksburg. The present Queen, Margrethe II, rules under a constitution granted in 1953. Norway and Iceland were once dependencies of Denmark.

The flag of Denmark is known as the *Dannebrog*, or Danish cloth. It is the form of flag used to identify the Christian warriors of the German Empire in the Middle Ages, although it acquired its distinctive Scandinavian form, with an extended arm to the cross, at an early date. Legend says that the flag appeared to King Valdemar II in 1219 during the conquest of Latvia, then a pagan land. The flag has unusual proportions, established by law of 11 July 1848. The flag for official use is a swallow-tail, known as the *splitflag*. In this the cross has arms of equal length but the proportions of the flag are different (56:107 as opposed to 28:37). Badges can be added to the canton, or to a white panel in the centre of the cross. The royal standard has the full royal arms in the white panel. The lesser arms are the crowned shield of Denmark, which also appears on the standard of Prince Philip, Duke of Edinburgh.

The Faroe Islands The islands belonged to Norway between 1380 and 1709, when they passed to Denmark. Home rule was achieved in 1948. The flag dates back to 1931 and is based on that of Norway, with the colours reversed. However, the blue was made a lighter shade in 1959. It uses the Scandinavian form of cross common to all these countries.

Greenland Greenland was claimed for Denmark in 1380 and was administered for many years by the Royal Greenland Trading Company. Home rule was introduced on 1 May 1979, with full internal self-rule in 1981. The latter has resulted in an Inuit government and a new name for the country: Kalaallit Nunaat. The flag was the result of a competition among local artists, and was officially adopted on 21 June 1985.

*The modern flag of Denmark (**left**) and standard of the King of Denmark in the eighteenth century (**above**).*

*The flags of Greenland (**top**) and the Faroe Islands (**above**).*

DJIBUTI, REPUBLIC OF

JAMHOURIYYA DJIBOUTI

Established 27 June 1977

***Above and above right:** The flag of Djibuti as from 1977, and as shown in a United Nations series of postage stamps.*

Tadjoura, a danakil sultanate on the Gulf of Aden, was taken over in 1888 by the French, who created the colony of French Somaliland. This was renamed the Territory of the Afars and Issas in 1967, since the population are partly Afars and partly Somalis (Issas). Independence was achieved in 1977 under the *Ligue Populaire pour l'Indépendance*.

The flag of the new republic is that of the LPAI, which in turn was based on that of an earlier nationalist party, the *Front de Libération de la Côte des Somalis*, dating from 1972. The light blue part of the flag refers to that of Somalia and the green to the Afars, or possibly to the Moslem faith. The white is for peace and the red star for unity. The triangle is said to stand for the words of the national motto: 'Unity, Equality, Peace'.

***Above:** The arms of Djibuti depicting native weapons beneath the star of unity.*

DOMINICA, COMMONWEALTH OF

Established 3 November 1978

Dominica was disputed for decades between France and Great Britain, finally passing to Britain in 1805. It was part of the Federation of the West Indies (1958-62), and became an Associated State on 1 March 1967. Independence as a republic was achieved in 1978.

The flag adopted on independence was basically similar to the present one, but some alterations have taken place since. The colours of the triple cross originally had the white in the centre, the stars originally had no yellow borders, and the parrot faced the fly. The order of the colours was changed in 1981 and the posture of the parrot in 1988. The parrot, a sisserou or imperial parrot, is taken from the arms, which were granted in 1961. The stars represent the parishes of the island, while the three parts of the cross stand for the Trinity. The flag of the President is 'scout' green, with the whole arms in the centre.

***Above and left:** The arms and flag of Dominica. The motto means "After the Good Lord comes the Land". The Sisserou Parrot is unique to Dominica.*

DOMINICAN REPUBLIC

REPÚBLICA DOMINICANA
Established 27 February 1844

The republic consists of the eastern part of the island of Santo Domingo, discovered by Columbus in 1492. Haiti was ceded to France in 1697, and the remainder of the island in 1795. Haiti freed itself from the French in 1804, and the Santo Domingans (or Quisqueyanos, as they call themselves) attempted to secure their freedom in 1821. In 1822 Santo Domingo was occupied by the Haitians, from whom the Quisqueyanos freed themselves in 1844. From 18 March 1861 to 11 July 1865 Santo Domingo was once more occupied by Spain. From 1916 to 1924 the country was occupied by the USA.

The independence movement of 1844 was led by the secret society, *la Trinitaria*. The flag of this group was based on that of Haiti, on which they placed a large white cross, within a ring of stars. The national flag was first hoisted on the Puerto del Conde in Santo Domingo on 27 February 1844, now celebrated as Independence Day. On 6 November Juan Pablo Duarte introduced the present flag, in which the blue and red are quartered by a cross throughout. The state flag has the national arms in the centre of the cross. These consist of a shield like the flag with a trophy of flags in the centre surmounted by a Bible and a cross. Above the shield is the Trinitarians' password, *Dios Patria Libertad*. Following the Spanish occupation, the national flag was re-established on 14 September 1863.

***Above and left:** The arms and flag. The Bible is open at the first chapter of St John's Gospel and the motto is "God, Country, Liberty".*

***Above:** The flag of the President is shown on a German cigarette card.*

ECUADOR, REPUBLIC OF

REPÚBLICA DEL ECUADOR

Established 13 May 1830

Ecuador was once part of the Spanish Viceroyalty of New Granada. The first call for independence was made in Quito on 10 August 1809, but it was not until 1822 that Ecuador was liberated by the decisive Battle of Pichincha. By the Agreement of Guayaquil of 26 July 1822, Ecuador became part of the Confederation of Greater Colombia. But on 10 August 1830 Ecuador finally severed its ties with Colombia.

The first distinctively Ecuadorean flag was hoisted on 9 October 1820 by the patriots of Guayaquil, and is still the flag of the department of Guayas. But following the accord made at Guayaquil between Bolívar and San Martín, the flag of Gran Colombia was adopted. Following the break with Colombia no new flag was adopted until 6 March 1845, when a flag of white, blue, and white in vertical strips, with three white stars on the blue part, was instituted. The number of stars was increased to seven on 6 November. On 26 September 1860 there was a return to the flag of Colombia. The present form of the flag is laid down by regulations of 5 December 1900, which give it proportions of 1:2 and prescribe the addition of the national arms in the centre. The arms date from 6 November 1845 and were revised by the law of 5 December 1900. Each department of Ecuador has a coat of arms and a flag.

See: Colombia and Venezuela

***Above and right:** The arms and flag of Ecuador. The arms always appear in the middle of the national flag and depict the first steam vessel ever to be used in Ecuador.*

Egyptian Arab Republic

JUMHURIYAT MISR AL-ARABIYA

Established as a Kingdom 28 February 1922

***Above and right:** The arms and the modern national flag.*

See: The Pan-Arab Colours

***Above:** The national flag prior to 1958.*

***Above:** The flag of the United Arab Republic (1958–1972).*

Egypt belonged to the Ottoman Empire from 1517 until 1914, when it was made a protectorate of the British, who had occupied the country in 1882. It became independent under King Fuad, a descendant of the former Khedive. On 23 July 1952 a military government took over, and King Farouk was deposed. On 18 June 1953 Egypt became a republic. On 22 February 1958 Egypt formed the United Arab Republic with Syria, which lasted until 28 September 1961. On 1 January 1972 the Federation of Arab Republics came into existence, combining Egypt, Syria, and Libya. This lasted until 1977.

Under the Khedives the flag of Egypt was red with three crescents and stars. When the country became independent, under the influence of the Wafd Party, the flag was changed to green, with a crescent and three stars in white. Following the coup of 23 July 1952 the Liberation Rally introduced a new flag and emblem, although these did not immediately supersede the previous ones. The new flag was of red, white, and black stripes, and the emblem, which appeared over all in the centre, was a gold spread eagle with a disc on its breast containing the crescent and three stars, and grasping two globes in its claws. The eagle is said to be the emblem of Salaheddin. The three colours are like those of the Arab Revolt.

The flag of the United Arab Republic was introduced on 10 April 1958 and was similar to the Liberation flag with two green stars representing Egypt and Syria. The emblem, introduced on 25 October, was the Salaheddin eagle with a shield on its breast reproducing the flag, and grasping a green scroll with the name of the state in Kufi script. After the secession of Syria, Egypt continued to use the flag and arms until 1 January 1972, when a common flag and arms for Egypt, Syria, and Libya were introduced. The flag was the same as before but with the arms in the centre, which were based on those of Syria. The arms were in plain gold. After the secession of Syria and Libya, Egypt retained these emblems until 4 October 1984, when the present version was introduced. The emblem is that of 1958, but the new title of the state now appears on the scroll. On the flag the emblem is in plain gold.

El Salvador, Republic of

REPÚBLICA DE EL SALVADOR

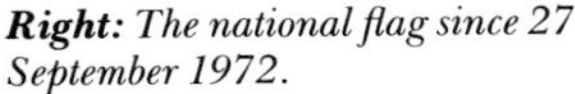

***Right:** The national flag since 27 September 1972.*

***Above:** The national flag, 1875–1912.*

El Salvador had a similar history to that of the other four members of the United Provinces of Central America. It resisted the Mexican annexation in 1822 and joined the federation in 1823. It declared its existence as a separate republic on 1 February 1841.

The flag of the United Provinces is said to have been designed in El Salvador by Manuel José Arce, who led the resistance to the Mexicans in 1822. It was very similar to the present flag and was first hoisted on 20 February 1822. The flag of the United Provinces was adopted on 21 August 1823 and continued to be used by several of the states, including El Salvador, after the dissolution of the federation.

On 28 April 1865 a flag like that of the USA was adopted, with a red canton and blue stripes, with nine stars and nine stripes. In 1875 the number of stars was increased to fourteen. The original flag of 1823 was readopted on 17 May 1912, with the emblem in the centre. This was altered in 1916 to the present form, and new regulations about the flags were issued on 27 September 1972. The state flag always has the arms in the centre, and the merchant ensign has the motto *Dios Union Libertad* in gold in the centre.

***Right:** The arms since 1912. They can be distinguished from those of Nicaragua by the trophy of flags and the surrounding inscription.*

Equatorial Guinea, Republic of

REPÚBLICA DE GUINEA ECUATORIAL

Established 12 October 1968

The republic consists of a territory (formerly known as Rio Muni) on the mainland of Africa and the two principal islands of Bioko (formerly Fernando Póo) and Annobón. The two sections were united as an autonomous region in 1963 and became independent as a federation in 1968. Since 1973 the constitution has been a unitary one.

The flag was first hoisted on the day of independence and has a blue triangle to represent the sea that links the various parts of the state. The green is for natural resources, red for the struggle for independence, and white for peace. The arms are derived from those of Bata, the capital of Rio Muni, and feature a silk cotton tree. This is the tree under which the first treaty was made between the Spaniards and King Bonkoro. The six stars are for the mainland and the five islands, and the motto is 'Unity, Peace and Justice'. Very different arms were in use during the period 1973-9 under the regime of Francisco Macia Nguema.

***Above:** The flag with the arms of the Nguema regime.*

***Above and left:** The arms and flag of Equatorial Guinea. The motto means "Unity, Peace, Justice". The arms appear in the middle of the state flag but not on the civil ensign.*

Ethiopia, People's Democratic Republic of

YE ITYOPIA HIZEBAWI DEMOCRACIYAWI REPUBLIK

Modern Ethiopia (formerly known as Abyssinia) was created by the Emperor Theodore (1855-68) and resisted penetration by the Europeans, although it was occupied by the Italians from 1936 to 1941. Eritrea was reacquired from the Italians in 1952, and has since been trying to free itself. In September 1974 the monarchy was overthrown. The present constitution was adopted on 10 September 1987. Both Eritrea and Tigre are in revolt against the central government.

The Ethiopian colours date from the 1890s and achieved their present form in a flag dating from 6 October 1897. The flag for popular use has always been plain, but for state purposes has the national emblem in the centre. Under the Empire this was the Lion of Judah, and the Lion and the Ethiopian tricolour gave rise to the emblems of the Rastafarian cult in Jamaica. After 1974 a new national emblem was introduced, but it was replaced by the present one in the new constitution of 1987. This also altered the proportions of the flag from 2:3 to 1:2. The national emblem now contains a representation of the obelisk of Axum, a large cogwheel, and a circular shield with weapons behind it. Above is a red star and around the emblem is a wreath of olive and palm branches.

The flag of the Eritrean People's Liberation Front is divided green over blue by a red triangle based on the hoist containing a gold star. The EPLF was formed in 1970.

The flag of the Tigre People's Liberation Front is red with a yellow triangle based on the hoist and a yellow star in the field. The TPLF began operations in 1975.

See: The Pan-African Colours, Aspirant and Colonial States

***Left:** The flag of Ethiopia since 1897 and a version of the Royal flag **(above)** as shown on a German cigarette card.*

*The reverse (**above left**) and obverse (**above**) of the standard of the Emperor Haile Selassie.*

FIJI, REPUBLIC OF

See: Flag Competitions

***Above and top:** The arms and flag of Fiji. The arms date from 1908 and the flag from 1970 and have not been altered despite recent political events.*

The Fiji island group was originally divided into separate chieftaincies, but in the mid-nineteenth century the island of Bau became predominant under chief Thakombau. He headed the short-lived confederation of chiefs formed in 1865, and then became King of the Bau confederacy in 1867. At the same time a Tongan chief ruled the Lau Confederacy. However, it was Thakombau who became King of all Fiji in 1871. On 10 October 1874 the islands were ceded to Britain. They regained self-government in 1937 and became independent as a Queen's Realm of the Commonwealth on 10 October 1970. Coups against the government took place in 1987, and on 6 October Fiji was declared a republic.

The flag of the Kingdom of Fiji was divided vertically into white and blue, with the shield of arms in the centre. The shield was red with a flying dove holding a palm branch in its beak. The state flag had the crown above the shield, and the royal flag was similar but on a plain white field. As a British colony Fiji was granted a coat of arms on 4 July 1908. In the shield the dove from the former flag is one of the emblems, and the motto is also the same as that of the Kingdom (it means 'Fear God and Honour the King').

On independence the present flag was hoisted, in which the Union Jack represents the Commonwealth. Blue, red, and white versions of the flag were also adopted. From 1970 to 1987 the flag for the Governor-General was blue with the royal crest and the name 'Fiji' on a *tabua*, or sperm-whale tooth.

***Above:** The flag of the Governor-General prior to 1987. The name is written on a sperm-whale tooth.*

FINLAND, REPUBLIC OF

SUOMEN TASAVALTA/REPUBLIKEN FINLAND

Established 6 December 1917

***Above, above right:** The arms and flag of Finland. A square version of the arms appears in the middle of the cross to make the state flag.*

Finland became a Grand Duchy in 1581 with its own arms, which are still in use today. In 1809 its was ceded to Russia, with the Emperor becoming its Grand Duke. Russian rule became increasingly unpopular, and the Bolshevik Revolution provided the opportunity to secede. As a result of further wars with the Soviet Union, Karelia and other areas were lost.

The flag of Finland emerged from various designs propounded by patriots in the late nineteenth century, starting with the design of Sakari Topelius in 1862. The blue cross appears to have been inspired by the ensign for Finnish yachts and is of course very similar in structure to those used in neighbouring countries. During the civil war of 1918 the provisional flag was a banner of the arms, ie, red with the lion and roses. The present flag was officially adopted on 29 May 1918, but has since been slightly modified, most recently on 26 May 1978. The shield appears in the centre of the state flag and the official ensigns.

The Aaland Islands (Ahvenanmaa) which have a large Swedish population, have had autonomy since 1921 and also a flag dating from the same period. It was officially adopted for use on land only on 7 April 1954. The colours combine those of the arms of Aaland, Finland, and Sweden.

***Above:** The flag of the Aaland Islands.*

FRANCE, REPUBLIC OF

REPUBLIQUE FRANÇAISE

Above left: *The Tricolore as adopted 15 February 1794.*
Above: *the first Revolutionary naval ensign (1790) and standard of the Emperor Napoleon (1805–1815) as shown on German cigarette cards.*

France is a country that has been through a great many constitutional changes. A kingdom until 1792, then a republic until 1804 (the First Republic), it was an Empire under Napoleon until 1814/15, and a kingdom again under the restored Bourbons until 1848. The Second Republic was formed on 12 March 1848 and

Above: *The flag of the French merchant marine prior to the Revolution. In practice the arms were often omitted.*

was succeeded by the Second Empire, under Louis Napoleon, on 2 December 1851. This fell in 1870, and the Third Republic was proclaimed on 4 September. This in turn fell with the German occupation of 1940. During the Second World War the *Etat Français* was ruled from Vichy. Then came the Provisional Government of 1944-6 and the Fourth Republic, inaugurated on 24 December 1946. This fell, over the Algerian problem, and was replaced by the present constitution on 4 October 1958.

The flags of the Kingdom of France were predominantly white, especially after the accession of the Bourbons in 1589. The royal arms were blue with the three golden fleurs-de-lis so characteristic of France. Blue and red were inaugurated in the Revolution of 1789, when the Bastille was taken and the Paris Militia organized. From then on, in combination with the Bourbon white, the revolutionary colours predominated and formed the basis of both naval and military flags.

The new naval ensign and jack were inaugurated on 24 October 1790, but were changed to the plain Tricolour on 15 February 1794, which lasted all through the Napoleonic period. The Bourbon flags were restored on 13 April 1814, but again replaced by the Napoleonic ones until Bonaparte's final defeat at Waterloo, after which the Bourbon colours were in use until the fall of Charles X in July 1830. From then onward the Tricolour became the permanent national flag, although there were subsequently variations in the military colours and the standards of the heads of state. In 1848 there was an unsuccessful attempt to replace the Tricolour with the Red Flag, and in 1871 there was an attempt to restore the monarchy under the Comte de Chambord. This attempt failed because the Count refused to accept the Tricolour as the national flag. There was no attempt to change the national flag under the Vichy regime, although during this period supporters of General de Gaulle added a red Cross of Lorraine to it, and there was a special jack for ships in the Free French navy.

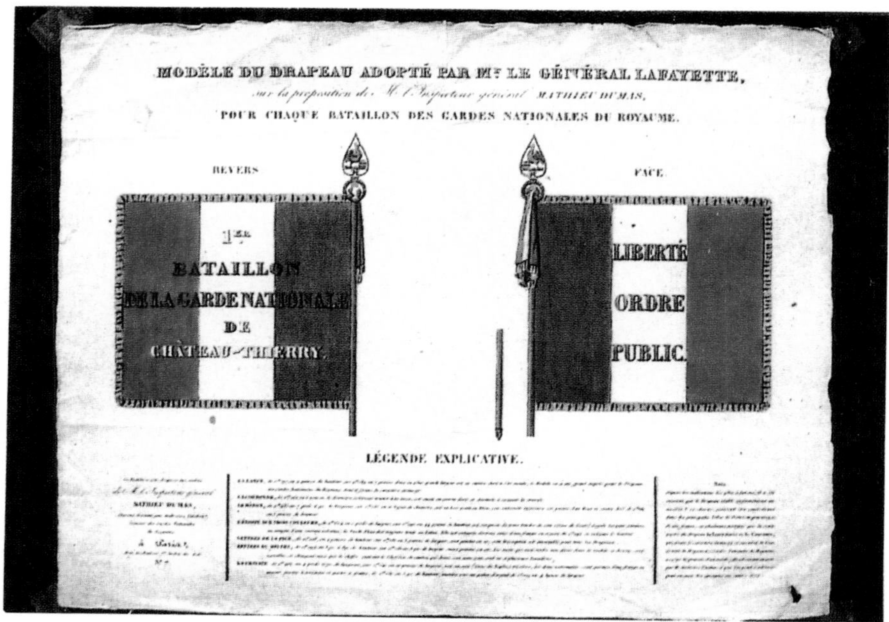

Above: *The Tricolore used as the basis of new military colours when it was restored in 1830.*

The President's standard is a square version of the national flag. Each President places his initials or emblem in the centre. General de Gaulle had both his initials and his Cross of Lorraine emblem. Giscard d'Estaing introduced a sort of republican device consisting of an axe and fasces within a wreath (France now

has no national arms, but the axe and fasces were used during the Third Republic). In 1982 the present President introduced the combined olive and oak tree device symbolic of northern and southern France.

Very few French dependencies have flags, although most of them have other local emblems. An official flag for Polynesia (Polynésie Française) was introduced on 23 November 1984; this flies alongside the Tricolour, on land only. New Caledonia may possibly acquire a flag in the near future, but, unlike the British system, the French relationship with the overseas dependencies does not normally allow for separate flags. The Marquesas Islands, the Tuamotu Islands, and St Pierre-Micquelon do have unofficial flags for local use.

Within France regional flags are becoming popular. These are mostly banners of the arms of the former provinces. The ones most frequently seen are those of Corsica, Languedoc, and Britanny. The latter flag is in fact an invention, although the ermine tails in the canton are derived from the arms of the ancient Duchy of Britanny.

The French *Tricolore*, once invented, made a massive impact on politically minded people throughout the world, and attempts were immediately made to imitate it. This first occurred in Italy at the time of Napoleon's invasion and then later on in Belgium and Germany. In the Year of Revolutions (1848) tricolours were adopted in Hungary, Romania, Slovakia, Croatia, Slovenia, Bosnia, Ireland, and Costa Rica, and these now form the basis of the flags of those countries. So common has the form become that it is almost compulsory for tricolours in some form or another to be adopted as the flags of revolutionary or radical movements, such as, for example, the Indian National Congress, the African National Congress, the Garvey colours, and many others. Tricolours used in Francophone countries tend to be vertically divided, elsewhere horizontally.

Above: *The official seal of France; France has no arms.*

GABON, REPUBLIC OF

REPUBLIQUE GABONAISE

Established 17 August 1960

Gabon was discovered by the Portuguese, but only colonized from 1839 onward by the French. From 1910 it formed part of French Equatorial Africa, and became an autonomous republic within the French Community on 28 November 1958. Independence was achieved in 1960.

The original flag was adopted on 29 June 1959 and was like the present one, except that the central strip was half its present width, and the French Tricolour was placed on the canton. The present plain tricolour was adopted on 9 August 1960, just prior to independence. The flag has the unusual proportions of 3:4. The President's flag is like the national flag, but with the arms on a white disc over all the centre.

*The arms (**far left**), flag (**above left**) and Presidential standard (**left**) of Gabon. The motto means "Union, Work, Justice".*

THE GAMBIA, REPUBLIC OF

Established 18 February 1965

The British colony was originally an offshort of Sierra Leone, but became separate in 1843. During the period 1866 to 1888 it was again linked with Sierra Leone, the Gold Coast, and Lagos. Self-government was achieved in 1963 and independence in 1965. The republic was declared on 24 February 1970.

The flag of the Gambia is based on a design submitted by a local person, Mr L. Thomasi. The red is said to stand for sunshine, the blue for the Gambia River, green for the wealth of nature, and white for unity and peace. The President's flag is the same with the whole arms over all in the centre. These were granted on 18 November 1964.

*The arms (**above**) and flag (**above right**) of the Gambia.*

GERMANY

See: Flag Conflicts, Some Famous Flag Incidents

Germany has been through many vicissitudes in modern times. The Germany left by the Congress of Vienna consisted of 39 states of various sizes, including part of Austria, and Prussia, which ultimately became the largest and most powerful one. There was no all-German government until 1848, when the Frankfurt Parliament was elected, but this was dissolved in 1850. Prussia then absorbed several of the states, including Hanover, and founded the North German Confederation (23 August 1866) and, after the Franco-Prussian War, the German Empire (18 January 1871). Austria was rigorously excluded.

The Empire lasted until 9 November 1918, when the republic was proclaimed. The Weimar constitution was adopted on 11 August 1919, consisting of 18 states, with Prussia still the largest. The Hitler regime began in 1933 and it lasted until May 1945, when Germany was defeated at the end of the Second World War. Germany was divided into several parts, according to arrangements made by the Allies at Yalta, London, and Potsdam, and was occupied by the USA, the USSR, France, Great Britain, and Poland. No peace treaty has been signed so far to legitimize these arrangements. The state of Prussia was abolished and new *länder* were created.

In 1949 two new regimes were created, the Federal Republic and the Democratic Republic, covering the zones occupied by the USA, France, and Great Britain on the one hand, and by the USSR on the other. The Federal Republic was recognized on 21 September 1949 and the Democratic Republic was established on 7 October 1949. The two regimes recognized each other on 21 September 1972 and both now sit in the United Nations. The status of Berlin, the Polish-occupied parts, and the Russian-occupied part of East Prussia remains undefined.

***Above:** The Nazi Hakenkreuz (swastika). See also "Flags in the Third Reich".*

***Above:** The traditional emblem of Germany, as shown on a cigarette card.*

***Above:** The arms of Prussia, combining the emblems of all its component parts.*

***Above:** The banner of the Grand Master of the Teutonic Knights.*

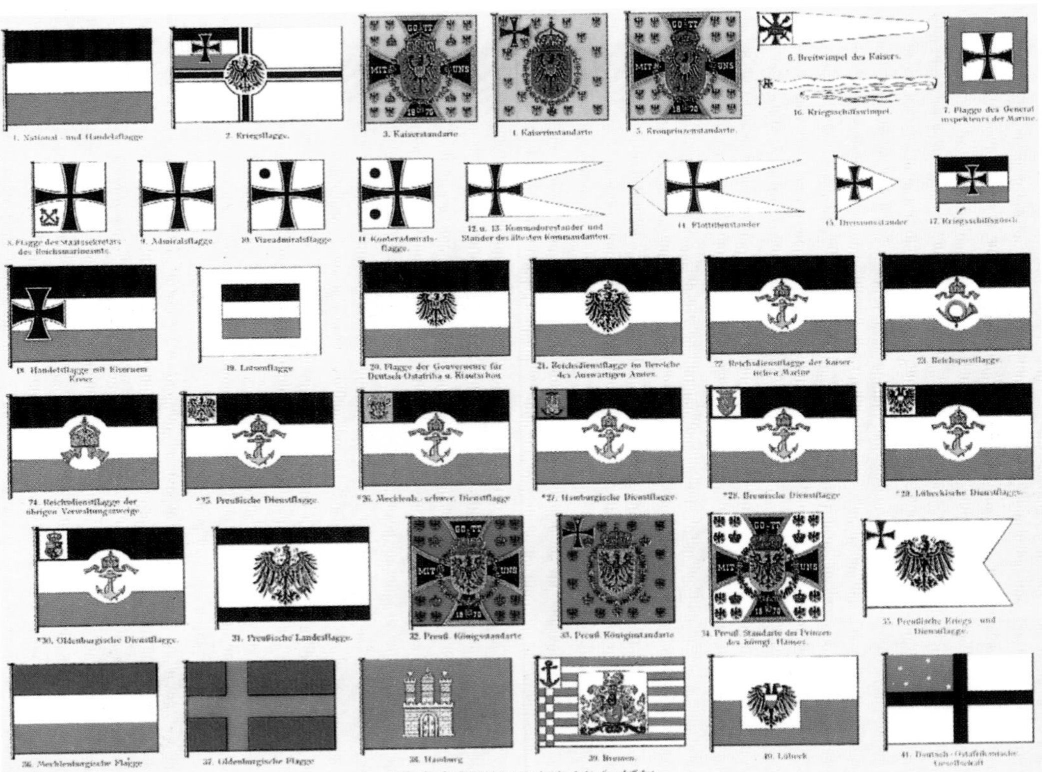

***Right:** A selection of flags from the Imperial period, as illustrated in a German encyclopedia.*

German Federal Republic

BUNDESREPUBLIK DEUTSCHLAND

The republic consists of ten federal states, or *Länder*, all with their own arms and flags, together with West Berlin.

The flag of the Federal Republic is the same as that adopted by the Federal Parliament at Frankfurt on 12 November 1848, which was itself based on the 'German Tricolour' widely used at previous but unofficial gatherings at Warburg Castle (1817) and Hambach (1832). The Federal Parliament and its works were abolished in June 1849. The initiative for union then passed to Prussia, and on 26 July 1867 the 'Bismarck Tricolour' of black, white, and red was introduced. This lasted until the fall of the subsequent German Empire in November 1918, although it remained the symbol of the right and its colours were re-employed in Hitler's swastika flags.

The German Tricolour was readopted by the Weimar constitution of 11 August 1919, but was replaced by the Bismarck version on 12 March 1933, following the appointment of Adolf Hitler as Reich Chancellor. The swastika flag was also made official on that day, and became the only flag on 15 September 1935. All Nazi symbols were abolished in 1945, and Germany remained without a flag until 12 November 1946, when the 'C' flag from the International Code of Signals, with a triangle cut out of the fly, was adopted by the Allied Control Commission for German vessels.

The Federal Republic readopted the German Tricolour on 8 May 1949, although it had already been in use unofficially for two or three years and had been adopted as the basis of the state flag by Rhineland-Palatinate on 15 May 1948. The Presidential flag of the Weimar period was also readopted, along with the arms (the black eagle on yellow) and many other symbols from the first republic. The flag of an admiral is the same as that used in the days of the Empire, and contains the Iron Cross, the badge of the Teutonic Knights from whom much of the heraldry of Prussia was derived. The flag for use by state authorities (*Bundesdienstflagge*) has the eagle shield over all set slightly toward the staff. With a triangle cut out of the fly this design is also used as the naval ensign and jack (this design is not one derived from the Weimar period). The command flags of the *Bundeswehr* are also new designs, although referring back to earlier ones. The flag of an army commander is the same as that of the Nazi period, ie, with the white part replaced by yellow.

***Above:** The arms of the German republic, adopted in 1921 and still in use today.*

***Above:** The German tricolour.*

The colours of the German flag are officially given as black, red, and gold, but the gold is really, when translated into flag terms, a deep chrome yellow. During the Weimar period opponents of the republic often scornfully referred to the flag as being black, red, and *yellow*, or even 'mustard' (*Senf*), hence the desire to give the colour a more dignified name.

A pre-Nazi flag that is still remembered and respected is the old Imperial *Reichskriegsflagge*, based on the naval ensign of Prussia, with a black cross and Iron Cross dating back to the Teutonic Knights. In the canton is the flag used as a jack in the Imperial Navy and in the centre is the eagle of Prussia. The actual design reproduced today is the pattern of 2 October 1903.

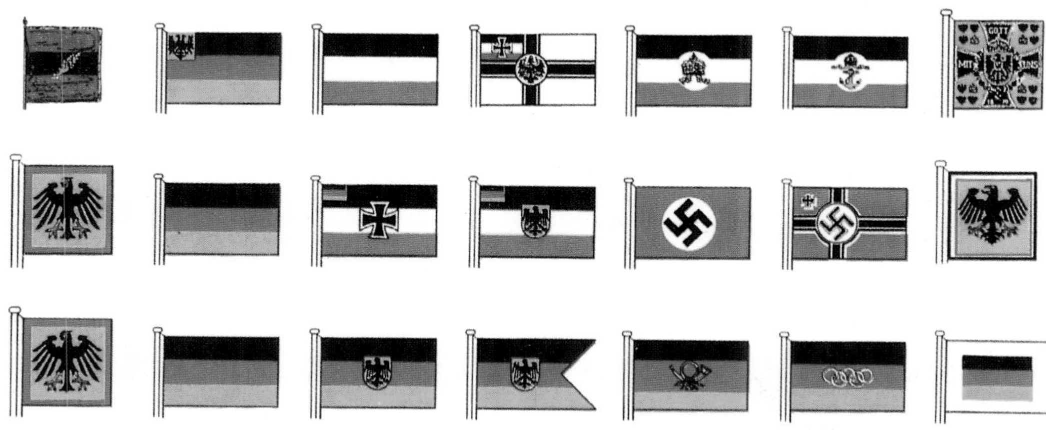

***Left:** Past and present flags of Germany as illustrated in a modern encyclopedia.*

Right: *A flag plate showing the arms of the Länder.*

Above: *The whole arms of Baden-Württemberg.*

Above: *The arms of Bavaria.*

Above: *Landeswappen of Bremen.*

Above: *The whole arms of Hamburg.*

BADEN-WÜRTTEMBERG

This *Land* is composed of three former German states: Baden, Württemberg, and Hohenzollern, which amalgamated in December 1951. Both the larger states had a long tradition of flags and heraldry, but when they amalgamated it was decided to revert to the original arms of Swabia, the black lions on yellow of the Hohenstaufen dynasty, which date back to the reign of Duke Heinrich (1216-20). The colours of black and yellow are derived from these arms. The plain flag is for popular use, while the *Landesdienstflagge* has the shield in the centre, following normal German practice. Above the shield are six smaller shields, representing component parts of the state; from dexter to sinister these are:
red and white divided in zig-zag: Franconia
white and black quarters: Hohenzollern (the homeland of the ruling family of Prussia)
yellow with a red diagonal: Baden
yellow with three black antlers: Württemberg
black with a gold lion: Palatinate (to which Heidelberg once belonged)
red with a white bar: Austria (which once held lands in Breisgau and Upper Swabia).

BAVARIA

Bavaria is the same as the pre-Nazi state, except for the loss of the Palatinate, and has the same coat of arms as those adopted for the Free State of Bavaria in 1923. As in some other German states, the arms have major and minor forms. The minor arms are the shield divided into blue and white lozenges (*Rauten*). These devices (strictly speaking, heraldic fusils) go back to the Counts of Bogen and have been known since 1204. They wre inherited by the Wittelsbach dynasty in 1242. The state flag consists of a banner of the lozengy sheild and is known as the *Rautenflagge*. Note that by tradition a white partial lozenge appears in the dexter chief of the shield containing the gold lion on black of the Palatinate; the red and white of Franconia; the blue panther of Spannheimer (inherited by the Wittelsbachs in 1248), and the Hohenstaufen lions (slightly different here from those of Swabia). The arms are supported by two golden lions, representing the Palatinate. The coronet is a *Volkskrone*, symbolic of demo-cracy, invented by Professor Hupps in 1923.

The plain flag is white over blue, and with the *Rautenflagge* was officially readopted on 14 December 1953. The flag for the Prime Minister is a white square with a blue border and the whole arms in the centre, and the flag for state officials is also square, white over blue with the whole arms on a white panel in the centre.

BREMEN

Freie Hansestadt Bremen

The state is an ancient Hansa city, ie, a port formerly belonging to the Hansa trading corporation. Its emblem is the key of St Peter, its spiritual patron. The minor arms consist of the shield with a white key on red, with a golden bejewelled coronet. The major arms have this supported by two golden lions on a platform. There are even more elaborate arms, with a helmet and crest (a lion holding a key), and red and silver mantling. These stand for the whole state, not just the city, and are known as the *Landeswappen*. The flags were regularized in 1891 and have remained unchanged since then. The ordinary flag is composed of eight red and white stripes, counterchanged by two vertical strips in the hoist. The state flag has a white panel in the centre with the minor arms thereon. A version with twelve stripes and the *Landeswappen* in the centre is also possible. The flag for vessels on state service was either of these designs with a blue anchor on a white square in the canton.

HAMBURG

Freie und Hansestadt Hamburg

Hamburg is another Hanseatic city, although it now has an area enlarged by former Prussian territory. The traditional arms are a white three-towered castle on red. In the major arms the shield has a helmet with crest and mantling and two lions as supporters. The flag for ordinary use is a banner of the arms, but the state flag is red with the whole arms on a white panel in the centre. These were stipulated by ordinances of 8 October 1897.

HESSE

Hessen

The present state consists of the old *Volksstaat* Hessen with districts from the former Prussian provinces, including Waldeck. In former times Hesse was divided into the Electorate (*Kurhessen*) and the Grand Duchy, each with similar arms. The main difference was that the lion of H-Darmstadt held a sword. The arms adopted for the *Volksstaat* in 1920 deprived the lion of the sword and his crown, and reduced his double tail to a single one. The Electorate as a Prussian province used a flag of red over white, but the general flags of H-Darmstadt and of the *Volkstaat* were red-white-red in 1:2:1. However, the

Above: *The banner of the Grand Duke of Hesse.*

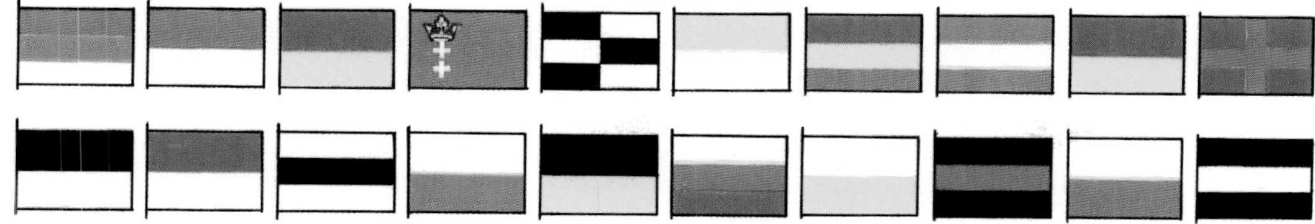

Above left: *A flag plate showing the flags of the pre-War states and provinces.*

flag for the new state, adopted on 31 December 1949, is red over white. The state flag has the arms in the centre, the shield being ensigned with a ducal coronet.

LOWER SAXONY
Niedersachsen

Lower Saxony consists of the former Prussian province of Hanover and the former states of Brunswick, Oldenburg and Schaumburg-Lippe. The emblem common to both Hanover and Brunswick is the prancing pony, which some equate with the emblem of Kent. It seems to have been adopted officially by the Guelphs in the fourteenth century. From them it passed to the British royal house in 1714 and became the main cap badge of British regiments in the eighteenth century. The white horse was resumed as arms in Brunswick and in Hanover in 1946 and on 3 April 1951 as the arms of Lower Saxony. At the same time it was decided to adopt the German Tricolour for the state, with addition of the arms. From 1946 to 1951, therefore, the state lacked both arms and flag. The state flag is the *Landesflagge*, with a triangle cut from the fly, like the national naval ensign. In square form this is used by government ministers. The flag of the Minister-Präsident is square, with a yellow field containing the arms and a red inner and a black outer border. On 13 October 1052 the *Landtag* gave permission for the renewed use of the flags of the previous component states.

NORTH RHINE-WESTPHALIA
Nordrhein-Westfalen

The state consists of the former Prussian provinces of Westphalia and the Rhineland (northern part) and the former state of Lippe. Its coat of arms reflects this, being a combination of the emblems of all three areas: the white wavy line on green for the Rhineland, the white horse of Westphalia (the same as that of Hanover and Brunswick), and the red rose for Lippe. The arms were adopted on 5 February 1948, after considerable debate, and comprehensive laws about the arms and flags were issued on 10 March 1953. The flag is theoretically derived from the arms, which appear in the centre of the state flag. It is interesting to note, however, that the same colour combination was used in the 1920s for the projected Rhineland Republic.

RHINELAND-PALATINATE
Rheinland-Pfalz

The state consists of the southern part of the Rhine Province and the former Bavarian province of the Palatinate. The arms were adopted on 10 May 1948 as part of the constitution. The tripartite shield contains a red cross on white for Trier, a white wheel on red for Mainz, and the golden lion on black of the Palatinate. The shield is ensigned with a coronet of vine leaves. The flag was adopted at the same time, an event which, as noted above, preceded its adoption by the Federal Republic. The Tricolour was chosen because it was on the territory of the state, at Hambach, that it first came into popular use in 1832, although the colours could be said to be derived from the arms.

The flag of the Minister-Präsident is square with the arms in the centre of the Tricolour, which has a yellow border. Similar flags are used by other notables.

SAARLAND
Saarland

The Saarland has twice been separated from Germany and administered by France and twice returned to the fatherland. During the first separation (1919-35) a flag of blue, white, and black stripes, derived from the then coat of arms, was introduced (28 July 1920). During the second separation a flag of blue and red, divided by a white Scandinavian cross and highly reminiscent of the French Tricolour, was used from 17 December 1947 to 10 September 1956. The present arms and flag were introduced on 9 July 1956 and became valid when the state entered the Federal Republic on 1 January 1957. The arms consist of four fields: blue, scattered with silver crosslets and charged with a silver lion, for Saarbrücken-Commercy; a red cross on white for Trier; yellow with a diagonal charged with three eaglets, for Lorraine, and the gold lion on black of the Palatinate. These are all places lying in or adjacent to the state. The flag is the same as the national Tricolour, with the arms in the centre within a white border. The flag of the Minister-Präsident is square with the arms on a yellow field with a red inner and a black outer border. Ministers use a square version of the state flag.

SCHLESWIG-HOLSTEIN
Schleswig-Holstein

The state was formerly a province of Prussia, having been disputed with Denmark in 1866. It now includes the former Free City of Lübeck. The arms consist of the combined emblems of Schleswig and Holstein. The two blue lions on yellow of Schleswig date from at least 1182 and are related to those in the arms of Denmark. The white nettle leaf on red of Holstein has been the subject of several speculative interpretations, but is also of very ancient origin. The combination of the two dates from the late fourteenth century. The shield was adopted by the new *Land* in 1948, having been used previously in the revolt of 1848-9 and by the Prussian province. The flag was officially adopted on 18 January 1957, and is in traditional colours. The flag of the Minister-Präsident is square with the shield of Schleswig-Holstein placed on the breast of a German eagle, on a red field with a white inner and a blue outer border. The flag for other senior persons is the same but oblong in shape.

Berlin

By the Declaration of 5 June 1945 Greater Berlin was made the responsibility of the four Commanders in Chief of the occupying Powers, the *Kommandatura*. The Soviet commander withdrew from this arrangement on 1 July 1948, and on 30 November 1948 the *Magisrat* became the municipal authority for the eastern eight boroughs, and the Berlin Senate was formed on 1 January 1949 to govern the twelve western boroughs. By the constitution of 1 September 1950 West Berlin claimed to be a *Land* of the German Federal Republic, whereas by the Constitution of the German Democratic Republic Berlin is its capital.

The arms of Berlin date back to the Middle Ages (they were first recorded in 1260). The arms were regularized by an ordinance of 12 June 1935, and this is the form still used in the DDR. The first flag was a horizontal tricolour of black, red, and white, introduced on 19 December 1861. But this led to confusion with the then national flag, and in 1913 a flag of red, white, red horizontal stripes replaced it, with the shield of arms in the centre. In 1943 the present tall mural crown was added above the crown. After the war the arms fell into desuetude until revived in the DDR in 1956. The flag itself now has the stripes in the proportions 1:1:8:1:1, and in practice only came into use during the anniversary celebrations of 1987.

In West Berlin a competition was held to find a new civic flag in 1952. The design for the arms and flag produced by the vexillologist Ottfried Neubecker was chosen and passed into law on 13 May 1954. The ordinary flag has the black bear alone in the white field. The state flag has the arms (the crowned shield), and the flag for members of the Senate is square with the arms in the centre and red border all round. Each of the twelve western boroughs has its own arms and flag, whereas the eastern ones have arms only.

German Democratic Republic

DEUTSCHE DEMOKRATISCHE REPUBLIK

Established 7 October 1949

Above and above right: *The arms and flag of the German Democratic Republic. The DDR flag has always had the emblem in the middle.*

The republic was established as a separate state in opposition to the Federal Republic in 1949 and assumed authority over the Soviet-occupied area. The five *Länder* of the republic were abolished on 23 July 1952 and replaced by city-regions.

The flag of the DDR is the same as that used in the Federal Republic, except that it has the state emblem in the centre. The arms originated in November 1950 and consisted originally of the hammer only, the badge of the wartime anti-fascist resistance, within a wreath of wheat ears. Later the ribbon in the national colours was added. The present form of the emblem dates from 1952. The dividers, hammer, and wheat ears symbolize the working class and its links with the factory workers and intelligentsia. The colours were adopted on 18 May 1948, at the same time as they were becoming widespread in the West. The arms were added on 1 October 1959, symbolizing that the two German states were each going their own way and needed separate flags. At the same time the civil ensign had the arms added in the canton. However, on 1 May 1973 the civil ensign was abolished altogether, although several new flags were introduced at this time. The flag of the Chairman of the Council of State, an office corresponding to President, was a red square with a corded border in the national colours and the state emblem in the centre. The naval ensign is red with the national colours in a band across the centre, with the state emblem superimposed on a large red disc within a wreath of laurel.

Since the events of November 1989 the plain German Tricolour has been widely flown on both sides of the Brandenburg Gate. The colours of the five former *Länder* which are now coming into use again are Brandenburg: red, white, red with the white half the width of the red stripes; Mecklenburg: blue, yellow, red; Saxony: white over green; Saxony-Anhalt: black over yellow, and Thuringia: white over red.

The flag of the Sorb population is a horizontal tricolour of blue, red, white.

Above: *The flag of the Head of State prior to November 1989.*

GHANA, REPUBLIC OF

Established 6 March 1957

Ghana was originally the British colony and protectorate of the Gold Coast, to which part of former German Togoland was added on the day of independence. The name is derived from that of a state on the upper Niger in the Middle Ages, said to be the original homeland of the dominant population. The country became a republic on 1 July 1960, and has since undergone several changes of regime.

The flag of Ghana is derived from that of Ethiopia by way of the Rastafarian movement of the West Indies, and has in turn given rise to many other flags of African states, so much so that its colours are now referred to as the 'Pan-African colours'. It was published on 10 October 1956 and officially adopted on the day of independence. The black star was said to be the 'lodestar of African freedom' and is also a device used in several other countries. The arms were granted on 4 March 1957 and were designed by the College of Arms in England.

Between 1 January 1964 and 28 February 1966, the central stripe of the flag was changed from yellow to white, to make it more like the flag of the then dominant Convention People's Party. The original design was restored after the overthrow of Kwame Nkrumah.

The flag of the President, which has not been used now for several years, was blue with the Presidential arms in the centre and the legend 'President of the Republic of Ghana' all around. Ghana has a wide range of other flags, more so than almost any other African country.

Above: *The flag of the President, employing a traditional symbol of authority.*

Above and left: *The arms and flag of Ghana. The arms have remained unaltered since independence.*

GREECE, REPUBLIC OF

ELLINIKI DIMOKRATIA

Established as a Kingdom 3 February 1830

Greece was part of the Ottoman Empire until 1821-9, when the independence movement liberated the heartland. Since then the state has expanded to its present dimensions. It was a kingdom from 1830 until 25 March 1924, under kings originating first from Bavaria (Othon, 1833-62) and Denmark (George I, 1863). George II was obliged to leave the country in 1923, but returned in November 1935. The country was occupied by the Germans from April 1941 to October 1944, followed by civil war until 1949. The monarchy was restored in September 1949, but in April 1967 there was a further coup and the king (Constantine) left the country. The second republic was formed in 1973, and in 1974 democracy was restored.

The flag of Greece dates from the earliest days of independence, although little is known about its origin. Crosses appeared on nationalist flags in the early nineteenth century, togethr with two popular mottoes: ευ τογτω υικα ('Conquer in this sign') and ελεγθεπια ι θαυατοα ('Liberty or Death'). A blue flag with a white canton containing a blue cross was in use by civil vessels from 1822 onward, thus preceding the accession of the Bavarian prince whose dynastic colours were blue and white. The striped flag appeared about the time of the declaration of independence (13 January 1822). It is said that the nine stripes stand for the nine syllables of the motto 'Liberty or Death', but the Stars and Stripes must have had some influence.

Other emblems dating from earlier times were the phoenix (used as the national emblem during the first republic and the Colonels' regime) and the black double-headed eagle on yellow (the emblem of Byzantium), still used as a banner by the Greek Orthodox Church and

Above and left: *The arms and flag of Greece as used since 1978.*

by the autonomous community of Mount Athos.

The shade of blue of the Greek flag has changed from time to time, often reflecting changes in political alignment. The present blue, adopted on 21 December 1978, and very similar to United Nations blue, reverts to the shade used during the first republic.

At one time two parallel national flags were in use: the plain cross flag and the striped flag. During the monarchy the first of these was used on land within the country only, and the second at sea and abroad. From 18 August 1970 to 23 July 1974 the plain cross flag was abolished, and the striped flag assumed a darker hue. The original situation was restored on 23 July 1974, but on 7 June 1975 the plain cross flag became the only national flag. On 21 December 1978 the striped flag was made the only national flag, and also merchant flag and naval ensign, although the plain cross flag is still used in connection with the Greek Orthodox Church.

The President's flag is a blue square with a gold fringe and the national arms in the centre. These also date from 1978, when they replaced the phoenix emblem.

Above: *The flags of Crete and the Ionian Islands as shown on German cigarette cards. These islands are now integrated into Greece.*

GRENADA

A QUEEN'S REALM OF THE COMMONWEALTH

Established 7 February 1974

The island of Grenada was captured by Great Britain in 1762, having been previously held by the French. It also includes some small islands in the southern Grenadine chain. 84 per cent of the population are of African origin. The colony became self-governing in 1951, and an Associated State on 3 March 1967. It became independent in 1974, and was invaded by the USA in November 1983.

The arms and flag of Grenada use the same colour combination. The arms came first, on 6 December 1973, and consist of a shield divided into red and green squares by a yellow cross, charged with an English lion, a lily badge of the Virgin Mary, and the ship of Columbus. The supporters are an armadillo and a Ramier pigeon. The flag, on the other hand, features a pod of nutmeg, symbolic of the island's nickname, 'The Isle of Spices', and was adopted on the day of independence. The seven stars stand for the seven parishes, and the colours, although based on those of the arms, recall the Rastafarian ones. As in one or two other states, the flag has different proportions for use on land (3:5) and at sea (1:2).

Prior to independence Grenada had another flag: a horizontal tricolour of blue, yellow and green with the nutmeg on a large oval in the centre, adopted on 19 January 1967. The three colours were used by all the Associated States in the West Indies at one time or another.

Top and above: *The national flag of Grenada for use on land, and as illustrated in a commemorative postage stamp.*

Above: *The arms of Grenada, showing the colour combination which influenced the flag design.*

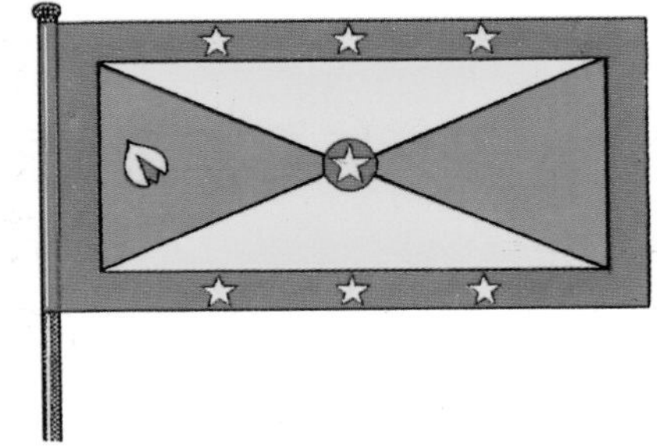

Above: *The flag of Grenada for use at sea (in proportions 1:2).*

GUATEMALA, REPUBLIC OF

REPÚBLICA DE GUATEMALA
Established 1839

Until 1839 Guatemala was part of the United Provinces of Central America, which had been formed in 1823 from the former Spanish Captaincy-General of Guatemala. Independence from Spain was proclaimed in Guatemala City on 15 September 1821, but the provinces were annexed by Mexico between 1822 and 1823. The federation of the five provinces was formed on 1 July 1823, but was dissolved by secessions in 1838-9.

The flag of the United Provinces was horizontal stripes of blue, white, blue, with the arms in the centre, and was adopted on 21 August 1823. The blue and white colours first appeared in El Salvador in February 1922. The arms consisted of a triangle with a depiction of five volcanoes surmounted by a Cap of Liberty and a rainbow. This appeared within a ring bearing the name *Provincias Unidas del Centro de America*. The civil ensign and the military colours bore the legend *Dios Union Libertad*, the watchword of the emancipation movement.

Guatemala adopted its own arms in 1825, which could be placed on the blue and white triband. A further version was introduced on 26 October 1843, and yet another on 14 March 1851. On this date the colours red and yellow were added to the triband. The fourth arms were adopted on 21 May 1858 and the flag was rearranged into stripes of blue, white, red, yellow, red, white, blue, thus making it more like the Spanish one. The fifth arms, very similar to those now in use, were adopted by decrees of 17 August and 18 November 1871,

***Left:** The flag of Guatemala.*

See: Costa Rica, El Salvador and Nicaragua

which reverted to the plain triband, but with the colours placed vertically. The arms were slightly revised on 15 September 1968. Their main feature is a scroll with the date of independence, and perching on this is a quetzal bird, symbolic of Guatemala's liberty. The state flag and ensign have the arms in the centre but the flag for civil use is plain.

***Above:** The arms of the United Provinces, and of modern Guatemala.*

GUINEA, REPUBLIC OF

REPUBLIQUE DE GUINEE
Established 2 October 1958

Guinea was made a French Protectorate in 1888, forming part of French West Africa from 1904 onward. Following the passing of the *Loi Cadre* by France, Guinea opted for total independence, under the leadership of Sekou Touré and the Democratic Party of Guinea (PDG). With Ghana it formed the Union of African States on 23 November 1958, which was extended to include Mali in December 1960. Following the death of Sekou Touré in 1984, the PDG was dissolved and the country is now ruled by the *Comité Militaire de Redressement National*.

The national flag was adopted in the constitution of 10 November 1958, and is like that of France but in the Pan-African colours already employed by Ghana, and which were also the party colours of the *Rassemblement Démocratique Africain* to which the PDG belonged. The national emblem was an elephant known as *Sili*. This appeared in green on a shield divided red and yellow, with a dove flying above and a

See: The Pan-African Colours

***Above and left:** The arms and flag of Guinea. The arms were altered after the coup of 1984.*

scroll bearing the national motto *Travail, Justice, Solidarité*. The arms appeared in the centre of the flag used by the President.

Following the coup of 1984 the elephant was removed from the shield and replaced by a rifle crossed with a sword. The olive branch now hangs down over the shield, and the motto scroll is divided into the national colours.

GUINEA-BISSAU, REPUBLIC OF

REPÚBLICA DA GUINÉ-BISSAU

Established 24 September 1973

See: The Pan-African Colours

This state adds the name of its capital to its title in order to avoid confusion with the neighbouring Republic of Guinea. It previously belonged to Portugal, whose explorers discovered the coast in 1446. The *Partido Africano da Independencia da Guiné e Cabo Verde* led the campaign for independence, which was secured in 1973 and recognized by Portugal on 10 September 1974 (see also Cape Verde).

The flag of Guinea-Bissau is based on that of the PAIGCV, the only difference being that the party flag has the initials underneath the black star, which is derived directly from that of Ghana. The party flag dates from August 1961.

Above and right: *The arms and flag of Guinea-Bissau. The motto is "Unidade, Luta, Progresso" meaning "Unity, Struggle, Progress".*

GUYANA, COOPERATIVE REPUBLIC OF

Established as a Queen's Realm of the Commonwealth 26 May 1966

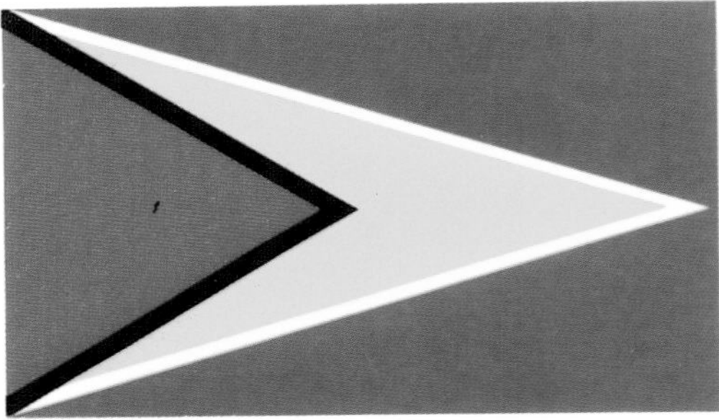

Above and above right: *The flag of the President and the national flag for use on land.*

Guyana was known as British Guiana until it became independent in 1966, having been captured from the Dutch in 1796. It became a 'Cooperative Republic' on 23 February 1970, a title that reflects the prevalence of this form of economic enterprise in the country.

The national arms were granted on 21 January 1966, and consist of a white shield with blue wavy lines; above these are a Victoria lily and below a Canje Pheasant, symbolic of the flora and fauna and the Essequibo River. The supporters are two jaguars, holding a pickaxe and a sugar cane stalk. The crest is a crown made of feathers, with large diamonds on either side, and sitting rather oddly on a medieval helmet.

The flag is based on a design submitted by the vexillologist Whitney Smith, and is known as the Golden Arrow. The original design had a red field and no fimbriations. These alterations were made by the College of Arms in England. The designer had the Pan-African colours in mind, although only 30 per cent of the population are of African origin. As in one or two other countries, the flag for use at sea is 1:2 and for use on land 3:5. The colours are now said to symbolize the forests and fields, the mineral wealth, and the zeal and dynamism of the young country. The Presidential standard was introduced in 1973 and is a banner of the arms with a green shield in the centre containing the crown of feathers. The flag of the People's National Congress, the ruling party, is based on the Garvey colours, with a palm tree on a white disc in the centre.

Above: *The arms of Guyana, which form the basis of the President's flag.*

Haiti, Republic of

REPUBLIQUE D'HAITI

Established 1 January 1804

Haiti, so-called after the Carib name for the island of Hispaniola, occupies the western end of the island now known as Santo Domingo. Originally Spanish, the area was acquired by France in 1697. The population rose against the French in the 1790s under the famous Negro general, Toussaint L'Ouverture. He was succeeded by Dessalines, who secured the independence of the country. In 1806 the latter was assassinated and the country divided into two parts, ruled by Christophe (the King Henri I, 28 March 1811) and Pétion. In 1820 Boyer united the two parts and in 1822 annexed the Spanish area. He was deposed in 1843 and many different regimes followed, including the Empire of Faustin (1847-59) and the American occupation (1915-34). The Duvalier regime commenced in 1957 and lasted until 7 February 1986.

In 1799 Toussaint L'Overture reported that he was using a white flag with a Negro's head, but after his demise rival flags were used during the war of independence, the blue and red and the black and red. The blue and red flag, originally in vertical form and said to be derived from the French Tricolour, was adopted on 18 May 1803. The red and black flag (the colours mean 'Liberty or Death') was adopted on 20 May 1805 for the Empire of Dessalines and was retained by Christophe. In the south Pétion used the blue and red in horizontal form, as now; this flag was also used by Boyer, and was confirmed by the constitution of 1843. They were also used by the Emperor Faustin, with the imperial arms overall. Duvalier reintroduced the black and red flag on 22 June 1964, and following his son's flight from the country the blue and red was readopted on 25 February 1986.

The arms date from the constitution of 1843 and consist of a trophy of arms grouped round a palm tree. They appear on a white panel in the centre of the state flag.

***Above and above right:** The Royal Standard prior to 1940 and the modern flag of Iceland.*

***Above:** The flag for the President and official usage.*

Honduras, Republic of

REPÚBLICA DE HONDURAS

Established 5 November 1838

Honduras was one of the five United Provinces of Central America (see Guatemala), but left the federation in 1838.

Honduras continued to use the flag of the United Provinces until 1866, when the present pattern of flags was introduced. These consist of the Central American flag with five blue stars in the centre (for civil use) or with the arms in the centre (for state use). The shade of blue was defined as somewhat darker than that used in the earlier flags. In 1949 the proportions were fixed as being 1:2, also unlike earlier flags, and it was also laid down that the five stars on the civil flag must be in a quincunx.

The arms also date from 1866, and are similar to those of Guatemala of 1825-43. The original triangle of Central America has become a pyramid with a volcano and two towers in front of it, and containing the rainbow above a sunrise. This is within an oval with a band around bearing the legend *República de Honduras Libre Soberana Independiente 15 de Septiembre de 1821*. Above this are two cornucopiae surmounted by the top part of a quiver of arrows. Below is a landscape strewn with tools and the entrances to mines, symbolizing the natural wealth of the country. An arc of five stars appears below the arms on the state flag.

See: Costa Rica, El Salvador, Guatemala and Nicaragua

***Top and above:** The arms and flag of Honduras. The state flag has the arms in place of the stars.*

HUNGARY, REPUBLIC OF

MAGYAR ÖRSAG
Established 16 November 1918

Above and above right: The arms and flag of Hungary. The arms in this form date from 1957.

Until the proclamation of the republic, Hungary was part of the Dual Monarchy of Austria-Hungary, the Hapsburgs having acquired the title of Kings of Hungary in 1687. During the Year of Revolutions (1848) Hungary achieved its own national government, and declared full independence under Lajos Kossuth in March 1849. In October of that year the nationalists were suppressed. Under compromise arrangements agreed upon in 1867, the Austrian Emperor formally became King of Hungary (a state much larger than the present one). The first republic of 1918 was followed by the Soviet Republic (21 March 1919), and when this fell Hungary became a kingdom again on 1 March 1920, with Admiral Horthy as Regent (a regime that lasted until October 1944, when he was deposed by the Germans). A provisional government took over on 23 December 1944 and the second republic was formed on 1 February 1946. On 18 August 1949 this became a People's Republic, which lasted until 1989 and included the period of the Rising of October-November 1956.

The national emblems of Hungary consist of what is now called the 'Kossuth' shield and the Crown of St Stephen. The shield is divided into red and white bars (the so-called 'Arpad' arms) and a red field with a white patriarchal cross standing on a green mound. These give rise to the national colours of red, white, and green, which go back to at least the early seventeenth century. The crown of St Stephen is characterized by a bent cross and was reputed to have been given to King Stephen in the year 1000 by Pope Sylvester II. The crown was captured by the Americans in 1945, but was returned to Hungary in 1978, after having lain for many years in Fort Knox.

Under Admiral Horthy the state flag had the crowned shield in the centre, but after his fall the shield only was used until the formation of the People's Republic. This introduced a Communist device: a hammer crossed with an ear of wheat within a wreath of wheat ears surmounted by a red star and tied with a ribbon of the national colours. In the Rising of 1956 this device was torn out of the flag by the patriots, and when Communist rule was restored it was decided to have no arms on the flag. The new arms introduced in 1957 were only used on special flags.

These arms have fallen into complete disuse since the events of 1989, and it is to be expected that a new national emblem will be introduced.

ICELAND, REPUBLIC OF

LYDVELDID ISLAND
Established as a Kingdom 1 December 1918

Iceland was an independent Norse republic from 930 to 1264, when it was taken over by the King of Norway. From Norway it passed to Denmark in 1381. On 1 December 1918, by treaty with Denmark, it became a separate realm of the Danish crown, but on 17 June 1944, the day that the treaty expired, it made itself into an independent republic once more. The ceremony was held at the *Thingvellir*, the site of the ancient parliament, or *Thing*. The language of Iceland is still much the same as it was in the days of the first republic.

Following the example of Norway, Iceland was inspired to obtain a separate flag, and the present design was introduced on 22 November 1913. It is very similar to that of Norway, with the blue and red reversed. The blue and white are said to be from the ancient arms of

Above and left: *The arms and flag of Iceland.*

Iceland, a silver falcon on blue. An ordinance of 1913 allowed the flag to be used on land and within the territorial waters. Regulations for the exact design were issued on 19 June 1915. With the creation of the separate realm the flag became the merchant ensign for use in all waters.

A national coat of arms (as opposed to the royal one) was introduced, as well as a government ensign. The ensign is the same as the merchant flag, but with a triangle cut out of the fly. The royal standard of the time was blue with the crowned silver falcon.

On the declaration of the republic the crown was removed from the national arms, which are now supported only by the four mythological figures, and rests on a slab of basalt. The arms appear on a white square in the centre of the government ensign to form the President's standard. The Regent, Sveinn Björnsson, had previously had a similar flag with a golden 'R' in the centre.

INDIA, REPUBLIC OF

BHARAT JUKTARASHTRA

Established as a Dominion 15 August 1947

The British assumed control of India in 1786 and brought more and more of it within the Raj until it was declared an Empire in 1877. The Empire, including Burma, had reached its final frontiers by 1890. Nationalist organization began in 1885 with the formation of the Indian National Congress, followed by the Moslem League in 1906. Although much of India was ruled directly by Great Britain, large parts remained in the hands of the Indian princes, who could be Moslem or Hindu. Agitation for emancipation increased after the First World War, and eventually led to independence in 1947. However, because of Hindu-Moslem enmity two rival states, India and Pakistan, came into existence (Burma had already been separated in 1937). India became a republic on 26 January 1950. It is divided into states based on ethnic-linguistic divisions. The former princely states were abolished in 1950.

The flag of the Indian National Congress developed gradually until 1931, when the final version was adopted. The central emblem is a blue spinning wheel known as the *charkha*. This symbolized the Gandhian ideal of self-sufficiency; it has always been stressed that the colours do not represent the religious divisions of India. The orange is said to represent courage and sacrifice, the white truth and peace, and the green faith and chivalry.

Above left and above: *The national flag of India and the capital of the Asoka pillar at Sarnath.*

A month before independence the national flag was chosen, based on that of the Congress. The only change made was to substitute a blue wheel, known as a *chakra*, for the spinning wheel. The wheel was taken from the Lion Column at Sarnath, erected by the first Buddhist Emperor, Asoka. The capital of this column, four conjoined lions, forms the national arms, adopted when the republic was declared.

The Presidential standard was adopted at the same time as the arms, and is quartered blue and red with gold emblems. The first is the national emblem, the second an elephant from the Ajanta frescoes, the third a balance as depicted on the Red Fort at Delhi, and the fourth a bowl of lotus flowers from Sarnath.

India has a wide range of other flags, usually based on British models. The civil ensign is red with the national flag in the canton, and the naval ensign is a red cross on white, also with the national flag in the canton.

Many of the flags of the former princely states are still remembered, but the only modern state to have a flag is Jammu and Kashmir. The emblem is a native plough, and the three strips stand for the three regions of the country. It was introduced in 1947 with the plough only, and with the three strips was officially adopted in 1952, as was a flag for the state President. Sikkim, a formerly independent state, was absorbed into India in 1975. It had a flag that included the *khorlo*, the Buddhist wheel of the law, analagous to the *chakra* on the Indian national flag.

Above: *The arms of India derived from the Sarnath column. The motto is "The Truth shall Prevail".*

INDONESIA, REPUBLIC OF

REPUBLIK INDONESIA

Established as United States of Indonesia 2 December 1949

Above and above right: *The arms and the flag of Indonesia.*

The Netherlands East Indies was the Dutch equivalent of the Indian Empire. Like it, Indonesia was taken over from the East India Company, in 1798. Unlike India, it was occupied by the Japanese from 1941 to 1945, during which period nationalist sentiment came to the fore. A republic was declared by the National Party on 17 August 1945, but the islands were reoccupied by the Dutch until 1949. Several states were organized in this period, which came together at the time of independence. However, in 1950 the states were abolished in favour of a unitary government. As in India a number of princely states existed, but these, too, were abolished in 1950, although there have been attempts to revive both them and the postwar states. The western part of New Guinea was ceded to Indonesia on 1 May 1963, after a period of self-rule, and in 1975 East Timor was annexed.

The flag of the National Party was red over white with a black buffalo's head in the centre, adopted in 1928. The red and white is based on the supposed flag of the medieval Empire of Majapahit, represented now by the jack of nine red and white stripes. The flag hoisted on 17 August 1945 was plain red over white, and the first one was fabricated by the wife of Dr Sukarno. The same flag was hoisted again on 17 December 1949, when Dr Sukarno was sworn in as the first President.

The arms were officially adopted on 1 February 1950 and have the buffalo's head in the first quarter. The shield is supported by the mythical bird *Sang Raja Valik*, a version of the *Garuda*, also used in Thailand. The seventeen wing feathers and eight tail feathers refer to the day independence was proclaimed in 1945. The motto is *Bhinneka Tunggal Ika* ('Unity in Diversity'). The President's flag is yellow and contains a star within a wreath of rice and *katoen* leaves, all in gold, and with a gold fringe.

The flag of West Irian was first used in December 1961 and abolished in 1963, when the area passed to Indonesia. However, it was revived on 1 July 1971 for the provisional government declared by the separatists.

IRAN, REPUBLIC OF

JAMHURIA-E-ISLAMI-E-IRÂN

Above and right: *The emblem and flag of Iran.*

Above: *The former emblem on an earlier state flag.*

Persia was the prey of many invaders during its long history, but with the accession of Shah Ismail in 1499 there was a national renaissance, and the Shi'a branch of Islam became predominant. Iran was a monarchy until 17 January 1979, when the Shah was forced to abdicate and to flee the country. On 11 February the Ayatollah Khomeini, the leader of the Shi'a sect, returned to Iran, and became head of the government. The Islamic republic was formed on 1 April 1980.

The traditional colours of Iran date back to at least the eighteenth century, but were only arranged in horizontal stripes in 1906. Regulations for the proportions and shades of colour were issued in 1933. Prior to these the flag was often shown in the proportions 1:3 and with pink instead of red. The former emblem, a lion holding a sword in front of a rising sun, dates from the order of the Lion and Sun founded in 1808, and appeared in the centre of the state flag.

The Shah had several ornate standards, employing the whole arms, but these disappeared with the Shah's abdication, as did all the flags bearing emblems relating to the Pahlavi dynasty.

A new national flag was introduced on 29 July 1980. This is in the traditional colours, but with the addition of emblems expressive of the Islamic Revolution. Along the edges of the green and yellow stripes appears the phrase *Allahu Akbar* repeated 22 times. These denote the date *22 Bahman*, or 11 February. In the centre of the flag is a red emblem that in some way symbolizes the following concepts: Allah, the Book, the Sword, the five principles of Islam, balance, unity, neutrality, and the universal government of the *Mostazafin* (the 'downtrodden'). When used apart from the flag, the emblem is green. So far, no other flags have been adopted.

IRAQ, REPUBLIC OF

AL-JUMHURIUYA AL-IRAQIA

Independdent as a Kingdom 14 December 1927

Iraq was for many centuries part of the Ottoman Empire. It was occupied by the British in 1916 and became part of the patrimony of the Hashemite dynasty (see also Jordan, Syria, Saudi Arabia). Faisal ibn Husain, who had just been expelled from Syria, was made King of Iraq on 23 August 1921. King Faisal II, his grandson, was killed in the revolution of 14 July 1958. Iraq then became a republic, but there have been several changes of regime and political orientation since then. The dominant party is the Arab Socialist Renaissance (or *Ba'ath*) Party, linked to the equivalent party in Syria.

The Sharif of Mecca, Husain, who made himself King of the Hejaz, had two sons who were also Kings, Abdullah and Faisal, and with them expected to rule all the Arab lands formerly in the Turkish Empire. The flag of the Arab Revolt was first raised in 1917 and contained the four colours of Arabism, including the red triangle that stood for the Hashemite dynasty. In about 1921 the order of the stripes was changed to black, white, red, as used today by the Palestine Arabs. The kingdoms of Syria, Transjordan, and Iraq used variations on the basic theme. In Iraq the red triangle became a trapezium, containing two stars of seven points.

Above and left: *The arms and flag of Iraq.*

The republicans rearranged the colours in vertical form, with a red star in the centre containing a yellow disc, rather like the stars that had appeared on the royal arms. This flag in turn was succeeded by the present one on 31 July 1963, which is based on the Nasserite flag of Egypt. The three stars presaged a union of Iraq, Egypt, and Syria, which has never occurred. The coat of arms is also very similar to that of Egypt, being based on the eagle of Saladin.

The flag of Kurdistan is a horizontal tricolour of red, white, and green, with a golden sun with eighteen rays in the centre.

IRELAND, REPUBLIC OF

POBLACHTA NA'EIREANN

Established 21 January 1919

Ireland gradually came under the sway of England over a number of centuries. Henry VIII eventually proclaimed himself King of Ireland in 1541, a title that remained with the English and British crowns until 1921. The Parliaments of Ireland and Britain were united on 1 January 1801, but a struggle for emancipation began at the same time. The Plantation of Ulster with Protestants made it difficult for the whole island to achieve independence as a united state, hence the Partition of 1921, whereby the Six Counties remained British when the Free State was formed. By the Constitution of 29 December 1937 Ireland became a republic, and on 18 April 1949 left the Commonwealth.

The modern flag of Ireland, known as 'The Tricolour', is modelled on that of France. The ancient flag is the well-known 'Green Flag', with a yellow harp, which dates back at least to the insurrection of 1798; but following the Rising of 1916 and the Troubles the Tricolour came to the fore as the prime symbol of the nationalists. It was eventually officially adopted in the Constitution of 1937. Its colours are said to be green for Ireland, orange for the Protestants, and white for peace, and the design was inspired by the French Tricolours used in the Revolutions of 1830 and 1848.

The Green Flag was readopted, for use as a jack, on 9 July 1947. The flag of the President was introduced on 24 May 1945, and is similar to the quarter for Ireland used in the British royal standard. The harp used on this flag and on the jack is the one now used as the national arms, based on a traditional Celtic design.

See: Revolutionary Tricolours

Above and left: *The arms and flag of Ireland.*

Left: *The life of Padraig Mac Piarais commemorated on a modern postage stamp.*

ISRAEL, REPUBLIC OF

MEDINAT ISRAEL
Established 14 May 1948

Israel was formed in 1948 in the mandated territory of Palestine, which had been entrusted to Great Britain after the First World War. The United Nations envisaged a partition of Palestine, but the actual boundaries were created by force of arms between Israel and its Arab neighbours in 1948, 1967, and 1973. The 'West Bank' and the Gaza Strip are Arab areas still occupied by Israel, and where agitation for an Arab state is intense.

The emblem of Israel emerged from the period of Zionism in the 1890s. It has been claimed on the one hand that the flag design first appeared at a Zionist meeting in Boston, Massachusetts, in 1891, and on the other that a flag like the modern one had already been displayed at the *kibbutz* of Rishon le-Zion in Palestine in 1885. Theodor Herzl, the first Zionist leader, had favoured a white flag with yellow stars, and a yellow star was used as a badge of opprobrium during the Nazi persecution of the Jews, but also appeared on Zionist flags and badges and those of Jewish volunteer forces. The actual modern design derives from the flag created by David Wolfsohn, Herzl's successor. It was first displayed at the First Zionist Congress in Basle in 1897 and was confirmed as the Jewish flag by the 18th Congress in 1933. The Star of David (*Magen David*) is an ancient emblem, used on Jewish flags since at least 1254. The blue and white are said to be derived from the colours of the *tallit*, or prayer shawl. The flag was officially adopted as the flag of Israel on 14 November 1948.

Modern Israel has a wide range of flags, which are often in a deeper blue than the national flag. The civil ensign is dark blue with the *Magen David* on a white oval near the hoist; the naval ensign is similar, but with the emblem on a white triangle based on the hoist. The national emblem is the *Menorah*, the seven-branched silver candlestick that stood in the Temple of Jerusalem until looted by the Romans. The actual form is modelled on the one to be seen on the Arch of Titus in Rome, with the name 'Israel' beneath in Hebrew letters, flanked by two olive branches.

Above and top: *The emblem and flag of Israel.*

Top and above: *The naval and civil ensigns with the Star of David on a triangle and oval respectively.*

Above: *Arab dissidents displaying their flag in Arab Palestine.*

ARAB PALESTINE

The flag universally employed by Arabs seeking to create a separate state in Palestine is that of the Arab Revolt, with the stripes in their revised order (ie, black, white, green). This flag is also used by the *Ba'ath* Party in Syria, and was used for the Gaza Strip when it was occupied by the Egyptians. It is very similar to the flag of Jordan, which has a white star in the red triangle. The display of this flag is a serious offence in the Israeli-occupied sectors, but despite this it is very widely used.

ITALY, REPUBLIC OF

REPUBBLICA ITALIANA
Established as a Kingdom 17 March 1861

Prior to its unification under the House of Savoy, Italy was a conglomeration of various states, although Napoleon had imposed a reorganization in the period 1796–1814, first by creating French-style republics, then by incorporating Italy into his Empire. The new Kingdom went on to unite the whole country, securing Venice in 1866 and Rome in 1870 (see also Vatican City State). Italy also acquired overseas possessions, including Libya, Eritrea, Somaliland, and the Dodecanese Islands. Under *Il Duce*, Mussolini, Italy also annexed Ethiopia and Albania. After the Second World War Italy became a republic (10 June 1946) and lost all her overseas possessions.

The Italian colours are derived from those of France and the flag is modelled on the *Tricolore*. This was first used in Milan on 6 November 1796 for the colours of the Lombard Legion. As a national flag it was adopted by the Cispadane Federation on 8 January 1797, although with the stripes laid horizontally. Green, white, and red flags continued to be used during the Napoleonic period, but were abolished after his fall. They came out again in the Year of Revolutions (1848) and the Italian tricolour was then officially adopted for the Kingdom of Sardinia (Savoy), with the arms of Savoy in the centre. This was the basis for the flag of united Italy. From 1851 onward the arms consisted of a red shield with a white cross and a blue border on the white central strip. The civil ensign had the shield only and the naval ensign the shield with the crown of Savoy above it.

Following the referendum of 2 June 1946, the arms of Savoy were removed from the flag on 18 June, and the national flag has been a plain tricolour ever since. However, it was then necessary to distinguish the flags at sea from those used by Mexico, and so a new shield was

See: Revolutionary Tricolours, The Year of Revolutions

decreed for the civil ensign on 9 November 1947. This is the quartered arms of Venice, Genoa, Amalfi, and Pisa, within a corded gold border. The naval ensign is similar, with a naval crown above the shield. On the naval version the arms of Venice are in a slightly different form, showing the lion of St Mark holding a sword, as on old naval ensigns of the Serene Republic. The jack is a square version of the shield in the naval ensign.

The arms of the state itself are a golden cogwheel surmounted by a star, all within a wreath of oak and olive leaves, and the name of the state on a ribbon beneath. A gold version of the arms appears in the centre of a square blue flag to form the President's standard (only used as a car flag).

During the Fascist regime the well-known emblem of the axe and fasces was in use. Fasces were bundles of rods carried before the magistrates of ancient Rome, often shown tied around the haft of an axe. These symbolized their powers to punish and execute wrongdoers. The symbol also came to stand for united strength and power.

***Above and left:** The arms and flag of Italy.*

IVORY COAST, REPUBLIC OF THE

REPUBLIQUE DE COTE D'IVOIRE
Established 7 August 1960

The French occupied the Ivory Coast in 1882 and made it a protectorate in 1889. From 1904 to 1958 it was a province of French West Africa. In the 1950s the *Parti Démocratique de la Côte d'Ivoire*, led by Félix Houphouët-Boigny, became dominant and is now the only legal party. The Ivory Coast became an autonomous republic within the French Community on 4 December 1958 and independent in 1960.

The national flag and emblem are based on those of the PDCI, whose colours are green and white and whose emblem is an elephant. The tricolour form is one common to Francophone countries and the orange stripe was added, it is said, to represent the northern savannah (cf Niger). The flag was first adopted on 3 December 1959. The colours are in the reverse order to those of the flag of Ireland, and the flag also has different proportions.

***Above and left:** The arms and flag of the Ivory Coast, a country now known by its French name, Cote d'Ivoire.*

JAMAICA

Established as a Queen's Realm of the Commonwealth 6 August 1962

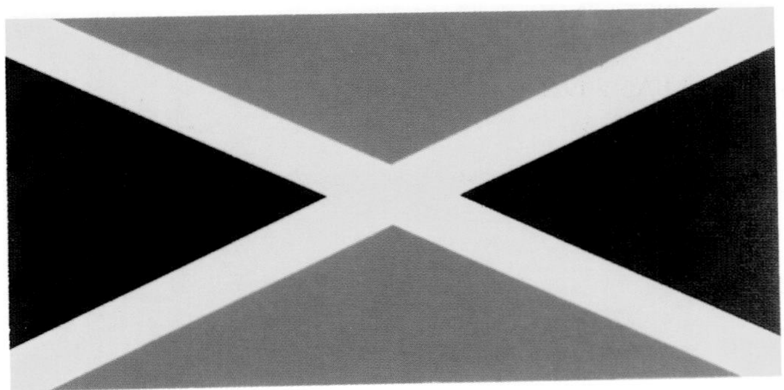

Above and top: *The arms and flag of Jamaica.*

Jamaica originally belonged to Spain, having been discovered by Columbus in 1494, but was captured by the English in 1655. In modern times it moved gradually toward independence, being the centre of the Federation of the West Indies from 3 January 1958 to 31 May 1962. Jamaica is the home of the Rastafarian movement, which began in the 1930s as a cult based on worship of the Emperor of Ethiopia, and was also the home of Marcus Garvey, who is now respected as an early leader of the black emancipation movement and the creator of the 'Black Liberation Flag'.

It was originally intended that the flag of independent Jamaica would be of green, black, green stripes separated by a yellow fimbriation, but it was discovered that this design had already been adopted by Tanganyika. On 20 June 1962 the present design was adopted instead. The colours are said to stand for agricultural and mineral wealth, and the hardships to be overcome.

The arms were originally granted in 1661 and are based on the red cross of England. An embellished form was granted on 8 April 1957, and the present motto was substituted on the day of independence.

The Queen's flag is a banner of the arms with the royal initial on a blue disc, within a chaplet of golden roses in the centre, following the pattern used in other Queen's Realms.

JAPAN, EMPIRE OF

NIHON

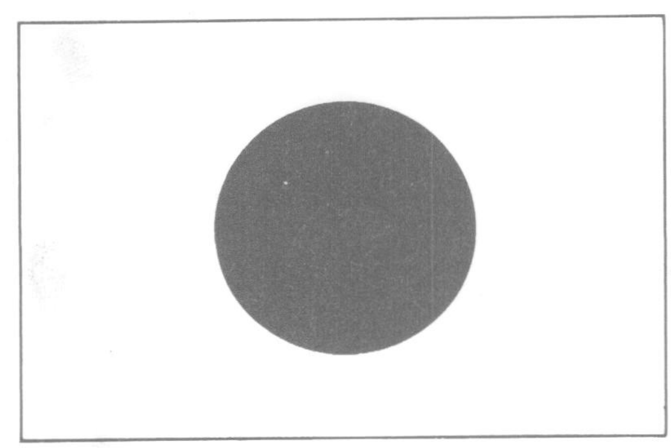

Above: *The emblem* (mon) *and flag of Japan.*

The Emperor of Japan claims to be a direct descendant of the sun goddess Amaterasu Omikami; in practice he and his predecessors descend from the House of Yamato, which united the country about AD 200. From 1186 until the 'Meiji Restoration' of 14 October 1867, the country was ruled by the shoguns, of which the last dynasty was the Tokugawa, inaugurated in 1603. In modern times Japan expanded into Formosa (1895), Korea (1910), the Pacific Islands (1920), Manchuria (1932), and eventually into China and Southeast Asia. All these gains were lost in 1945.

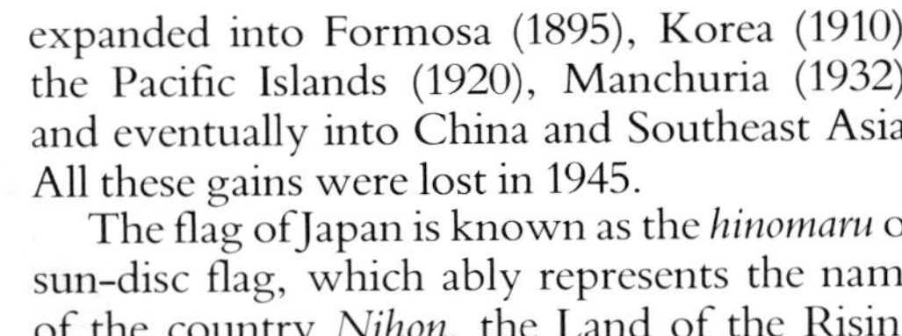

The flag of Japan is known as the *hinomaru* or sun-disc flag, which ably represents the name of the country *Nihon*, the Land of the Rising Sun. The flag dates back to medieval times as part of the Imperial heraldry, and was used as a naval ensign in the time of the shoguns. It was agreed that it would be a general marine flag on 9 July 1854. It was in fact confined to civil vessels by the law of 27 January 1870, and a range of other flags was introduced for government and military purposes.

The Imperial standard is red with the *mon* (or heraldic device) of a chrysanthemum flower. The naval ensign is the famous 'Rising Sun' flag with red rays extended from the disc to the edges of the flag.

All the prefectures of Japan have their own emblems and flags.

Above: *The Rising Sun naval ensign of Japan.*

Above: *The military colours of Japan.*

JORDAN, THE HASHEMITE KINGDOM OF

AL-MAMLAKA AL-URDINIYA AL-HASHEMIYA

Established as Amirate of Transjordan 1 April 1921

Transjordania was originally part of the Ottoman Empire and became a British mandate in 1920. Abdullah, the second son of King Husein of the Hejaz, was appointed Amir in 1921. The country became nominally independent on 20 February 1928 and fully independent on 22 March 1946. Between 1948 and 1967 the West Bank area of Palestine was incorporated into the kingdom, although claims to the area were abandoned in 1988. The name 'Jordan' was adopted in 1946.

The flag of Jordan is the flag of the Arab Revolt in its revised form, adopted in 1921. A white star of seven points, as previously used in the flag of Syria, was added on 16 April 1928. The seven points represented the provinces of 'Greater Syria' to which the Hashemites laid claim. They distinguish the flag from the form used in Arab Palestine.

The royal standard is composed of pieces coloured alternately in the national colours, with a white oval in the centre charged with another flag, which is like the national flag but with a crown in place of the star, added when the Amir became a King in 1946. The elaborate field was necessary to distinguish the royal standard from that of Iraq, prior to 1958.

The flag of the Arab Legion, the irregular force raised in Jordan, was red with the national flag in the canton and a device of two crossed swords beneath a crown in the fly. A flag based on this is now the ensign of the Jordan Army.

See: The Pan-Arab Colours

***Above and above left:** The arms and flag of Jordan.*

KENYA, REPUBLIC OF

JAMHURI YA KENYA

Established as a Queen's Realm of the Commonwealth 12 December 1963

Kenya was developed by the British East Africa Company until it became a crown colony on 23 July 1920. The coastal strip was nominally in the possession of the Sultan of Zanzibar until the day of independence in 1963, when it was incorporated into Kenya. Kenya achieved self-government and then independence under the leadership of the Kenya African National Union, led by Jomo Kenyatta. It became a republic, of which Kenyatta was the first President, on 12 December 1964.

The flag of KANU formed the basis of the flag of independent Kenya. The party flag was in the Garvey colours of black, red, and green, with white shield and two crossed spears in the centre. The national flag has a more elaborate form of shield in the centre, and white fimbriations to the central strip. The white parts are said to refer to the flag of the rival Kenya African Democratic Union, but it is more likely that they were inserted by the College of Arms in the cause of heraldic purity. The dark red colour is known as 'Kenya Red'.

The arms feature the KANU party badge, a cockerel, on a shield of the national colours based on a representation of Mount Kenya. The motto *Harambee* means 'Pull Together!' The lions refer to the former colonial ensign-badge, which was a rampant lion.

***Left:** The arms and flag of Kenya. The shield is of traditional African shape, as in several other African countries.*

KIRIBATI, REPUBLIC OF

Established 12 July 1979

Above and above right: *The arms and flag of Kiribati; the flag is a heraldic banner of the shield.*

Pronounced 'Kiribass', Kiribati is the Gilbertese pronounciation of the name given by the British to the former Gilbert Islands in the Pacific. Together with the Ellice Islands (now Tuvalu), the islands became a British protectorate in 1892 and a colony on 12 January 1916. The two groups were separated in 1975, and independence for Kiribati followed in 1979.

The flag of Kiribati is a banner of the arms granted to the Gilbert and Ellice Islands Colony on 1 May 1937, one of the few examples of an armorial banner being used as a national flag, but it was the choice of the government following a competition held prior to independence. The arms now carry the motto *Te Mauri Te Raoi Ao Te Tabomoa* ('Health, Peace, Prosperity'), in place of the original 'Fear God and Honour the King' written on the scroll in both Gilbert and Ellice languages. The bird in the arms and flag is a frigate bird.

KOREA

HAN KUK

Korea was originally a kingdom ruled since 1392 by the Yi dynasty, but it was annexed by Japan on 29 August 1910. At the end of the Second World War it was occupied simultaneously by Russian and American forces and partitioned along the 38th Parallel. Eventually two rival states were set up in the north and south. The Korean War between these two states lasted from 25 June 1950 to 27 July 1953. Since 1984 there have been serious moves toward reunification.

KOREA, REPUBLIC OF

DAEHAN MINKUK

Established 15 August 1948

South Korea emerged from the National Assembly held in 1948 following the general elections called for by the United Nations, but only controls the former American Zone. It is recognized by most countries outside the Soviet bloc as the legitimate government of Korea. It belongs to most United Nations agencies, but because of the partition neither it nor North Korea has been able to join the UN as full members.

South Korea uses a flag based on that of the former kingdom, adopted on 25 January 1950. In the centre is the yin-yang symbol of the reconciliation of opposites, and around this are four characters from the *I Ching*, which in this case represent four polarities, such as the points of the compass and the four seasons. The whole flag is known as the *T'ae Gük*, or 'Great Polarity'.

The flag of the President is blue with a golden hibiscus *mon* flanked by two 'Wonder Birds'. The naval ensign is also blue, with a white canton in which the yin-yang surmounts two crossed black anchors.

Above and above left: *The arms and flag of the Republic of Korea. The scroll carries the name of the country.*

Korea, People's Democratic Republic of

CHOSUN MINCHU-CHUI INMIN GONGHOA-GUK

The Provisional Government was set up by the Russians on 8 August 1945. The People's Democratic Republic emerged from general elections held in 1948 and was established on 9 September 1948. The ruling party is the Korean Workers' Party, formed in July 1946 by a merger of the Communists and other parties.

Above and above right: *The arms and flag of the People's Democratic Republic. The scroll bears the name of the country.*

The only flag of North Korea is that adopted on 9 September 1948. This is in the red, white, and blue colours of the former kingdom, but the *yin-yang* has been replaced by the Red Star.

North and South Korea agreed to field a joint team for the All-Asia Games in 1990, under a common flag depicting a blue map of Korea on a white field.

Kuwait, Amirate of

DOWLAT AL-KUWAIT

Kuwait was first settled in the late seventeenth century by Anaiza Arabs. In *c*1750 Sabah bin Jabir became Sheik, and members of the House of Al-Sabah have ruled the state ever since. While still nominally part of the Ottoman Empire (until 1914), on 23 January 1899 Kuwait became a British Protected State. This treaty was abrogated on 19 June 1961, the date reckoned as that of the restoration of independence. Iraq renounced its claim to Kuwait on 4 October 1963. The Sheik Sabah III assumed the title of Amir in 1971

Before 1961 the flags of Kuwait were all red and white, like those of other Persian Gulf states. The usual flag had the name 'Kuwait' in white on a red field, with a vertical white strip in the hoist. On 7 September 1961 the present flag was instituted, which is in the Pan-Arab colours, albeit arranged rather like the tricolour of Iran, and with a trapezium like that in the pre-1958 flag of Iraq. The national arms depict a hawk with outspread wings containing an Arab *dhow* on stylized waves with the name of the state on a ribbon above.

See: The Pan-Arab Colours

Left and above: *The arms and flag of Kuwait.*

LAO PEOPLE'S DEMOCRATIC REPUBLIC

SATHALAMALID PASATHU'PAAIT PASASIM LAO

Established as an Independent Kingdom 7 December 1956

Above: *The arms of Laos with the name of the state on the scroll.*

Above: *The national flag shown on a postage stamp.*

Above right: *The national flag of Laos.*

The Kingdom of Laos became a French protectorate in 1893 but was occupied by the Japanese from 1941 to 1945. An independent government was set up by the Lao Issara movement, but this was suppressed when the French returned. The Patriotic Front (*Pathet Lao*) campaigned against the government until 1973, but entered a coalition with the royalists in 1974. On 29 November 1975 the King abdicated and the People's Democratic Republic was proclaimed on 2 December.

The traditional flag of Laos, officially adopted in the constitution of 11 May 1947, is red with a triple elephant standing on a pedestal beneath a parasol. This symbolizes the old name of the country, *Muong Lan Xan Hom Khao*, or the Land of the Million Elephants and the White Parasol. Prior to 1947 the flag also had a French *tricolore* in the canton. The 1947 flag is still in use by the faction trying to overthrow the *Pathet Lao*.

The flag of the *Pathet Lao* was adopted as the national flag on 23 December 1975, having been in use unofficially for some time.

Above: *The flag of the Kingdom of Laos.*

LEBANON, REPUBLIC OF

AL-JUMHOURIYA AL-LUBAṆANIYA

Established 26 November 1941

Right and below right: *The flag and arms of Lebanon depicting one of the famous Cedars of Lebanon.*

Lebanon was part of the Ottoman lands mandated to France in 1920, but was separated out by them as a distinct entity from Syria. An independent government was proclaimed in 1941, but it only became fully operational on 1 January 1944. The constitution, first adopted in 1926, allows for the various religious sects to have a constitutional role. Despite this, the country has been in a state of intermittent civil war for more than a decade.

Each of the units in the French-mandated area had a distinct flag: the one adopted for the Lebanon was the *tricolore* with a depiction of a cedar tree in the centre. This was a natural choice since the cedars of Lebanon have been famous since the time of King Solomon, and had previously been used by the Christian governor of the area under the Turks. The present design was introduced on 7 December 1943 and seems to be based on the earlier flag. No explanation is available for the addition of the red stripes.

The various factions in the civil war have their own flags, often referring to the national flag. The Palestine Liberation Organization (PLO) flag is also widely used.

Lesotho, Kingdom of

'MUSO OA LESOTHO
Established 1829

Chief Moshoeshoe established Lesotho on the mountain Thaba Bosiu in 1829. His country became a British protectorate (known as Basutoland) on 12 March 1868, although for a period, from 1871 to 1883, it became part of Cape Colony. Independence was restored and the country became a kingdom on 4 October 1966. The Prime Minister was deposed on 20 January 1986; since that time the country has been ruled by a military council.

The traditional emblem of Lesotho is a crocodile, the totem animal of Moshoeshoe the Great. This now forms the charge on the national arms adopted on independence, and previously was used in the arms granted on 20 March 1951. The present arms are on a distinctive Basotho shield, backed by a feathery spine.

The supporters are Basotho ponies and the motto is *Khotso Pula Nala* ('Peace, Rain, Plenty'); the whole stands on a representation of Mount Thaba Bosiu.

The flag adopted on independence was in the colours of the then dominant National Party – blue, white, red, and green – with a Basotho hat in the blue part. After the coup of 1986 it was decided to introduce a new design that did not refer to the former party colours. In the present flag the three colours refer to the national motto, and the emblem is now a silhouette version of the shield and weapons from the arms in brown. This was adopted on 20 January 1987. A new royal standard was also introduced, with the whole arms in colour in place of the brown silhouette.

Above: *The flag of Lesotho, 1966–87.*

Above and above left: *The arms and flag of Lesotho. The emblem on the flag is an outline version of the shield and weapons from the arms.*

Liberia, Republic of

Established 26 July 1847

Liberia was a state established by the American Colonization Society on the west coast of Africa, largely to serve as a home for freed slaves. Monrovia was founded in 1822 and in 1833 the Republic of Maryland was formed further along the coast. Maryland united with Liberia in 1857.

The first flag of Liberia was like that of the United States, but with a cross in place of the stars in the canton. This was adopted on 9 April 1827. We have no information about what flag, if any, was flown in Maryland. When Liberia became independent it was decided to have a more distinctive flag, and the number of stripes was reduced to eleven, to stand for the eleven signatories of the declaration of independence. The cross in the canton was replaced by a white star, said to be 'a shining light in the Dark Continent'. The flag was introduced on 27 August 1847, and although it has often been proposed to exchange it for a design more distinctively African, no alteration has taken place since then.

The President's flag is a blue square with a shield in the centre containing the pattern of the national flag, and a white star in each corner.

Above and above left: *The arms and flag of Liberia.*

Left: *The Liberian flag depicted on a cigarette "silk".*

LIBYAN ARAB JAMAHIRYA, SOCIALIST PEOPLE'S

AL-JAMAHIRIYA AL-ARABIYA AL-LIBIYA AL-SHABIYA AL-ISHTIRAKIYA AL-UZMA

Established as Kingdom 24 December 1951

Above and top: *The arms and flag of Libya. The shield on the hawk's breast has been deliberately left blank.*

Originally part of the Turkish Empire, Libya was ceded to Italy on 19 October 1912. It traditionally consists of three areas: Cyrenaica, Tripoli, and Fezzan. Cyrenaica was the home of the Senussi sect, led by the descendants of the holy Mohammed Al-Sanusi. These led the resistance to the Italians, and after the war Muhammed Al-Idris became first Amir of Cyrenaica, and then King of Libya when the country became independent. He was deposed on 1 September 1969 and a military government under Muammar Qhadafi was formed. On 1 January 1972 Libya entered the Federation of Arab Republics, along with Syria and Egypt, but left in 1977, when the 'Jamahiriya', or Commonwealth, was formed.

The flag of Idris as Amir of Cyrenaica was the black flag of the Senussi, bearing a white crescent and star. When he became King this remained as the royal standard, with a white crown in the canton. The national flag, adopted on independence, was like that of Cyrenaica, but with a red band above the black part and a green band below it. The three parts were said to represent the three parts of the country, and the whole was in the Pan-Arab colours.

With the formation of the republic a flag in the Nasserite colours of red, white, black was adopted, but with no stars in the centre. A coat of arms almost identical to that of Egypt was also adopted. On 1 January 1972 the national flag became that of the Federation, which was common to all three countries, and was a horizontal tricolour of red, white, black with the arms of the Federation in gold in the centre. The only mark of difference was the name of the country on the scroll beneath the hawk.

When Libya became the Jamahiriya in 1977 the present flag was adopted, consisting of a sheet of plain green only. The arms remain the same as before, but all green, with a blank shield and the title 'Libyan Arab Republic' on the scroll. No satisfactory explanation for the plain green flag is forthcoming.

LIECHTENSTEIN, PRINCIPALITY OF

FÜRSTENTUM LIECHTENSTEIN

Established 23 January 1719

Above and right: *The arms and national flag of Liechtenstein.*

The principality consists of the two former counties of Vaduz and Schellenberg, which passed to the House of Liechtenstein in 1699 and 1712. The state was part of the Holy Roman Empire until 1806 but has been legally independent since 1866 when the German Confederation was dissolved. A constitution was adopted in 1921, and the country is divided into Vaduz and ten other communes.

The traditional colours of the state are blue and red, but they do not have any heraldic origin. They have been known since at least 1764, and were adopted as the national flag in the form of a horizontal bicolour by the Constitution of 5 October 1921. However, this was identical with the flag of Haiti, and for the sake of distinction the ducal coronet was added in the hoist on 24 June 1937.

New flag laws were brought in on 30 June 1982. The Prince's flag is blue over red with the whole arms in the centre and a yellow border all round. Without the border this is the state flag. The arms are those of the House of Liechtenstein and have no relationship with the local heraldry. A flag in the colours of the princely house, yellow and red, is often flown by loyal citizens.

Above: *The Prince's flag, as from 1982.*

LUXEMBOURG, GRAND DUCHY OF

GRAND-DUCHE DE LUXEMBOURG/GROßHERZOGTUM LUXEMBURG/GROUSHERZOGDEM LETZEBUERG

Established 9 June 1815

The ancient Duchy of Luxembourg became a Grand Duchy in 1815, within the German Confederation, but ruled by the House of Orange-Nassau, which also ruled the United Netherlands. Following the formation of an independent Belgium, Luxembourg ceded its French-speaking area to Belgium in 1839. In 1890 the personal union with the Netherlands came to an end and since then the country has been fully independent.

The arms of Luxembourg date back to medieval times and have given rise to the national colours of red, white, and blue, only coincidentally the same as those of the Netherlands. They first appeared in the form of cockades in 1787, but there was no flag as such

Above: *The armorial flag and civil ensign.*

until 1830, when patriots were urged to display the national colours. The flag was defined as a horizontal tricolour of red, white, blue on 12 June 1845 in the proportions 3:5, but the flag was not officially adopted until 16 August 1972. No exact specifications have ever been issued.

From 1890 to 1912 the flag was flown in conjunction with the blue and orange colours of the House of Nassau-Weilburg, and the banner of arms was in use as a military colour.

The standard of the Grand Duke is square with the crowned shield of arms on a blue field on the obverse. The shield is surrounded by the collar of the Order of the Royal Crown, and the field contains seven gold billets as in the arms of Nassau. On the reverse is the national tricolour. Since 1972 the banner of arms has been in use as a civil ensign.

Above and above left: *The whole arms of Luxembourg and the national flag.*

MADAGASCAR, DEMOCRATIC REPUBLIC OF

REPOBLIKA DEMOKRATIKA N'I MADAGASCAR

Established 26 June 1960

Although Madagascar is usually classed as part of Africa, it is really a distinct mini-continent, and its people are of Malayo-Polynesian origin. The dominant inhabitants are the Merina, who achieved suzerainty over most of the island in the early eighteenth century. The French were anxious to annex the island and conquered it in 1894–6. The last reigning Queen, Ranavalona III, was deposed on 28 February 1897. The autonomous Malagasy republic was formed on 14 October 1958, and it became fully independent in 1960. On 30 December 1975 the present constitution and title came into effect.

The flags of the Merina monarchs were all red and white, and several examples have survived from that period. It is interesting to note the correspondence with the red and white also used in Malaya, Indonesia, and Polynesia. The flag of Queen Ranavalona III was diagonally red over white with her crowned intials over all. The insurrection of 1947–8 used a similar flag but with eighteen blue stars on the white part.

The flag adopted on 21 October 1958 is also red and white, but with a green panel in the lower fly. This is said to stand for the *Hova*, the mass of the people. On 9 February 1976, the coat of arms was superseded by the present seal, which contains the name of the state and the motto, *Tanindrazana Tolom-Piavotana Fahafahana* ('Fatherland, Revolution, Liberty'). At the centre is a trident composed of a rifle, a spade, and a pen.

Above and left: *The emblem and flag of Madagascar.*

Above: *A flag from the time of Queen Ranavalona, with her royal cypher.*

MALAWI, REPUBLIC OF

MFUKO LA MALAWI

Established as a Queen's Realm of the Commonwealth 6 July 1964

Malawi came under European control as the Central African Protectorate on 15 May 1891, and was renamed Nyasaland in 1907. It was part of the Federation of Rhodesia and Nyasaland from 1953 to 1963 but achieved self-government on 1 February 1963, becoming independent in 1964 and a republic on 6 July 1966.

The flag of Malawi is based on that of the Malawi Congress Party, which was the dominant party at the time of independence (and still is today). The party flag, like that of the Kenya African National Union, was derived from the Black Liberation flag invented by Marcus Garvey, and was adopted in 1953. The rising sun is also part of the coat of arms, granted on 30 June 1964, and previously also part of the arms of Nyasaland. It expresses the idea of *Kwacha*, the dawn of a new age.

The President's flag is red with a gold lion, as in the central part of the coat of arms, and the name 'MALAWI' beneath on a gold scroll.

Above: *The President's flag.*

Above and above right: *The arms and flag of Malawi. The leopard on the arms is from the former badge of Nyasaland.*

MALAYSIA, FEDERATION OF

PERSEKUTAN TANAH MALAYSIA

Established as Malaysia 31 August 1957

The federation was formed on 27 May 1950 from the peninsular Malay States and the two former Straits Settlements of Penang and Melaka. Four of these states had already been in federation, from 1895 to 1941, but this did not survive the Japanese occupation. The Straits Settlements had consisted of Singapore, Penang, Melaka, and Labuan, but Singapore became a separate colony after the Second World War, and Labuan was ceded to North Borneo.

On 16 September 1963 the federation was enlarged to include Singapore and the two Borneo states of Sabah and Sarawak, but Singapore seceded on 9 August 1965. The federation has a head of state who is elected every five years from among the rulers of the peninsular states. Islam is the predominant religion.

The flag of the Federated Malay States was four horizontal stripes of white, red, yellow, and black, derived from the dominant colours of the state flags. In the centre was a white oval with a leaping tiger. All the Malay states had their own flags, including ones for the Rajas, the members of the royal families, the ministers, and in some cases for their provinces or districts. Most of them had flags for use as civil ensigns. The state of Kelantan is credited with no less than 31 distinct flags, and at one time had a very distinctive ensign consisting of a blue inscription in the shape of a tiger.

The flag adopted for the Federation seems to be inspired by the red and white colours of Malayo-Polynesia (see also Indonesia and Polynesia) and by the Stars and Stripes. A proposed flag of two *kris* (Malay swords) and a ring of stars was rejected at the last moment. Instead, the flag has a crescent and star, and the star had eleven points to represent the states. When the Federation of Malaysia was formed in 1963 the number of points, as well as the number of stripes, was increased to fourteen. This was not altered when Singapore left the Federation, and the extra point and stripe are now said to stand for the federal territories.

The arms are based on the colours of the old Federated States, with quarters for Melaka and Penang and a chief containing five *kris* for the Unfederated States. In 1963 quarters were added for Singapore, Sabah, and Sarawak. After 1965 the quarter for Singapore was replaced by a red hibiscus flower. Every time

Above and top: *The arms and the flag of Malaysia. The motto on the arms is "Unity is Strength".*

the arms of the states change, their quarters on the federal arms have to change, which has happened quite often. The flag of the *Yang Di-Pertuan Agong* (Head of State) is yellow with the arms within a wreath of rice ears in the centre.

Malaysia has a range of ensigns, including distinctive civil and naval ensigns. Each state still has its own arms and flag. The flag of Sarawak uses the same colours as used by the Brooke family, the 'White Rajas' who ruled Sarawak from 1841 to 1946. The flag of Sabah includes an outline of Mount Kinabalu, and that of Penang depicts a *pinang* tree, while that of Melaka is a variation on the national flag. The rulers of the traditional states also have distinctive flags, such as that of the Raja of Perlis, which is yellow with a blue canton containing the royal arms.

BRITISH EMPIRE
FEDERATED MALAY STATES
ENSIGN

Above: *The flag of the Federated Malay States as shown on a cigarette "silk".*

MALDIVES, REPUBLIC OF THE

DIHEVI JUMHURIYA

Established as a Sultanate 26 July 1965

The state consists of 1,200 coral islands in the Indian Ocean, and indeed the name Maldives means 'The Thousand Islands'. It became a British Protected State in 1887, attached to Ceylon until 1949. From 1953 to 1954 it was a republic, but then the Sultan was restored and the country became independent in 1965. The second republic was declared on 11 November 1968. Islam is the state religion.

The flag of the islands was originally red, as with other offshoots of Oman. It gradually acquired a vertical strip of black and white pieces in the hoist, and then a crescent that faced the hoist. In the 1930s the civil ensign was red with a green panel in the centre. The flag of the Sultan was the same but with a crescent and star in the green panel, and the flag for government service was like this but with a crescent only. The system was reorganized after the independence of Ceylon, so that the government service flag became the national flag, and the crescents were changed so that they faced the fly. When the country became independent the only change was that the vertical stripes of black and white were omitted from the hoist. The former Sultan's standard is now the Presidential standard.

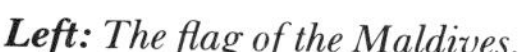

Left: *The flag of the Maldives.*

Above: *The flag of the Sultan prior to 1965.*

Above: *The arms of the Maldives.*

MALI, REPUBLIC OF THE

REPUBLIQUE DE MALI

Established as Mali Federation 20 June 1960

Formerly the French Sudan, what is now Mali came under French jurisdiction in the period 1881-95 and was a province of French West Africa. It became an autonomous republic on 24 November 1958, and formed the Mali Federation with Senegal on 4 April 1959. After independence, on 22 August 1960, Senegal seceded but Mali continued to use the name, derived from that of a medieval empire on the headwaters of the River Niger.

Mobido Keita, the former President of Mali, was sympathetic to Kwame Nkrumah's notion of a United States of Africa, and symbolized this by using the red, yellow, green, and black colours initiated by the flag of Ghana. The flag of Mali was adopted on 4 April 1959 and contained a black *kanaga*, or man-figure, adopted at the suggestion of Léopold Senghor,

See: The Pan-African Colours

Above and above left: *The flags of the Mali Federation, with the* kanaga *emblem, and of Mali.*

the Senegal leader. After the split with Senegal Mali continued to use this, but dropped the symbol from the flag on 1 March 1961.

The *kanaga* is a powerful symbol of the world-view and philosophy of the people of this part of Africa, and was used for many years as the logo for Senghor's journal, *Présence Africaine*.

MALTA, REPUBLIC OF

REPUBBLICA TA'MALTA

Established as a Queen's Realm of the Commonwealth 21 September 1964

Malta was ruled by the Knights of St John of Jerusalem from 1530 until they were expelled by Napoleon in 1798. It was taken over by Great Britain in 1802 and became independent in 1964. The republic was declared on 13 December 1974.

Much of the heraldry of Malta is influenced by the colours and devices of the Knights of Malta. Their badge was the characteristic Maltese cross and their arms were a white cross on red. From these colours came the red and white shield that was used during the colonial period. The shield had an augmentation of honour, the medal of the George Cross, added on a small blue square in the canton in 1943. On 5 September 1947 the banner of arms, including this augmentation, was adopted as the flag of Malta. On independence in 1964 the only change made was that the blue square was omitted from behind the George Cross.

The civil ensign of Malta, adopted on 11 November 1965, is the Maltese cross on a red field with a white border. The President's flag, introduced at the same time as the new coat of arms on 28 October 1988, is blue with the arms in the centre and a gold Maltese cross in each corner. The present arms supersede a graphic device adopted in 1975 to replace the original coat of arms, which dated from 1964.

The Knights of St John now have their headquarters in Rome.

***Right and above right:** The arms of Malta, introduced in 1988, and the flag of Malta.*

MAURITANIA, ISLAMIC REPUBLIC OF

EL DJUMHIRIYA EL-MUSLIMIYA EL-MAURITANIYA

Established 28 November 1960

The territory was taken over by France in 1903 and became a province of French West Africa in 1926. It became an autonomous republic on 28 November 1958 and independent in 1960. From 1976 to 1979 Mauritania occupied part of the former Spanish colony of Western Sahara.

The flag was adopted on 1 April 1959 and is completely expressive of the name of the state. The construction of the crescent and star is a very neat geometric diagram. The emblem is the obverse of the seal, containing the crescent and star together with the top of a palm tree and an ear of millet. In the encircling band is the name of the state in French and Arabic.

***Right and above right:** The seal and flag of Mauritania.*

Mauritius

Established as a Queen's Realm of the Commonwealth 12 March 1968

The island group was at one time occupied by the Dutch, who named it after the Stadholder Maurice of Orange, but in 1715 it was annexed by France, under the name *Ile de France*. It was occupied by Great Britain in 1810 and became independent in 1968.

Mauritius acquired a coat of arms on 25 August 1906, consisting of a quartered shield charged with a ship, three palm trees, a key, and a star above a triangle. The key and the star are referred to in the motto, *Stella Clavisque Maris Indici* ('The Star and the Key of the Indian Ocean'). The supporters are a dodo, the characteristic bird of the island, now extinct, and a deer, each holding a sugar-cane stalk. The flag is derived from the colours of the shield, although not the white. It was designed by the College of Arms. The civil ensign is red with the national flag in the canton and the arms on a white disc in the fly, rather like an old colonial ensign. The ensign for armed vessels is white with blue and red vertical strips and an anchor in the centre surmounted by a gold star. The Governor-General's flag is blue with the royal crest and the name of the state on a gold scroll. The Queen's personal flag is a banner of the arms, with the royal initial on a blue disc in the centre, enclosed within a chaplet of golden roses. It was first used in 1988.

Above and above left: *The arms and flag of Mauritius.*

Mexico, United States of

ESTADOS UNIDOS MEXICANOS

Established as an Empire 28 September 1821

Mexico was conquered by the Spaniards in the period 1512-27 and became the centre of their central American empire, called New Spain, which extended over much of what is now the southwestern United States and south as far as Costa Rica. The independence process began with the *Grito de Dolores* on 16 September 1810, but only became effective under Iturbide's Army of Three Guarantees in 1821. The *Plan de Iguala* (24 February) guaranteed freedom of religion, independence, and unity within a monarchical constitution. Independence was reproclaimed on 28 September. Iturbide's empire fell in 1823, and Mexico became a republic under varying constitutions, except for the period 1864–7 under the Emperor Maximilian. The present constitution is a federal one. Mexico consists of 31 states and the federal district.

The flag of the Army of Three Guarantees had three diagonal stripes of white, green, and red, each with a gold star, and an oval in the centre containing a crown. The tricolour form, based on the French model, was proclaimed on 2 November 1821, with a crowned spread eagle in the centre. The eagle is standing on a cactus, an unusual posture that is derived from the Aztec ideogram for Mexico City. This is explained by the legend that their city was to be founded at the spot where they saw an eagle on a cactus on an island. A flag form similar to Iturbide's was revived for the Empire of 1864–7, but at other times the eagle has been crownless. From 14 April 1823 the eagle has been depicted as also holding a snake in its beak. The latest form of the arms was laid down on 17 September 1968 and ensures that the arms appear in the flag for civil use as well as the state flag (necessary to distinguish it from that of Italy). The national flag is also the President's standard and the naval ensign. A flag similar to that of the Army of Three Guarantees is now the naval jack. All the Mexican states have arms, but none has a flag.

Above and above right: *The arms and flag of Mexico, as of 17 September 1968.*

MONACO, PRINCIPALITY OF

PRINCIPATO DI MONACO

Established 1297

Right and below right: *The arms and state flag of Monaco.*

The Grimaldi family established themselves in Monaco in the thirteenth century and existed by licence from neighbouring potentates, most recently that of the French head of state (1861). The area containing Monaco was transferred to France from Savoy in 1860. The principality has been ruled by the Grimaldi family since 1297 but received a constitution in 1911.

The arms of Grimaldi are lozenges of red and white, and these have given rise to the national flag. The princely arms are supported by two friars holding swords, referring to the ruse whereby the Grimaldi first gained possession of the citadel. The motto, *Deo Juvante* ('With God's Help') also refers to this incident. The shield is surrounded by the collar of the Order of St Charles and is placed on a pavilion ensigned with a princely crown. The Prince's standard and flag for state officials is the arms on a plain white flag. The national flag is red over white stripes. Both were laid down in regulations of 4 April 1881. The proportions set then were 4:5, but in practice they are made 2:3. The Prince's personal flag is white with his crowned cipher in gold. The town flag is white with a crowned shield depicting a friar holding a sword and a Grimaldi shield.

MONGOLIAN PEOPLE'S REPUBLIC

BÜGD NAYRAMDAKH MONGOL ARD ULS

Established 13 March 1921

See: The Red Flag.

After having been the centre of the Mongol Empire in the Middle Ages, Mongolia declined into a province of China. It sought to obtain its freedom at the time of the Chinese Revolution in 1911. China reasserted its authority in 1919, but at that time the area was occupied by Whites hostile to the Bolsheviks. These were expelled by the national hero Sukhe Bator in 1921 and a People's Republic was proclaimed on 26 November 1924. This was recognized by China on 5 January 1946.

The *soyonbo* emblem of Mongolia first appeared on the flag used in 1911, in blue on a yellow field. The emblem is a complex one, depicting the Buddhist world-view, and is said to have been created by Dzanbadzor, an alleged reincarnation of Buddha, in the seventeenth century. The form used by the Communists under Sukhe Bator was red with the emblem in blue and with black inscriptions. This was simplified in the Constitution of 26 November 1924, and was replaced on 30 June 1940 by the present design. In this the *soyonbo* has lost the lotus flower that formed its base, has acquired a gold star, and is now yellow on red. The blue stripe is said to represent the Mongol race. The arms of Mongolia reached their present form in 1960.

Above and top: *The arms and flag of Mongolia. On the scroll are the initials of the republic.*

Above: *The flag of Mongolia prior to 1940.*

MOROCCO, KINGDOM OF

AL-MAMLAKA AL-MAGHREBIYA

Established 6 June 1666

The royal family of Morocco is descended from Mulay Al-Rashid of the house of Filali, who established himself as Sultan in 1666. The house claims to be descended from the Prophet Mohammed via Fatima and Ali, and the ruler is styled *Amir El-Muminin* ('Commander of the Faithful'). The country was partitioned between France and Spain in 1912, but independence was restored in 1956. The International Zone of Tangier was handed back to Morocco; part of Spanish Sahara was ceded in 1958 and Ifni in 1969. The ruler took the title 'King' on 18 August 1957. In 1975 Morocco occupied the northern part of the former Spanish Western Sahara and the southern part in 1979. Morocco's possession of Western Sahara is disputed by the Sahrawi Arab Democratic Republic.

The flag of Morocco was originally plain red, despite the numerous fanciful designs attributed to the country by European flag chart publishers. On 17 November 1915 the green pentacle was added to the centre to make a flag for use by the Sultan's armed forces. It is said that the French Marshal Lyautey was repsonsible for this. The red field is said to symbolize the Sharifian claims of the royal family, ie, their descent from the Prophet. During the French occupation the *Tricolore* appeared in the canton. The civil ensign for the Spanish Zone was red with the pentacle in white in a green canton. A hexagram was also in use for some flags, not unlike the one on the present flag of Israel.

***Above:** The flag of Sahrawi Arab Democratic Republic formed on 28 February 1976. This regime seeks to gain control of the territory of the Western Sahara.*

See: The Pan-Arab Colours.

Morocco has few other national flags today. The naval ensign is like the national flag, but with a crown in the canton, and the jack is the national flag with a yellow border. On the other hand, all the provinces have distinctive arms and flags, mostly designed by a French heraldist resident in the country.

The royal arms were also designed by French heraldists, on the basis of the old emblems of the Sultans. The shield depicts the pentacle against a background of the Atlas Mountains with the sun rising over them. The supporters are two lions and the shield is ensigned with the royal crown. Underneath is a scroll with a motto that means 'If ye aid God He will aid you' (a quotation from the Koran).

***Above and above left:** The arms and national flag of Morocco.*

SAHRAWI ARAB DEMOCRATIC REPUBLIC

This regime, formed on 28 February 1976, is based in Algeria and seeks to gain control of the former Spanish territory of Western Sahara. Its flag is very like that of the Palestine Arabs, but with a red crescent and star on the white part.

MOZAMBIQUE, PEOPLE'S REPUBLIC OF

REPÚBLICA POPULAR DE MOÇAMBIQUE

Established 25 June 1975

The Portuguese first came to Mozambique in 1498 and began to settle there in 1506. The colony of Portuguese East Africa was set up in 1752, and it was transformed into an overseas province of Portugal on 11 June 1951. The *Frente de Libertação de Moçambique* (FRELIMO) led the struggle for independence. A joint government was established in 1974, which led to independence in 1975. Since then FRELIMO in turn has been challenged by the South African-backed *Resistência Nacional Moçambicana* (RENAMO), which now holds large parts of the country.

***Left:** The flag of Mozambique.*

Above: *The arms of Mozambique.*

The original flag of FRELIMO was based on that of the South African National Congress, being a horizontal tricolour of green, black, yellow, with the black fimbriated in white and a red triangle over all based on the hoist. The flag adopted for independent Mozambique used these colours but in a new arrangement, radiating out from the upper hoist, and with a simplified version of the arms in black and white superimposed. A new version of the flag was introduced on 1 May 1983, much more like the original FRELIMO flag, with a large yellow star on the red triangle, over which are laid a hoe, a rifle, and a book, emblems taken from the coat of arms, which was itself altered in 1982. The party flag is now red with a crossed hoe and hammer beneath a star in the canton, all yellow.

The President's flag is red with the national arms on a yellow disc in the centre. The flag of RENAMO is horizontally blue over red with the party emblem set slightly toward the hoist over all. The five arrows are taken from the colonial arms of Mozambique.

Above: *The first flag of Mozambique, 1975–83.*

NAMIBIA

Established 21 March 1990

Above and above right: *The arms of Namibia under South African rule and the flag is adopted on independence in 1990.*

South West Africa was annexed by Germany in 1884, except for Walvis Bay, which had already been seized by Great Britain. It was occupied by South African forces in 1915 and given to South Africa as a mandated territory in 1920. In 1966 the General Council of the United Nations terminated South Africa's mandate. Despite this, South African forces remained there, and faced armed resistance from the South West Africa People's Organization (SWAPO). A settlement was reached in August 1988 to provide for elections to a constituent assembly and independence, which was achieved in 1990.

The flag adopted by the new constitution, which came into effect on the day of independence, is based on the colours of SWAPO, whose flag is a horizontal tricolour of blue, red, and green. To this were added white fimbriations and a gold sun, bringing in colours used in the flags of other parties. The sun is like that on the flag of Taiwan, and its twelve points may stand for the country's twelve ethnic groups.

NAURU, REPUBLIC OF

NAOERO

Established 31 January 1968

Above and right: *The arms and flag of Nauru.*

Nauru is a small island in the Pacific, almost entirely composed of phosphate. It was annexed by Germany in 1888, taken over by Australia in 1914, and mandated to the British Empire in 1920. The mandate was transferred to Great Britain, Australia, and New Zealand jointly in 1947. Self-government was achieved on 31 January 1966 and independence in 1968.

The flag was adopted shortly before independence, and is intended to depict the island's geographical position, ie, just below the equator, represented by the yellow stripe across the blue of the Pacific. The star of twelve points represents the island and its twelve tribes. There is also a coat of arms, consisting of two palm branches enclosing a field divided into three. On the upper part is the alchemist's symbol for phosphate. The lower part contains a frigate bird on a perch, and a branch of *tomano*. Above the field is the star of twelve points, flanked by cult objects made of feathers and shells. The name is on a scroll above the motto, 'God's Will First', on a scroll beneath.

NEPAL, KINGDOM OF

NEPAL ADHIRAJYA

Established 1768

Nepal became part of the Gurkha empire in 1768, but accepted British protection in 1816. By the Kot massacre of 15 September 1846 Jung Bahadur became master of the country, and his family remained as hereditary first ministers until 18 February 1951, while the senior branch of the Rana family remained as titular monarchs. After 1951 the king ruled directly, but constitutional government was established in 1962.

The flag of Nepal is the only national flag that is not a rectangle. It seems to have begun life as a sort of double pennant. The emblems represent the sun and the moon, and until 16 December 1962 they had human faces. The red of the field is officially described as 'crimson', the colour of the rhododendrons that are a salient feature of the country. It has been said that the sun and moon represent the rival branches of the Rana family, but both emblems appear on the royal standard, which is red with a rampant lion holding a flag and the sun and moon in the upper corners. There are also flags for other members of the royal family.

A new national emblem was also introduced in 1962, consisting of a landscape strewn with symbolic objects, and surmounted by crossed *kukris*, flags, the footprints of Gorakhnath (the god of the Gurkhas), and a crown. The supporters are Gurkhas in ancient and in modern dress. The scroll bears the name of the country in Sanskrit.

***Above and left:** The arms of Nepal as from 1962, and the flag.*

THE NETHERLANDS, KINGDOM OF

KONINGKRIJK DER NEDERLANDEN

Established as the Republic of the United Netherlands 26 July 1581

The Netherlands at one time formed part of Burgundy and after that of the Spanish domains. From 1566 onward there was agitation and rebellion against Spain, culminating in the formation of the Union of Utrecht in 1579. A leading role was taken by William of Orange, Count of Nassau, who became the first *Stadhouder* of the republic formed in 1581. The council of the republic, known as the States-General, prevented him from becoming a monarch. In 1579 the southern Catholic provinces broke away from the union (they now form the Kingdom of Belgium). The independence of the remaining United Netherlands was recognized in 1648. In 1975 the country was occupied by France, which created the Batavian Republic, followed by the Kingdom of Holland. By the Treaty of Vienna the country became a monarchy and then included Belgium and Luxembourg, both of which subsequently broke away.

The Netherlands developed a substantial overseas empire, including Indonesia, Surinam, and the Dutch Antilles. Of these only the Antilles remain, including the island state of Aruba. Other colonies, such as New York, Ceylon, Mauritius, and the Cape of Good Hope, were taken over by Great Britain.

The Netherlands is a semifederal state, consisting of twelve provinces that elect members to the First Chamber of the States-General and have a measure of self-government.

See: The Dutch Tricolour, Revolutionary Tricolours

The Netherlands Antilles and Aruba are corealms of the Dutch crown, on the basis of a statute of 29 December 1954.

The heraldry of the Netherlands is derived from two main sources: the arms and colours of Orange and Nassau on the one hand, and the medieval arms of the provinces on the other.

***Above and above left:** The whole arms and the flag of the Netherlands.*

***Left and far left:** The royal standard, and the standard of Prince Claus.*

From the top: *The new provincial and dependency flags of Flevoland, South Holland, Curacao, Bonaire, Saba and Sint Maarten.*

The main charge in the arms of the Principality of Orange was a blue hunting horn on yellow and of Nassau a yellow lion rampant on a blue field covered with gold *billets* (rectangular shapes). Another lion – red on yellow – formed the arms of Holland. The States-General took as its arms the reverse of this, a yellow lion on red holding a bunch of arrows (originally seventeen, but after 1559 only seven) and a sword. A flag like this was used on Dutch ships up to the French Revolution, and there was also a jack with the arms in the centre. The motto of the United Netherlands was *Eendracht maakt Macht* ('Unity is Strength').

The famous Dutch Tricolour, known as the *Prinsenvlag*, was used by the privateers in the service of William of Orange as early as 1572. Its stripes represent his livery colours of orange, white, and blue, derived from the arms of Orange and of Nassau. The main use of the Tricolour was at sea, and probably because orange was a difficult colour to maintain in a sea flag, the upper stripe of the flag gradually changed to red, although orange continued to be used as a national colour. The Tricolour formed the basis of the flags used by the overseas trading companies, and later inspired the flags of New York and South Africa.

With adaptations, the Tricolour continued as the flag of the Batavian Republic and the Napoleonic Kingdom; it became the flag of the United Kingdom in 1815 and has remained so ever since. In modern times standards have been developed for members of the royal family, using the colours orange and 'Nassau Blue' and the hunting horn of Orange. The arms of the kingdom are a combination of those of Nassau and of the States-General. The blue field bears the billets of Nassau and the rampant lion holds the arrows and sword of the original seal. The motto *Je Maintiendrai* ('I will maintain'), is that of Prince William who became King of England and Scotland in 1689.

The modern jack of the Dutch Navy is derived from those used in the seventeenth century, in *gyrons* of red, white, and blue, but without the shield of the States-General.

The provinces all have arms and flags of their own, as does every locality in the Netherlands. The flags of the provinces, with one or two exceptions, are modern inventions, and some have been introduced quite recently, eg, South Holland and Flevoland. The Antilles and Aruba also have arms and flags and likewise four of the five parts of the Antilles. When Aruba was separated from the Antilles, the flag of the latter had to be changed from depicting six stars to five.

These are the dates of introduction of the various flags:

Drenthe: 19 February 1947
Flevoland: 1 January 1986 (the date Flevoland, a region won from the polders of the Ijsselmeer, became the twelfth province)
Friesland: 9 July 1957
Gelderland: 13 April 1953
Groningen: 17 February 1950
Limburg: 28 July 1953
North Brabant: 21 January 1959
North Holland: 22 October 1958
Overijssel: 21 July 1948
South Holland: 1 January 1986 (previously the flag was a horizontal triband of yellow, red, yellow)
Utrecht: 15 January 1951
Zeeland: 14 January 1949
Antilles: 1 January 1986
  Curaçao: 2 July 1984
  Vonaire: 15 December 1981
  St Maarten: 17 November 1982
  Saba: 6 December 1985
  St Eustatius still has no flag

Aruba: 18 March 1976

NEW ZEALAND

Established as a Dominion 26 September 1907

Above: *The flag of New Zealand.*

New Zealand was first settled by Europeans in the early nineteenth century. In 1840 some of the Maori chiefs ceded sovereignty to Great Britain in the Treaty of Waitangi. Self-government was achieved in 1856 and by 1871 the last Maori armed resistance was suppressed. In 1907 came *de facto* independence, which was legalized by the Statute of Westminster, 1931. New Zealand has acquired the dependencies of the Cook Islands, Tokelau, and the Ross Dependency, and previously administered Western Samoa. The British High Commissioner in Wellington administers the Pitcairn Islands.

New Zealand had a flag prior to the cession of sovereignty to Britain, borrowed from the Church Missionary Society. This was white with a Cross of St George and a further cross in the canton fimbriated black on a blue field, and the four quarters of the blue each charged with a white star. This is the so-called 'Waitangi' flag. When New Zealand became a British colony it used the normal colonial flag system, which developed in the later part of the nineteenth century: a Union Jack with a badge within a garland for the Governor, a Red Ensign for civil vessels, and a Blue Ensign for government ships. The first badge, for the Blue Ensign in 1867, was the letters 'NZ' in red, fimbriated white. This was followed in 1869 by a design like the present one, of four red stars, fimbriated white, representing the Southern Cross. In 1899 a Red Ensign was created with four red stars on a white disc in the fly. By the New Zealand Ensign Act of 1901 (effective 27 June 1902), the Blue Ensign became the national flag, and exact specifications were laid down that defined the size and location of the stars. It is perhaps unfortunate that at exactly this time Australia was adopting a very similar flag. In 1903 the Red Ensign was changed so that the stars were white on the red field. This flag can also be used on land by Maoris. The Governor's flag was changed in 1874 to the standard form with a badge of four stars around the letters 'NZ'.

The arms of New Zealand were first granted on 26 August 1911, but were revised in 1956 with the addition of the royal crown. The flag of the Queen of New Zealand is a banner of the arms with the crowned royal initial on blue within a chaplet of roses. This dates from 11 October 1962. Since the Statute of Westminster, Governors-General of the Queen's Realms have had blue flags with the royal crest on them, and the name of the country beneath, usually on a scroll, and this pattern is used by the Governor-General of New Zealand The following dependencies have flags.

Above: *The first flag of New Zealand, the "Waitangi Flag".*

COOK ISLANDS

The flag is like that of New Zealand but has a ring of fifteen stars in the fly. The previous flag was green with the stars only, but was altered on 4 January 1979, following a change in political control. The flag of the Prime Minister is blue with the islands' logo in white.

NIUE

The flag is yellow with the Union Jack in the canton. On the Union Jack are four yellow stars representing the Southern Cross, and in the centre a yellow star on a blue disc, standing for Niue itself. The flag dates from October 1974.

TOKELAU

A flag is under consideration, consisting of a blue field with a triple ring of yellow, broken to contain three white stars, one for each island, and a green palm tree, the whole design suggesting a coral atoll.

Above: *The arms as embellished, 1956.*

Above: *The flag of the Governor General.*

NICARAGUA, REPUBLIC OF

REPÚBLICA DE NICARAGUA

Established 1838

Nicaragua was one of the five United Provinces of Central America, formed in 1823 after secession from Mexico. Between 1856 and 1860 William Walker tried to set up a secessionist government. Until 1893 the British-protected Mosquito Coast remained outside the government's jurisdiction. The USA had a military presence in Nicaragua from 1912 to 1933. In 1934 General Sandino was assassinated and two years later the Somoza regime began, which was ousted by the modern Sandinistas in 1979. The 1986 Constitution provides for the autonomy of the two Moskito Coast provinces.

The flag and arms of Nicaragua are almost identical with those of the United Provinces of Central America, the only difference being in the inscription around the triangle. They were established by regulations of 4 September 1908. On earlier flags the triangle was surrounded by a trophy and a wreath of oak and laurel. On 21 April 1854 Nicaragua changed from the Central American colours to a tricolour of white, yellow, red with a new emblem in the centre, a single volcano. In 1873 the colours were changed to yellow, white, and *nacar* (light blue) but evidently reverted to blue-white-blue soon afterward.

The colours of Sandino appeared in 1927 to represent the idea of Liberty or Death. They were afterward taken up by the *Frente Sandinista de Liberación National*, with their initials in white over all.

The flag of the Moskito Coast, from 1834 onward, consisted of blue and white stripes with the Union Jack in the canton. The Nicaraguan flag was substituted for the Union Jack after the cession of 1860.

See: Costa Rica, El Salvador, Guatemala, Honduras

Above: *The arms of the United Provinces of Central America.*

Above and above left: *The arms of Nicaragua, as from 1908. The arms always appear in the middle of the flag.*

Niger, Republic of

REPUBLIQUE DU NIGER
Established 3 August 1960

Niger was acquired for France about the year 1900 and became a province of French West Africa. It became an autonomous republic on 18 December 1958 and independent in 1960. Niger is an arid country, except for the area around the river after which it is named; its people are related to those of northern Nigeria.

Niger has only ever had one flag, the present one, adopted on 23 November 1959. It is said that the three stripes represent the three geographic zones: the riverside, the savannah, and the desert, and that the orange disc symbolizes the sun. It seems likely, however, that the colours are related to those of the Ivory Coast, with which the country was once in alliance. Although often depicted as a squarish flag, the proportions are in fact 2:3.

Niger has a seal and a coat of arms. The sun is the central feature of the arms, adopted on 1 December 1962, consisting of a green shield supported by four crossed flags. The other objects are a spear crossed by two Tuareg swords, ears of millet, and a buffalo's head.

***Above and above left:** The arms and flag of Niger.*

Nigeria, Federal Republic of

Established as a Queen's Realm of the Commonwealth 1 October 1960

See: Flag Competitions

Originally consisting of several distinct British colonies, Nigeria was organized and reorganized several times between 1861, when Lagos was ceded to Great Britain, and independence in 1960. Reorganization has also occurred several times since then. The original three states are now 21, and from 1967 to 1970 the eastern region, then known as Biafra, maintained an independent existence. Part of the former British mandated territory of Cameroons was merged with Nigeria on 1 October 1961, and Nigeria became a republic on 1 October 1963.

The flag of Nigeria emerged from a competition held prior to independence. The designer envisaged the green land divided by the shining river Niger, an idea that was also in the minds of the designer of the arms, granted on 28 April 1960, although they coloured the land black, perhaps to stand for 'Nigeria'. The Y-shape of the river on the shield represents the confluence of the Niger and the Benuë. The flag was announced on 16 October 1959 and has remained unchanged since then.

The arms have acquired a new motto, with the words 'Faith' and 'Progress' being added to the origir.al. The states have coats of arms, but no flags, although the three original states did have flags. The flag of Biafra was a horizontal tricolour of red, black, green, with a gold rising sun in the centre.

The state flag of Nigeria is like the national flag, with the arms in the centre. The naval ensign is white, with the national flag in the canton and the navy badge in the fly.

***Above and left:** The national flag, and the arms of the original three regions of Nigeria.*

NORWAY, KINGDOM OF

KONGERIKET NORGE

Established 26 October 1905

Norway lost its independence to Denmark in 1387, when the male line of kings died out, and in 1814 was transferred to Sweden as a corealm of the Swedish Crown. After a long period of agitation the union was ended by mutual agreement in 1905. Prince Carl of Denmark then became King of Norway under the name Haakon VII.

The traditional emblem of Norway is the lion holding an axe, said to be the arms of King Haakonsson in the early thirteenth century, while the axe is the attribute of St Olav, the founder of Christanity in Norway. During the crisis of 1814, patriots added the lion and axe to the canton of the Danish flag. After the union with Sweden the Swedish flag was in use with a red canton bearing a white saltire. On 17 July 1821 a distinct Norwegian flag was adopted, the same as the present one, but it was some time before Sweden accepted it. In 1844 a 'Union Mark' was created, consisting of the combined Swedish and Norwegian crosses, and parallel flags were introduced, each with the Union Mark in the canton. Eventually, on 11 October 1899, the Norwegian flags without the Union Mark were permitted. Further, but temporary, changes were instituted under the Quisling regime (1940–45).

The design of the Norwegian flag is derived from that of Denmark, with the addition of a blue cross, although the proportions and construction of the flag are very different. It is said that the colour combination was inspired by the French *Tricolore*. The royal standard is a banner of the arms. As in other Scandinavian countries, the official flags have swallow-tailed flies with the cross extended into a tongue. This is the form of the Norwegian naval ensign, which can have a variety of emblems added to the canton to form specialized and departmental flags.

Most of the counties of Norway have distinctive arms and flags, but none of the country's dependencies has any distinctive emblems.

Above and left: *The arms and flag of Norway.*

Below: *The flags of some of the counties of Norway.*

OMAN, SULTANATE OF

SALTANAT OMAN

Established 1649

Oman has had a chequered history, for most of which it was dominated by the Imams. The present dynasty of Albu Said acceded in 1744 and called themselves Imams and Sayyids of Oman and later Sultans of Muscat and Oman. The reference to Muscat has been dropped by the present Sultan, who acceded in 1970. In 1954–5 there was an attempt by the Imam to set up a separate state of Oman in the interior. Oman joined the United Nations in 1971.

The traditional flag of Muscat was plain red and was the origin of similar flags used in Zanzibar, the Maldives, and elsewhere. The present Sultan instituted a series of changes immediately after his accession, effective from 16 December 1970. The red field acquired panels of green and white, and the national emblem, the badge of the Albu Saids, was added in the canton. The badge is two crossed scimitars and a dagger, known as a *gambia*, linked by an ornate horse bit. At first this was plain white, but in 1985 it was altered to red with white fimbriations. The white panel on the flag is said to represent the old Oman, which the Imam had tried to revive in 1954, and the green panel is symbolic of the fertile province of Dhofar.

The Sultan's standard is red with a green frame and the Saidi emblem in gold.

Above and left above: *The emblem and flag of Oman.*

PAKISTAN, ISLAMIC REPUBLIC OF

ISLAMI JAMHURIYA-E-PAKISTAN
Established as a Dominion 14 August 1947

Above and top: The flag of the President of Pakistan, and the national arms.

Pakistan originally consisted of two blocks of territory representing the mainly Moslem areas of India at the time of Partition. A conflict with India over the State of Jammu and Kashmir began at that time and has never been settled. Pakistan became an Islamic Republic on 23 March 1956. War began in East Pakistan in March 1971, leading to the secession of Bangladesh. When this state was recognized by Great Britain Pakistan left the Commonwealth, but re-entered in 1989.

The flag of Pakistan is based on the flag of the Moslem League, which led the agitation for a separate Moslem state when India became independent. The Moslem League flag, plain green with a white crescent and star was adopted on 30 December 1906. The present flag adds a white vertical strip in the hoist, intended to represent the non-Moslem minority, and was adopted on 11 August 1947. For use at sea as a naval ensign the flag is in the proportions 1:2. A civil ensign was introduced on 17 March 1956, of blue with a white canton containing a green crescent and star, but this was replaced on 22 October by a Red Ensign with the national flag in the canton.

The President's flag was originally blue with a gold emblem in the centre, consisting of a crescent and star within a wreath of olive leaves, with the name 'Pakistan' below in Urdu. This was altered to a design like the national flag, but with the same emblem in place of the crescent and star on 8 February 1967; the name of the country was also included in Bengali. The Bengali title was removed on 15 August 1973, following the secession of Bangladesh. The crescent and star face upward and to the hoist, as on the national arms. The arms were adopted when the country became an Islamic Republic on 23 March 1956. The shield contains quarters depicting the country's natural wealth (cotton, tea, wheat, and jute) within a wreath of narcissus, the national flower. The scroll bears the motto, *Imân Itehad Nazm* ('Faith, Unity, Discipline').

AZAD KASHMIR

The flag of 'Free Kashmir', ie, the part controlled by Pakistan, consists of three parts: the lower half is of nine stripes of green and white; the upper hoist is orange, and the upper fly is green with a white crescent and star. The four white stripes represent the four rivers of Kashmir, the orange quarter the Hindus and Sikhs, and the crescent and star the dominant Moslem population.

*The civil ensign **(above)** and the national flag **(top left)** of Pakistan.*

PANAMA, REPUBLIC OF

REPÚBLICA DE PANAMÁ
Established 3 November 1903

Above and right: Two flags of Panama, one of them from a United Nations postage stamp series.

See: The Heritage of the Stars and Stripes

Panama was originally a department of the United States of Columbia, but had long been earmarked as one of the two possible sites for a canal to link the Caribbean with the Pacific ocean (the other being Nicaragua). In 1901 the United States secured the sole right to build such a canal. Negotiations with Colombia broke down in 1903, and the province of Panama chose to make a unilateral declaration of independence, which was immediately recognized by the USA, and then went on to make the Canal Treaty with America. By a more recent treaty the United States will hand over the canal to Panama at the end of 1999.

Sovereignty over the former Canal Zone was restored to Panama on 1 October 1979; prior to that the Canal Zone had been administered exclusively by the USA.

Not unnaturally the flag of Panama reminds one of the flag of the USA, although it is said that its colours stand for the *Colorados* (the 'Reds', or radical party) and for the Conservatives, the traditional parties of the time, with white for peace. It was designed by the first President, Manuel Amador Guerrero, and first hoisted on 20 December 1903. Bunau-Varilla, another of the promoters of independence, is said to have created a rival version in October 1903, consisting of seven red and yellow stripes with a blue canton (thus in the Colombian colours), and with two linked suns or globes in the canton. However, he then abandoned this in favour of Guerrero's design, and in fact his wife purchased the material in New York and sewed the first flag, which Guerrero smuggled into Panama. In the 1960s there was considerable trouble over Panama's right to fly its flag in the Canal Zone, which was only resolved by the Treaty of 1977.

***Above:** The arms of Panama. The motto is "For the Benefit of the World".*

PAPUA NEW GUINEA

PAPUA NIUGINI

Established as a Queen's Realm of the Commonwealth 16 September 1975

Papua New Guinea consists of two former territories: Papua, which was first annexed by Queensland in 1883, and New Guinea, consisting of the northeastern part of the island and several groups of adjacent islands, which were obtained by Germany in 1884–9. Papua passed to Australia in 1901 and after the First World War Australia received the Mandate for New Guinea. After the Second World War New Guinea was united with Papua as a single unit. It became self-governing on 1 December 1973 and independent in 1975, although the desire of the island of Bougainville to secede is still a live issue.

***Above and left:** The arms and flag of Papua New Guinea depicting the bird of paradise.*

The Germans introduced the idea of the bird of paradise as a badge for New Guinea, and it remained a useful local emblem. Under the British and Australians Papua had ensign-badges, but there was no proper flag until 1970, when a flag of blue, yellow, and green vertical stripes, with a Southern Cross on the blue part and a bird of paradise on the green part, was introduced. These colours did not meet with favour locally, and on 12 March 1971 the House of Assembly voted to adopt the present design. This became the flag of an independent state in 1975.

Each of the provinces has its own emblem and provincial flag, many of which are extremely colourful and generally based on local art forms. The naval ensign of Papua New Guinea is white with the national flag in the canton.

PARAGUAY, REPUBLIC OF

REPUBLICA DE PARAGUAY

Established 14 May 1811

Following the moves toward independence from Spain in Argentina, there was a similar development in Paraguay, where a government independent of both Spain and Argentina was established in 1811. The first dictator, Dr Francia, took over in 1814 and ruled until 1840. In later years Paraguay fought very costly wars against her neighbours, one result of which was to tip the balance of the population toward the Guaraní Indian element.

The star in the centre of the arms on the obverse side of the flag of Paraguay is known as the Star of May, to celebrate the declaration of independence. Several designs were used in the early years, and the red, white, and blue tricolour first appeared in 1812. It was not until 25 November 1842 that the present design was instituted, which kept up the tradition of having a different emblem on each side. During Francia's dictatorship the emblems had been

***Above left:** The national flag (obverse side) of Paraguay.*

***Above:** The emblem from the reverse side of the Paraguayan flag.*

the arms of Asunción and of Spain, although the arms date from his regime (1821), but in 1842 it was decided to use the national arms on the obverse and a device known as the Treasury Seal on the reverse.

The President's flag is based on an earlier model of that of the USA, and has the arms in the centre and a gold star in each canton. There is a very wide variety of flags for the various branches and officers of the armed forces.

PERU, REPUBLIC OF

REPÚBLICA DE PERÚ

Established 28 July 1821

***Above and right:** The arms and flag of Peru.*

See: Central and South America

The struggle for independence in Peru began with the landing of José de San Martín on 8 September 1820, and he became the first Protector of the republic declared in 1821. He was succeeded by Don José Bernardo Tagle and then by Simón Bolívar who, with the help of Sucre, defeated the Spaniards in 1824. Bolivia was formed into a separate state, named Upper Peru, in 1825. On the other hand, Peru has gained considerable territory from Ecuador and Chile.

The flag of the Peruvian Legion formed by San Martín was divided diagonally into red and white triangles, with an emblem in the centre showing the sun rising over the Andes, all within a wreath. In 1822, however, the national flag, as it had then become, was altered by the Marquis of Torre Tagle to one of horizontal red and white stripes, with a radiant sun in the centre. Finally, on 25 February 1825, these stripes, were turned into vertical ones, perhaps to avoid confusion with the flag of Spain.

The arms of Peru appear in two forms, each with the same shield, which were adopted at the same time as the flag. The shield depicts the wealth of the country: a vicuña, a quinine tree, and a cornucopia. The shield is supported by national flags and crowned with a laurel wreath. This is the form in which the arms appear on the President's flag, which is otherwise white and has four gold suns in the corners. On the naval ensign and state flag, however, the shield is without the flags and instead has a wreath of laurel and palm around it, tied with red and white ribbons. Peru has a wide range of departmental and rank flags.

THE PHILIPPINES, REPUBLIC OF

REPUBLIKA NG PILIPINAS

Established 4 July 1946

***Above and right:** The arms and flag of the Philippines.*

The Philippine Islands were acquired by Spain in 1565 and remained in their hands until the defeat of Spain by the USA in the war of 1898. The United States then controlled the archipelago until 1946, apart from the Japanese occupation of 1941-5. The nationalist movement began in the 1890s and under the Americans the Philippines gained an increasing amount of home rule, becoming a Commonwealth on 14 May 1935. Independence was postponed until after the Second World War, due to the Japanese intervention.

The nationalist emblems were mostly derived from Masonic sources and employed red and white flags. The sun emblem first appeared in 1896, and was added to the flag designed in 1898 for the republic declared at Cavite on 12 June 1898. The eight rays on the sun are said to represent the eight provinces in revolt against Spain, and the three stars the three main groups of islands.

The Americans allowed the flag to be used until 1907, when it was outlawed, but it was revived in 1920 and became the flag of the Commonwealth in 1935. The Japanese also adopted an ambiguous attitude to the flag, and it was not until 1945 that it became legal again.

The President's flag is blue with the sun in the centre surmounted by a red triangle bearing a golden sea lion and three stars. Around this is a ring of stars like those on the American Presidential standard. These are supposed to stand for the departments of the republic, but in fact do not correspond with their number.

POLAND, REPUBLIC OF

POLISKA RZECZPOSPOLITA

Established 10 November 1918

In the great period of Polish history the country included what is now Lithuania, Byelorussia, and the western Ukraine, but successive partitions reduced its size until it was finally extinguished in 1795. Napoleon created a Duchy of Warsaw, but in 1815 this passed to Russia, and it was not until the end of the First World War that Poland was able to free itself and win back territory from Germany. Germany invaded and conquered the country in 1939 and partitioned it with the Soviet Union, and in 1945 it was entirely occupied by the USSR. A provisional government was formed, which was followed in 1947 by the People's Republic. The Communist Party lost power in 1989, and a government was formed by 'Solidarity'.

The traditional emblem of Poland is a white eagle on red, which has been depicted in various ways over the centuries. During the period of the Poland-Lithuania Commonwealth it was impaled with the White Knight emblem, which is now in use again in Lithuania. The national emblem was revived in 1918, and the present shield is based on one designed in 1927, although the crown was removed in 1952, only to be restored in 1990. The shield gave rise to the national colours of white and red, which were officially readopted as the national flag on 1 August 1919.

Before 1952 there was a flag for the President, which was a banner of the arms with an ornate white border. It is possible that this flag will also be restored. The civil ensign is like the national flag, but with the national shield in the centre of the white strip. The naval ensign has a similar design, but the flag is 1:2 and swallow-tailed. The jack has an arm with a sabre on a red disc in the centre, which recalls the sixteenth-century naval ensign, while the cross pattée form recalls the pattern of pre-Communist military colours.

Above and above left: *The arms and flag of Poland, with the crown restored to the white eagle. As of early 1990, this shield has been used on the state flag and civil ensign in the middle of the white strip.*

PORTUGAL, REPUBLIC OF

REPÚBLICA PORTUGUESE

Established 5 October 1910

As a result of being the first country to explore the world beyond Europe, Portugal acquired a huge overseas empire, which at one time included Brazil, Angola, Mozambique, Guinea, Timor, and many smaller places. A constitutional union was formed with Brazil on 16 December 1815, called the Kingdom of Portugal, Brazil, and the Algarve, but in September 1822 Brazil renounced its allegiance to Portugal. This was followed by the civil war between rival claimants to the throne of Portugal. The monarchy was overthrown in 1910, and was followed by the Salazar dictatorship (1933-74). After the restoration of democracy the remaining overseas empire was emancipated. The Azores and Madeira remain autonomous within the Portuguese republic.

Above: *An early flag of Portugal with the armillary sphere.*

See: Portugal and Brazil

Portuguese national heraldry contains several intriguing items. One is the blue shield with five white discs, known as the *quinas*, dating from 1139. This is perhaps the oldest emblem, and represents Portuguese victories over the Moors. Another is the cross of the Order of Christ (founded in 1317), a distinctive crimson cross containing a silver cross. The order is one of Portugal's oldest and most respected. A third object is the *armilla*, or sphere, a model of the motion of the earth that demonstrates Copernican theory. The red border around the Portu-

Above and above left: *The arms and flag of Portugal.*

guese shield, with seven castles, is known as the 'Bordure of Castile' and commemorates the marriage of Alfonso III with Beatrice of Castile in 1252.

Early Portuguese flags had the blue and white shield only. Later ones bore the whole royal arms, and by the seventeenth century also employed the cross of the Order of Christ, crosses of other orders and the armillary sphere. This emblem, together with the colours green and white, was used from the reign

***Right:** The banner of the Order of Christ as shown on a German cigarette card.*

of Henry the Navigator. The flag adopted for the United Kingdom on 13 May 1816 was white with the Portuguese shield placed on a crowned *armilla* (then the official emblem of Brazil). The colours of blue and white were officially adopted on 23 August 1823 for the national cockade. During the civil war a flag of blue and white was adopted by the supporters of Queen Maria in the Azores (18 October 1830), and after their victory became the national flag of Portugal. The crowned shield only was placed on the partition line of the blue and white panels.

After the revolution the crown was dropped from the shield and replaced by a simplified version of the *armilla*. The colours were changed to red and green: red for revolution and green from the ancient flags. This flag was decreed on 19 June 1911 and has remained the same ever since.

The flag of the President is plain green with the shield and sphere in the centre. The cross of the Order of Christ continued to be used on flags for overseas governors, and is still in use on the flag of the Governor of Macao, Portugal's only remaining colony. The cross is also used on the flag of Madeira, adopted on 12 September 1978. The flag of the Azores, adopted on 2 April 1979, commemorates the fact that the first flag was designed there, and also carries a hawk, symbolic of the islands' name (*açor* means hawk).

Qatar, State of

DAWLAT QATAR

Established 12 September 1868

Qatar was originally closely linked to Bahrain, but in 1868 the British imposed a settlement whereby Qatar became nominally independent. From 1871 to 1915 the country was occupied by the Turks who in turn were driven out by the Saudi Arabians, who then recognized Qatari independence. Qatar was in treaty relationship with Great Britain from 1916 to 3 September 1971. The rulers, of the House of Al-Thani, now bear the title Amir.

***Above and above right:** The emblem and national flag of Qatar. Note the unusual proportions of the flag.*

The flag of Qatar is probably derived from that of Bahrain, but has experienced some changes over the years. The serrated border is still there, but the colour of the red has become deeper, to a shade now known as 'Qatar maroon', and the flag's proportions have become extended. These changes were made official in 1949. At one time there were red diamond shapes on the white part near the points of the serrations, and also the name in Arabic script on the red part.

Qatar is in the process of adopting a range of flags for its armed forces. These are white for the army and blue for the navy, with their respective badges. The national emblem is a disc with two crossed swords and a dhow sailing near a coast with two palm trees.

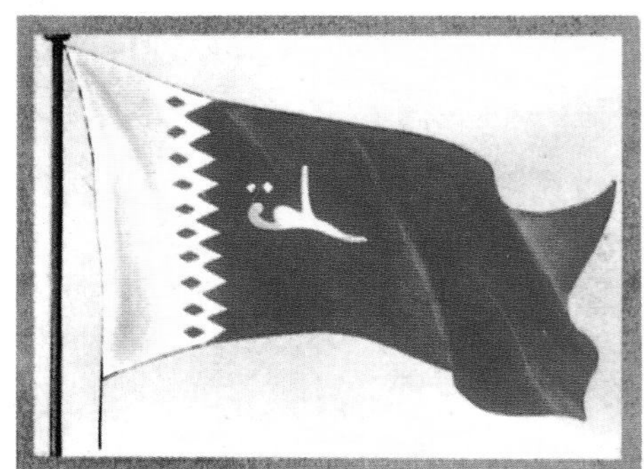

***Above:** An earlier version of the national flag with the name in Arabic.*

***Above:** Another early version in a different shade of maroon.*

Romania, Republic of

REPUBLICA ROMÂNIA
Established as United Principalities 17 January 1859

Romania was originally two provinces of the Ottoman Empire, Wallachia and Moldavia, which secured a measure of autonomy in 1834. They became united under a single prince in 1859 and achieved international recognition in 1880. On 22 May 1881 the country became a kingdom under a prince of the Hohenzollern dynasty. After the First World War 'Greater Romania' was formed by adding territory from Hungary and Russia. In 1940, Bessarabia was regained by the Soviet Union, which occupied the whole country in 1944. The King abdicated in December 1947 and the People's Republic was formed. In December 1989 the Communist dictator Ceausescu was overthrown and a National Salvation Front formed.

See: The Year of Revolutions

Above: The standard of Ceausescu, when he was Head of State.

The joint colours of Moldavia (blue and red) and of Wallachia (blue and yellow) became popular in the attempts to unite the two principalities and the tricolour flag appeared in 1848, probably based on the French *Tricolore.* The tricolour in this form was adopted officially in April 1867, when Prince Charles of Hohenzollern became joint prince, with the combined arms in the centre of the yellow strip. The arms changed their form over the years, and in 1948 were replaced by the Communist emblem, which was of typical allegorical landscape form. The details of this emblem also changed over the years, the most recent form dating from 21 August 1965, when the separate civil ensign (without the arms) was abolished.

***Above and left:** The former emblem of Romania and the basic tricolour, now without the emblem.*

Rwanda, Republic of

REPUBLIKA Y'U RWANDA
Established 1 July 1962

Rwanda is a former kingdom in central Africa once dominated by the Watutsi. It was part of German East Africa from 1897 until 1916, when it was occupied by Belgian forces from the Congo. It was a Belgian mandated territory until it achieved independence. The Tutsi Mwami Kigeri V was deposed by the dominant PARMEHUTU party, representing the majority population, on 2 October 1961. A PARMEHUTU government was formed on 1 January 1962, and independence was achieved on 1 July that same year.

The first flag of Rwanda was introduced by PARMEHUTU on 28 January 1961 and was a simple vertical tricolour of green, yellow, red. However, this turned out to be identical with the flag of Mali, once this country had removed the *kanaga* (black outline of a man) from its flag (1 March 1961). In September 1961 the flag was altered so that the red and green changed places, and a large black 'R' was added to the centre. This was the flag hoisted on the day of independence, and it has been in use ever since.

During the revolution of December 1989 the people followed the example of the Hungarians in 1956 and cut the emblem from the centre of the flag. Since then the plain tricolour only has been in use, although in this form it is identical with the flag of Chad. Prior to the revolution there was a wide range of specialized flags. That of the Head of State (Ceausescu) was a square tricolour with the arms over all in the centre, and a white inner border all round, and a red outer border, usually with a wide gold fringe.

See: The Pan-African Colours

***Above and left:** The arms and emblem of Rwanda: the motto is "Liberty, Co-operation, Progress".*

St Christopher-Nevis

Established as a Queen's Realm of the Commonwealth 19 September 1983

St Christopher, or St Kitts, and its adjacent islands were discovered by Columbus in 1493 and settlement began in 1623, although it was not until 1713 that the island became officially British. For most of its history St Kitts was linked with Nevis and Anguilla and the group was a component part of the Leeward Islands Federation from 1871 to 1956. From 1958 to 1962 they were part of the Federation of the West Indies. In 1967 Anguilla unilaterally seceded and has been ruled directly by Great Britain since 1969. The other two islands became an Associated State on 27 February 1967 and independent in 1983.

On 4 June 1957 St Kitts acquired a coat of arms, which emphasized the tripartite nature of the colony; a further version was adopted on 16 February 1967. The present arms are based on those of 1967. The chief contains a Carib's head between a lily and a rose (for France and England). The main charge is a chevron with two poinciana flowers and a schooner. The supporters are two pelicans and the crest is three arms and hands holding a torch. On independence the motto was changed from 'Unity in Trinity' to 'Country Above Self'.

The flag of the Associated State was a vertical tricolour of green, yellow, and blue, with a black palm tree of three branches in the centre. These colours were also used in Grenada at one time, as well as in St Vincent.

The flag adopted on independence is in colours like those used by the Rastafarians (although not officially described as such) and was designed by a schoolteacher, Edrice Lewis. The two stars stand for hope and liberty.

***Above and right:** The flag and arms of St Kitts.*

Saint Lucia

Established as a Queen's Realm of the Commonwealth 22 February 1979

***Above and right:** The arms and flag of St Lucia.*

St Lucia was discovered by Columbus in 1502 but was not colonized until about 1650, when French settlers arrived. Great Britain acquired the island in 1814. From 1958 to 1962 it was part of the Federation of the West Indies, and became an Associated State on 1 March 1967. Independence was achieved in 1979.

St Lucia has had several badges and coats of arms during its history. A black shield with a cross of sugar cane separating quarters charged with roses and lilies was granted on 19 August 1939. When the island became an Associated State, the arms were changed to black charges on yellow, with the addition of a gold African stool on a black disc in the centre, and supporters, crest, and motto, all in gold. On independence the arms were changed again: the field became blue, and the charges, supporters ('Jacquot' parrots), and crest were changed to more natural colours, similar to those in the national flag.

The flag was designed by a local artist and adopted on 21 February 1967. The design is a stylized representation of the twin peaks of the Pitons rising from the sea. The construction of the flag was slightly altered on the day of independence.

St Vincent and the Grenadines

Established as a Queen's Realm of the Commonwealth 27 October 1979

St Vincent was discovered by Columbus in 1498. It became an English colony in 1627, although it continued to be disputed with France until 1783. After a period in the Federation of the West Indies, St Vincent became an Associated State on 27 October 1969, and independent ten years later.

St Vincent acquired a coat of arms on 29 November 1912. It shows two figures ('Peace' and 'Justice') sacrificing at an altar, with a crest consisting of a sprig of cotton. This was the basis of the flag-badge used on the Blue Ensign. Although a flag in the standard colours of blue, yellow, and green was designed for St Vincent as an Associated State, it was never brought into use. This flag also included a sprig of breadfruit, to commemorate tht fact that these plants were first brought there from the Pacific.

The flag adopted on independence had the same colours arranged vertically with the coat of arms placed on a large breadfruit leaf. The flag was designed locally, but white fimbriations were added by the College of Arms. On 12 October 1985 a new design was introduced. The leaf, arms, and fimbriations have been removed and replaced by three diamonds. These alterations were made by a Swiss graphic designer, and the idea is that the diamonds form a V standing for 'Vincent'.

Above: *The former colonial ensign of St Vincent.*

Above and top: *The present national flag of St Vincent and a spurious version on a postage stamp.*

Above: *The arms of St Vincent, with the motto "Peace and Justice".*

San Marino, Serene Republic of

SERENISSIMA REPUBBLICA DI SAN MARINO

Established 301

San Marino was founded, according to tradition, by St Marinus in AD 301. It is centred on Mount Titano, just inland from Rimini. Around the hilltop are three towers – the Guaita, the Cesta, and the Montale – which symbolize the republic's powers to defend itself. Its independence was recognized by the Pope in 1631, by Napoleon in 1799, and by Italy by a treaty on 22 March 1862.

The traditional arms of San Marino were regularized by legislation of 6 April 1862. They are based on the three towers of Mount Titano, each topped with an ostrich feather, such as once decorated the actual towers. This is contained within a heart-shaped shield with a princely crown above. Around is wreath of oak and laurel, and the motto is 'Liberty'. The flag is in the colours of the arms, and dates in this form from 1797. The state flag has the arms over all in the centre.

Left: *The arms and flag of San Marino; note the distinctive crown.*

São Tomé and Príncipe, Democratic Republic of

REPÚBLICA DEMOCRATICA DE SÃO TOMÉ E PRÍNCIPE

Established 12 July 1975

See: The Pan-African Colours.

The islands were discovered by the Portuguese in 1471 and made into a colony in 1522. The *Movimento de Liberación de São Tomé e Príncipe* led the struggle for independence, which was agreed on with the Portuguese in November 1974 and took place the following July.

The MLSP was formed in 1972 and used the present colours from the outset, although in flags of a rather different design. There is no doubt that the colours and the black stars are derived directly from the model set by the flag of Ghana. The eventual party flag was like the present national flag, but with equal horizontal stripes. The two black stars stand for the two main islands. A coat of arms was also adopted, with a shield in the shape of an almond containing a cocoa tree; above this is a blue or black star. The supporters are two parrots, and the lower scroll bears the motto, *Unidale Disciplina Trabalho* ('Unity, Discipline, Work').

***Above and left:** The arms and flag of São Tomé: the motto is "Unity, Discipline, Work".*

Saudi Arabia, Kingdom of

AL-MAMLAKA AL-ARABIYA AS-SA'UDIYA

Established under present title 23 September 1932

***Above and right:** The arms and flag of Saudi Arabia; the inscription means "There is no god but Allah and Mohammed is the Prophet of Allah".*

The Saudi royal family began as rulers of Dar'iya in central Arabia, becoming Amirs in 1630. Muhammad Ibn Sa'ud became the patron of Muhammad Al-Whahabi, founder of the Whahabite movement, which inspired the Sa'udis to expand their control over all Arabia. In 1891 they were defeated by the Rashidis of Jebel Shammar, and again in 1901, but Abd Al-Aziz ibn Sa'ud began the reconquest of Nejd (Central Arabia) the following year. In 1913 Al-Hasa was annexed, in 1920 Asir, and Jebel Shammar was conquered in 1921. In 1924-5 he conquered the Hashemite kingdom of Hejaz, taking the title himself on 8 January 1926. In 1932 the two states of Hejaz and Jejd were merged to form the Kingdom of Sa'udi Arabia.

The flag favoured by the Whahabi sect was green, with the *shahada* (the Islamic creed) in white. This flag in various forms was known from the late nineteenth century, and in earlier times it generally had a narrow white strip in the hoist. The sword was added in 1902 to commemorate the bequest of the Sa'udi cause to Ibn Sa'ud, and has also been depicted in many forms. The modern form of the flag has the sword laid horizontally, with a simple hilt. The obverse and reverse of the flag are an absolute mirror image, which means that the sword points to the hoist on the obverse side and to the fly on the reverse, while the inscription reads correctly from right to left on both sides. This is usually achieved by sewing two identical flags back to back.

The royal standard is like the national flag, with the national arms (two crossed swords and a palm tree) in the lower canton near the sword hilt. The naval ensign is like the national flag, with a vertical strip in the hoist separated from the main field by a white stripe and charged with the yellow badge of the Royal Saudi Navy.

SENEGAL, REPUBLIC OF

REPUBLIQUE DU SENEGAL

Established 22 August 1960

Senegal began to be settled by the French in 1659 and it became a province of French West Africa in 1902. It became an autonomous republic within the French Community on 25 November 1958, and on 4 April 1959 formed the Federation of Mali with the former French Soudan. This state became independent on 20 June 1960; two months later Senegal seceded to become independent in its own right.

Up to the time of secession, Senegal shares the flag history of Mali, although it should be noted that there was an unofficial flag for the autonomous republic of 1958-9 of green with a yellow star. After the break with Mali, Senegal kept the same basic design but added a green star in the centre after Mali had removed the *kanaga* (black man-figure) from its flag.

The President's flag is the same as the national flag, but with his initials (currently 'A D') in black on either side of the star. The arms were designed in 1965 by a French vexillologist on the basis of the emblems on the state seal and depict a gold lion rampant and a baobab tree. The motto is *Un Peuple-Un But-Une Foi* ('One People, One Goal, One Faith'), the motto of the Mali Federation. Behind the shield is the collar and star of the Order of Senegal.

See: The Pan-African Colours

***Above and left:** The arms and flag of Senegal: the motto is the same as that of Mali, "One People, one Goal, one Faith."*

THE SEYCHELLES, REPUBLIC OF

REPUBLIK SESEL

Established 29 June 1976

The Seychelles archipelago was colonized by the French from 1756 onward, but seized by Great Britain in 1794 and attached to Mauritius. A separate colony was formed in 1903 and self-government was granted on 1 October 1975. The islands became an independent republic in 1976 and experienced a *coup d'état* on 5 June 1977. Creole, a dialect of French similar to that of the West Indies, is the native language.

The Seychelles colony acquired a badge in 1903, consisting of a disc portraying a landscape with palm trees, a tortoise, and the motto, *Finis Coronat Opus* ('The End Crowns the Work'). This was later made rather more artistic, placing a larger tortoise in front of one palm tree and depicting a ship sailing off the coast, the whole thing being enclosed in an oval with the name and the motto on it. On independence this was further simplified to just the tortoise and palm tree within a wreath of palm leaves. At the same time a coat of arms was granted, showing much the same scene on a shield supported by two sailfish and with a crest of a *paille en queue* bird.

The flag adopted on independence was in the colours of the then coalition parties, in the form of blue and red triangles separated by a white saltire cross. After the coup of 1977 the present flag was adopted, which is like that of the People's United Party (now the People's Progressive Front), but without the rising sun that appears on the party flag. The President's flag is like the national flag, but with the whole arms on a white disc in the centre and a gold border all round the flag.

***Above:** The colonial badge of the Seychelles, depicting a giant tortoise.*

***Above and left:** The arms and flag of the Seychelles: the motto means "The End Crowns the Work".*

SIERRA LEONE, REPUBLIC OF

Established as a Queen's Realm of the Commonwealth 27 April 1961

Above and right: *The arms and flag of Sierra Leone.*

Sierra Leone was obtained in 1787 as a home for freed slaves – hence the name of its capital, Freetown – and it thus set a pattern for the later creation of Liberia and Libreville (see Gabon). The coastal area became a crown colony in 1808 and the hinterland became British in 1896. A constitution was granted in 1924. The country became independent in 1961 and a republic on 19 April 1971.

Sierra Leone acquired a coat of arms on 30 July 1914. The chief depicted the pre-1801 flag to denote the settlers of 1787 and the dexter an African waving to a British ship. The motto, *Auspice Britannia Liber* ('Free Under Britain's Protection'), completed the picture. This was also used as an ensign-badge. On 1 December 1960 a new coat of arms was granted, depicting a gold lion passant, on a green field with a chief *dancetty* (with a zig-zag border), thus representing the 'Lion Mountains'. In the base are wavy lines for the sea, and three torches represent enlightenment.

The flag adopted on the day of independence uses the main colours from the arms, but they are here said to stand for agriculture and the mountains, unity and justice (part of the national motto), and the contribution made by Sierra Leone's unique natural harbour. The first of the special royal standards, composed of a banner of the country's arms with the crowned royal initial within a chaplet of roses, was designed for Sierra Leone in 1961.

Above: *The former royal flag of Sierra Leone, based on the arms.*

SINGAPORE, REPUBLIC OF

XINJIAPO GONGHEGNO

Established 9 August 1965

Above and right: *The arms and flag of Singapore; the motto means "Let Singapore Flourish"*

Singapore was acquired by the East India Company in 1819 and became a British colony in 1857. It achieved self-government in 1959, and entered the Federation of Malaysia in 1963. Singapore withdrew from the Federation and became an independent republic in 1965. The majority of the population of Singapore are of Chinese origin.

Singapore acquired a coat of arms on 13 September 1948, depicting a lion on top of a tower, symbolic of it name ('City of the Lion'). The present coat of arms dates from 26 November 1959 and was adopted at the same time as the flag. The arms depict a crescent and five stars, with supporters of a lion (for Singapore) and a tiger (for Malaya). The motto is *Majulah Singapura* ('Let Singapore Flourish').

On the flag the crescent and stars are placed in the upper hoist of a red over white bicolour. The crescent and stars have nothing directly to do with Islam. The crescent represents a growing young country, and the five stars stand for democracy, peace, progress, justice, and equality. The flag dates from 3 December 1959 and has remained in use ever since.

The flag of the President is a banner of the arms, with the crescent and stars turned sideways, as in the national flag. This was originally introduced for the *Yang di-Pertuan Negara* (Head of State). A civil ensign was introduced on 6 September 1966, with a red field; the crescent and stars are in the arms in white in the centre, within a white ring. This distinctive flag provides a contrast with the civil ensign of neighbouring Indonesia.

Above: *The civil ensign of Singapore (for use by merchant and private vessels).*

SOLOMON ISLANDS

Established as a Queen's Realm of the Commonwealth 7 July 1978

The Spaniards were the first Europeans to come to the Solomon Islands in 1568, but there was very little other contact until the late nineteenth century. The Germans annexed the northern islands in 1885 and in 1893 the British took over the southern islands. In the following three years all the German islands except Bougainville and Buka (now part of Papua New Guinea) were ceded to Great Britain. They were all occupied by Japan in 1942-5. The British colony became self-governing (dropping the word 'British') on 2 January 1976 and independent in 1978.

The Solomon Islands have had three coats of arms in their short existence as a state. One was granted on 10 March 1947, consisting of a shield only, depicting a turtle and a chief divided into black and white triangles. This was replaced on 24 September 1956 with another shield with an English lion in the chief, and quarters with emblems representing four of the districts into which the Protectorate was then divided: eagle (Malaita District), turtle (Western), trophy of weapons (Central), and flying frigate birds (Eastern). Some of these items were carried over into the arms granted on 18 November 1977, in which the shield was now yellow with a blue chief and a green saltire. It is supported by a crocodile and a shark, and the crest is a radiant sun above a native canoe.

Prior to independence there was a local competition to find a flag design, but in the end the flag was chosen by the Legislative Assembly. The five stars represent the then five districts, while the yellow band represents sunshine, blue the sea, and green the land (these colours also appear in the arms). The flag was adopted on 18 November 1977. There is a range of other flags, including a civil ensign that is red with the national flag in the canton. The Governor-General's flag is blue with the royal crest above the yellow silhouette of a frigate bird bearing the name of the state.

Above and above left: *The arms and flag of the Solomon Islands.*

Left: *The Solomon Islands emblem on stamps commemorating the Royal Visit of 1982.*

SOMALIA, DEMOCRATIC REPUBLIC OF

JAMHURIYADDA DIMUGRADIGA SOMALIYA

Established 1 July 1960

Somalia consists of an amalgamation of the former British and former Italian Somaliland. The British part was acquired in 1886 and the Italian in 1889. After the Second World War the Italians were allowed to keep their section as a Trusteeship. British Somaliland became independent on 26 June 1960, merging with the Italian area to form an independent state on 1 July. The Democratic Republic was formed on 23 September 1979.

The flag now in use is the same as that adopted on 12 October 1954 for Italian Somaliland. Its colour refers to the flag of the United Nations, under whose authority the country was governed, and the five-pointed star to the five areas inhabited by Somalis (British, French, Italian Somaliland, Kenya, and Ogaden). The coat of arms also depicts a white star on a blue shield, supported by two leopards. Beneath are crossed spears and palm branches and a scroll that, unusually, bears no inscription. The leopards were used in the badge of Italian Somaliland.

The flag of the West Somali Liberation Front, which operates in the Ogaden, is divided vertically red and green with a white star over all in the centre.

Above and above left: *The arms and flag of Somalia. The scroll is unusual in not carrying a motto.*

South Africa, Republic of

REPUBLIEK VAN SUID AFRIKA

Established as Union of South Africa 31 May 1910

Right and below right: *The arms and flag of South Africa: the motto means "Strength from Unity".*

Above and top: *The flags of a volunteer unit from the Transvaal during the Boer War and that of the Orange Free State, as shown on German cigarette cards.*

South Africa is a federation of the two former Boer republics of Transvaal and the Orange Free State, conquered in the Boer War (1899-1902), and the British colonies of the Cape and Natal. The Transvaal, later known as the South African Republic, was founded in the 1850s. It was annexed by Great Britain in 1877 and regained its independence in 1884. The Orange Free State was founded in the 1830s and was recognized by Britain in 1854. It was annexed by Britain in 1900. The Cape Colony was founded by the Dutch in 1652 and acquired by Britain in 1795 and 1806. Natal was originally a Boer colony, but was annexed to the Cape in 1844. Zululand was annexed to Natal in 1897, and parts of the Transvaal in 1903. The combined state became a Dominion of the British Empire in 1910, and a republic outside the Commonwealth on 31 May 1961.

The heraldry of South Africa is almost all derived from Dutch sources. The motto of the arms, adopted in 1910, was a Latin translation of the motto of the Dutch republic. The four quarters of the arms represent the four parts of the state, but these use emblems created for them by the British (figure with anchor – Cape of Good Hope; two wildebeeste – Natal; orange tree – Orange Free State; covered wagon – Transvaal). A more elaborate form of arms was granted on 21 September 1932.

Before they were taken over by the British, the Boer republics had arms and flags of their own, all of Dutch inspiration. The flag of the Transvaal, known as the *Vierkleur* ('Four Colour') flag was the Dutch flag with a green vertical strip in the hoist. This was adopted on 6 January 1857. The flag of the Orange Free State was eight stripes of white and orange with the Dutch flag in the canton.

At first South Africa had no special flag of its own apart from the civil ensign, which used the shield of arms as a badge, and in the 1920s the National Party began moves to create one. This led to considerable controversy, but eventually the present design was approved and adopted on 31 May 1928. It is based on the *Prinsenvlag*, known in South Africa as the Van Riebeeck Flag, since it is supposed that this was the flag used by the early Dutch settlers. In the centre is a Union Mark consisting of the flags of Britain, the Orange Free State, and the Transvaal. At first this flag was flown side by side with the Union Jack, on land, but in 1957 this provision was removed, and the South African flag became the only national flag and civil ensign.

The flag of the President is like this, but has the colours arranged in triangles, with the whole coat of arms on the white triangle, with the letters 'SP' (for 'State President') above. This was introduced on 3 September 1984 and replaced an earlier design. The naval ensign is white with a green Scandinavian cross and the national flag in the canton. There is a wide range of departmental and special flags.

The Homelands, or 'Bantustans', set aside for the majority population, also have arms and flags, except for Kangwane, which has only a coat of arms. One of these, the flag of Kwazulu, or Zululand, bears the black, green, yellow colours of the *Inkatha* movement, which are also those of the African National Congress. In the red strip are Zulu weapons. The flag of Kwandebele bears a knobkerrie and four axeheads, that of Gazankulu two linked spoons, that of Ciskei a crane, and of Qwaqwa (Basuto people) a pony like the ones in the arms of Lesotho. These flags have mostly been designed or inspired by the office of the State Herald. Four of these states are claimed to be independent (Bophuthatswana, Ciskei, Transkei, and Venda), but are not recognized as such by any other government.

Above: *The emblem of the African National Congress, adopted on their 75th anniversary.*

SPAIN, KINGDOM OF

REINO DE ESPAÑA

See: Suppressed Nations

Spain has been a united kingdom since the time of Ferdinand and Isabella (the Catholic monarchs) except for the periods of the two republics (1868-74 and 1931-9) and the dictatorship of Franco (1939-75). The kingdom was officially restored on 6 July 1947, and King Juan Carlos acceded on 22 November 1975. Since then there has been a deliberate attempt to restore power to the traditional regions of the country, now known as autonomous communities, and sixteen of these have been set up, together with the Canary Islands.

The present arms of Spain are a much simplified version of the traditional quarterings. The main ones shown on the contemporary shield are: a gold castle on red for Castile, a *morado* (mulberry-coloured) lion on white for León, four vertical bars of red on yellow for Aragon, and a pattern of gold chains on red for Navarre. The pomegranate is for Granada. In the centre of the shield is a blue red-edged cartouche with three fleurs-de-lis. This is the badge of the House of Bourbon, to which the monarch belongs. Above the shield is the royal crown and the supporters are columns representing the Pillars of Hercules. They carry the motto, *Plus Ultra* ('More Beyond'), referring to the greater Spain.

The flag of Spain that is so well known today was adopted on 28 May 1785. Previous flags were predominantly white, the livery colour of the House of Bourbon, but there were too many white flags in the naval wars of those days and something more effective was required. The red and yellow are the predominant colours of both Castile and Aragon, the homelands of the Catholic monarchs, and so were a natural choice. In 1785 the arms on the flag consisted only of a crowned cartouche with the emblems of Castile and León.

When the second republic was formed a new flag was adopted, of equal stripes of red, yellow, and *morado*, the latter colour being taken from the lion of León. The republican arms appeared in the centre of the state flag. During the civil war the old flag was used by the Nationalists, and when Franco took over in 1939 he restored this flag with a new coat of arms. The arms included a large black spread eagle and the badge of the *Falange Español*, the yoke and arrows. The arms were altered in 1977, and then on 19 December 1981 the present arms were introduced. These are to some extent a compromise, as some elements wanted a complete return to the republican arms of 1931, while others wanted to retain the trappings introduced by Franco. Following the tradition of the flag of 1785 the arms are set near the hoist, not in the centre of the flag. The civil ensign is without the arms.

The royal standard is like the pre-1931 model, being dark blue with the royal version of the arms in the centre. These include the ragged saltire of Burgundy and the collar of the Order of the Golden Fleece.

All the autonomous regions have arms and flags, several of which are traditional designs. Those of the Basque Provinces and of Catalonia were used by the autonomous governments set up under the Second Republic.

La Rioja

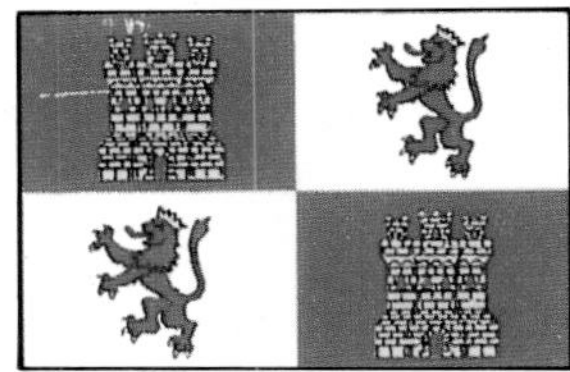

Castilla-Leon

Madrid

Top and above left: *The arms and flag of Spain (the arms appear on the yellow stripe in the state flag).*

SRI LANKA, DEMOCRATIC SOCIALIST REPUBLIC OF

SRI LANKA PRAJANTANTRIKA SAMAJAWADI JAMARAJAYA

Established as a Dominion 4 February 1948

The island of Ceylon was colonized first by the Portuguese and then by the Dutch. The British seized it in 1796 and made it into a colony in 1802. The inland kingdom of Kandy was annexed in 1815. Ceylon achieved independence in 1948 and became a republic under the name Sri Lanka on 22 May 1972. The present title was assumed on 7 September 1978. Between 1983 and 1989 there was armed conflict with the Tamil separatists.

The first flag of independent Ceylon was an almost exact replica of the flag of the old state of Kandy. This was not popular with the non-

Left: *The flag of Sri Lanka.*

Sinhalese and non-Buddhist part of the population, and it was agreed to amend it to represent their interests. This was done in 1951 by adding the green and orange panels in the hoist. When the republic was declared the flag was altered by making the objects in the corners of the red panel into *bo* leaves (they had previously been 'ancient Ceylonese pinnacles or spires'). The *bo*, or *pipul*, tree is the one under which the Buddha received enlightenment. When the Democratic Republic came in the leaves were again altered slightly. The red in the lion panel is now a rather dark colour.

The President's flag is a red flag with a stylized lotus flower in the centre, green *bo* leaves in each corner, and an ornate border of white, red, and green. This was introduced by the present President; there had formerly been two previous designs. The arms date from the institution of the republic and portray the Kandy lion within an ornate frame.

The flag of the Tamil United Liberation Front is red with a yellow sun rising from the lower edge.

Above: *The arms of Sri Lanka*

SUDAN, REPUBLIC OF

JAMHURYAT ES-SUDAN

In the course of the nineteenth century the Sudan was conquered by Egypt. General Gordon did two tours of duty as Governor and was killed in 1885 defending Khartoum from the Mahdi. The Mahdi himself died soon afterward and was buried at Omdurman. The Khalifa's army was defeated by the joint British-Egyptian army at Omdurman in September 1898. Thereafter the Sudan was ruled as a condominium until it became independent on 1 January 1956. For several years the government has been challenged by a secessionist movement in the south.

The flag adopted on independence was a horizontal tricolour of blue, yellow, green, but this was abolished after the Democratic Republic was formed on 25 May 1969. Following a competition the present flag was adopted on 20 May 1970 and is closely related to the Arab Liberation colours popularized by Nasser. They are also the same as the colours of the Umma party, which sees itself as the successor to the Mahdist movement. The President's flag is the same but with the national arms in the centre on the white strip. The arms are a secretary bird with a native shield on its breast; above it is a scroll with the motto, *Al Nasr Nilâ* ('Victory is Ours'), and beneath it the name of the country.

Above and right: *The arms and flag of Sudan.*

SURINAM, REPUBLIC OF

REPUBLIEK VAN SURINAME

Established 25 November 1975

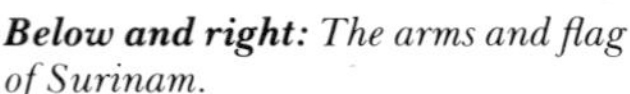

Below and right: *The arms and flag of Surinam.*

In 1667 England exchanged Surinam with the Netherlands for New York, but afterward twice reoccupied the country. It returned to the Netherlands in 1816 and afterward became a corealm of the Dutch crown. It became self-governing in 1954 and independent in 1975.

Surinam had a coat of arms from earlier times, depicting a ship at sea, supported by two Indians holding bows, with the motto, *Justitia Pietas Fides* ('Justice, Piety, Faith'). The modern arms were a revised form of this, introduced on 15 December 1959, with a sinister side portraying a green palm tree, and a star on a diamond in the centre. These arms were slightly modified on independence.

Surinam also had a flag, introduced at the same time as the modern arms, of white with five stars of white, black, brown, yellow, and red joined by an oval line. These five stars represented the racial composition of the population. An even earlier flag was the Dutch tricolour with the old arms in the centre. On independence a flag was adopted combining the colours of the then principal political parties. The large yellow star symbolizes unity and hope for the future. The President's flag has a square white panel containing the arms.

Swaziland, Kingdom of

UMBUSO WE SWATINI

Established c1750

Both the Transvaal and Great Britain guaranteed the independence of Swaziland in the nineteenth century, but in 1890 they established a joint protectorate over the country. In 1894 this passed to the Transvaal alone, but then reverted to Britain in 1902. From 1903 the King was recognized only as Paramount Chief, but regained his title on 25 April 1967. On 6 September 1968 full independence was regained. The traditional title of the King is *Ngwenyama* (The Lion) and he rules jointly with the Queen Mother, the *Ndlovukazi* (The She-Elephant).

The arms of Swaziland, adopted on 30 April 1968, are a blue shield containing a Swazi shield of the type used by the Emasotsha Regiment, and behind this a stick and two spears. The crest is the headdress of the regiment, a band of otter skin decorated with the tail feathers of the widow bird (*lisakabuli*). The supporters are a lion and an elephant (the King and Queen Mother) and the motto, *Siyinqaba*, means 'We are the Fortress'.

Above and left: The arms and flag of Swaziland. The motto is "We are the Fortress".

The flag was adopted on 30 September 1967. The background is that of the flag of the Swazi Pioneer Corps raised during the First World War. The charges are the same shield and weapons as in the arms. They bear *tinjobo*, or tassels, of feathers of the widow bird and the lourie (*ligwalgwala*). The royal standard has a gold lion passant in the upper blue stripe.

Sweden, Kingdom of

KONUNGARIKET SVERIGE

Sweden has been a kingdom since earliest times and at one time controlled wide territories around the Baltic Sea. Finland, Estonia, Latvia, and Pomerania have all since gone their separate ways. From 1815 to 1905 Norway was a corealm of the Swedish Crown.

The basic arms of Sweden are three gold crowns on blue, which have given rise to the national colours. The whole arms contain quarters for the old royal dynasties of Sweden divided by a gold cross. On the central shield are the arms of Vasa and Bernadotte. Around the shield is the collar of the Order of the Seraphim. The achievement is placed on a crowned ermine pavilion. The arms were revised in 1906 following the end of the union with Norway.

Above and left: The royal arms and flag of Sweden.

Above: The former Royal Standard showing the Union Mark.

The flag with the colours as a Scandinavian cross dates from 1523, when Gustav I of the House of Vasa came to the throne, and like the arms was revised on 22 June 1906. Prior to that it had the same Union Mark in the canton as was used in Norway.

The naval ensign is a swallow-tailed version of the national flag, with the cross extended into a tongue. The royal standard is the ensign with the arms on a white panel in the centre of the cross. Sweden has a wide range of departmental and special flags.

Above: The Royal banner of arms, used by the Commander-in-Chief of the Armed Forces.

Above: The banner of Albrecht of Mecklenberg, King of Sweden, 1363–89, as shown on a German cigarette card.

SWITZERLAND, CONFEDERATION OF

CONFEDERATIO HELVETICA

Established 1 August 1291

Right: *The national flag of Switzerland.*

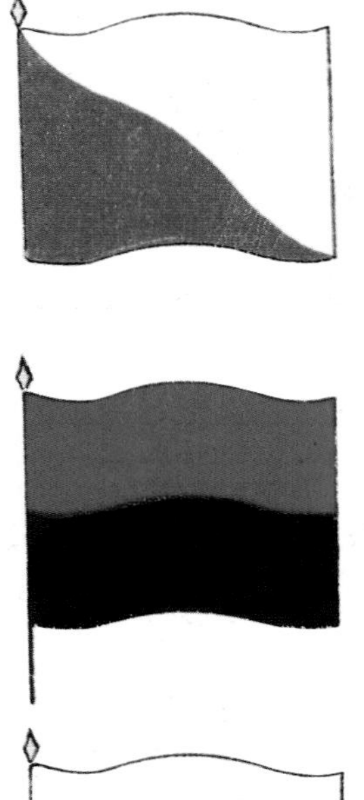

Above: *The flags of Zurich, Berne and Lucerne.*

Switzerland was formed with the oath taken by the men of Schwyz, Unterwalden and Uri in 1291 for mutual self-defence against feudal oppressors. The original three cantons were eventually joined by others, until the confederation grew to its present size. In 1798 Switzerland became the Helvetian Republic, under the protection of Napoleon. The present form of government was adopted in 1848. The cantons still retain very wide powers, and in 1979 a new canton – Jura – was formed out of Berne. German, French, Italian, and Romansch are the official languages.

The arms and flag of Switzerland are derived from the symbol used by the canton of Schywz, a white couped cross (one whose arms do not reach the edges of the shield or flag) on red. The Swiss soldiers adopted it as their badge at the Battle of Laupen (1339), and it became the official banner of the confederation in 1480. The cantons kept their own arms and flags throughout their history, but they could show their allegiance to the confederation by flying a red pennant with the couped cross above their own flag, or using a white cross on their flags, whose quarters would be filled with patterns in their own colours. Similar flags to these were used by mercenary regiments in the service of foreign powers. The national flag as such was only adopted in 1848. It is a square flag for use on land, but on water it has the proportions 2:3. Today the cantons use square banners of their arms, with one or two variations. For decorative purposes streamers in their colours can be used.

Above: *The flag of Switzerland from 1798–1803.*

SYRIA, ARAB REPUBLIC OF

AL-JAMHURIYA AL-AARABIYA AS-SURIYA

Right: *The flag of Syria.*

See: The Pan-Arab Colours

Syria was liberated from the Turks in 1918. For two years the Hashemite Prince Faisal ruled there (as King from March to July 1920), until he was forcibly expelled by the French. The French divided Syria into six areas, of which three formed a federal government in 1922. An autonomous republic was formed on 14 May 1930, and it became independent on 12 April 1946. On 22 February 1958 Syria joined the United Arab Republic with Egypt, but left on 28 September 1961. It again joined with Egypt (and Libya) in the Federation of Arab Republics on 1 January 1972, but left this in 1977.

Syria has one of the most complicated flag histories of any country in the modern world. Its first flag, dating from 1922, was a horizontal triband of green-white-green with the *Tricolore* in the canton. On 1 January 1932 a national flag was adopted of green-white-black horizontal stripes with three red stars on the white stripe. These colours referred deliberately to the flag of the Arab Revolt as used by the Hashemites. The flag remained in use until Syria joined the UAR, when the common flag (see Egypt) was used. Syria then used the 1932 flag until 8 March 1963, when a flag like that of the UAR – both with three stars – was adopted. This flag symbolized an intended union with both Egypt and Iraq and is still in used in Iraq. It was replaced in Syria by the flag of the Federation in January 1972. The federal flag had a gold hawk in the centre with the name of the country on a scroll beneath. The present flag dates from 29 March 1980.

Except for the period 1958-61 the arms have remained much the same. They are the badge of the tribe of the Prophet, the Quraish. The shield on the hawk's breast has changed according to the current flag, and the scroll beneath has borne the varying titles of the country.

TANZANIA, UNITED REPUBLIC OF

JAMHURI YA MUUNGANO WA TANZANIA

Established as Tanganyika 9 December 1961

Tanganyika was part of German East Africa from 1884 until the First World War, after which it was mandated to Great Britain. Self-government was achieved on 1 May 1961 and independence on 9 December of that year. Tanganyika became a republic on 9 December 1962. The Sultanate of Zanzibar was originally part of the Omani domains in East Africa, but became a British protectorate in 1890. Independence was regained on 10 December 1963 but on 17 January 1964 the Sultanate was abolished in favour of a People's Republic. On 26 April 1964 this republic united with Tanganyika to form the present state. The name 'Tanzania' was adopted on 29 October 1964.

The flag of Tanganyika was based on the horizontal triband of the Tanganyika African National Union, of green, black, red. On independence the national flag was formed by adding fimbriations of yellow to the black stripe. The flag of Zanzibar was originally plain red, like that of Oman, but on independence a green disc bearing two yellow cloves was added, this spice having been part of the reason for the islands' prosperity. The flag of the Afro-Shirazi party, which took over in January 1964, was a horizontal tricolour of blue, black, green, with a yellow hoe in the centre. After the coup Zanzibar had a flag in the same colours but without the hoe and with a narrow white vertical strip in the hoist. On the formation of the United Republic this Zanzibari flag was amalgamated with that of Tanganyika to form the present national flag. The colours were rearranged to give them equal status.

The flag of the President is based on an earlier one, the arms including the hoe from the Afro-Shirazi flag. The motto is *Uhuru na Umoja* ('Freedom and Unity').

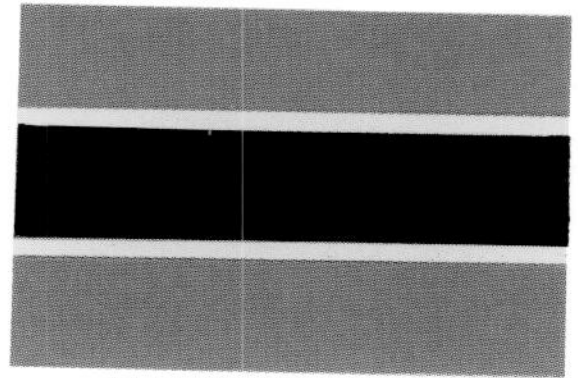

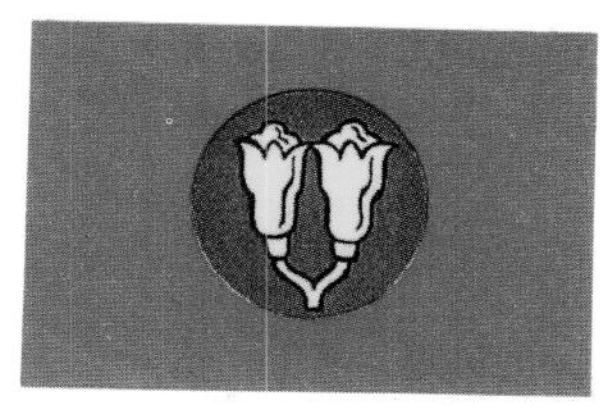

***Above left:** The flag of Tanzania.*

***Top (downwards):** The arms of Tanzania, the Tanzania flag of 1963–64, and the flag of Zanzibar when it became independent.*

THAILAND, KINGDOM OF

PRATHES THAI/MUANG THAI

Established 1782

Modern Thailand dates from the accession of Phaya Chakri in 1782, who founded the currently ruling dynasty. Despite encroachments by the Europeans, Thailand managed to preserve its independence, although territories were ceded to France and Great Britain (regained temporarily during the Second World War). The name of the country was officially changed from Siam to Thailand on 26 June 1939. During the First World War Thailand sided with the Allies, but in the Second World War was occupied by the Japanese.

The emblem of the ruling family, from which they took their title, is the *chakra*, or Buddhist wheel, which in Siam took the form of a revolving disc with flamelike blades on its rim. The first distinctive flag was red with a white *chakra*. In 1817 a white elephant was added to the centre of the wheel, but in 1855 the white elephant alone came to be used. This is the famous 'White Elephant' flag so widely associated with Siam. White elephants were valued trophies, and a triple-headed elephant, like that of Laos, was already the national emblem. The caparisoned form of elephant, ie, one with harness and trappings, was introduced in 1891 for use on the naval ensign.

A simplied form of flag, of red with two horizontal white stripes, was introduced in 1916, after the declaration of war on Germany in 1917 blue was added to the centre in order to express solidarity with the Allies, whose flags were mostly red, white, and blue. This flag is known as the *Trairanga* (tricolour) and was adopted on 28 September 1917.

The royal standard contains an emblem derived from Hindu mythology, the *garuda*, or bird-man. The present design, of a red garuda on a field of royal yellow, was introduced in 1910. The garuda also forms the national arms of Thailand. Most of the departmental flags are based on the national flag, using either the caparisoned elephant or the *chakra* emblem, or both. The naval ensign has the elephant on a red disc in the centre of the national flag, while the jack is the national flag with the navy badge: a crowned anchor and *chakra* in yellow.

***Above and left:** The emblem and flag of Thailand. The emblem is the garuda or bird-man of Hindu mythology.*

TOGO, REPUBLIC OF

REPUBLIQUE TOGOLAISE

Established 27 April 1960

***Right:** The flag of Togo.*

See: The Pan-African Colours

The German colony of Togoland was created in July 1884. After the First World War the territory was divided into mandates held by Great Britain and France. The British part was amalgamated with Ghana in March 1957. The French part, the present state, became autonomous on 30 August 1956, and independent in 1960.

The autonomous republic had a flag of green, with the *Tricolore* in the canton and two yellow stars on the green field. The significance of these is unknown. Four days before independence the present national flag was inaugurated and has remained unchanged ever since. It is in the same red, yellow, green as used in other West African states, but is unusual in having a white star instead of a black one.

The national emblem was instituted on 14 March 1962 and modified in 1980, principally by altering the motto from *Travail, Liberté, Patrie* ('Work, Freedom, Fatherland') to *Union, Paix, Solidarité* ('Union, Peace, Solidarity'). The central emblem was originally a shield with the letters 'R T', but it is now a radiant sun.

***Above:** The pre-independence flag of Togo.*

TONGA, KINGDOM OF

Established 1820–45

The Tonga Islands were once known as the Friendly Islands, having been so named by Captain Cook in 1777. The Kingdom of Tonga was formed by the amalgamation of the three groups of islands by King Taufa'ahau Tupou, the ancestor of the present King. A constitution was granted in 1875, and has remained largely unaltered ever since. In 1899 Tonga became a British Protectorate, but independence was regained on 4 June 1970.

King Taufa'ahau Tupou became a Christian in 1831 and used Christian symbolism in the flags of his country. The first flag, introduced about 1850, was white with a red and blue cipher in the centre and red and blue couped crosses in the cantons. The present flag originated in 1864 and was designed by the King's European First Minister, the Rev S. W. Baker. The cross and the red colour of the flag signified the sacrifice of Christ's blood. The flag was incorporated into the Constitution of 1875.

The royal arms and standard were designed in 1862. The three stars stand for the three original ruling dynasties; the crown represents the monarchy; the dove is for peace (an original missionary emblem, as also used in Fiji), and the three swords for the three kingdoms united by Taufa'ahau Tupou. The motto is *Koe 'Otua Mo Tonga Ko Hoku Tofi'a* ('God and Tonga Are My Inheritence').

The naval ensign was introduced in 1985 and recalls that of Imperial Germany. It is flown alongside the Defence Services flag, which is white with the badge of the services in red in the centre.

***Above and left:** The arms and flag of Tonga. The standard is a banner of the arms.*

Trinidad and Tobago, Republic of

Established as a Queen's Realm of the Commonwealth 31 August 1962

The islands were discovered by Columbus in 1498 and remained Spanish until 1797, when they were captured by Great Britain, to which they were ceded in 1802. They were put under a single administration in 1889, and formed part of the West Indies Federation from 1958. The break-up of this in 1962 led directly to their independence. The state became a republic on 1 August 1976.

The islands acquired a coat of arms, based on their ensign-badge, on 13 October 1958. This showed a ship anchored off a jetty, and bore the motto, *Miscerique Probat Populus et Foedera Jungi* ('He approves the mingling of peoples and their being joined by treaties').

***Above:** The colonial badge of Trinidad as used on the Blue Ensign.*

***Above and left:** The arms and flag of Trinidad and Tobago.*

The present coat of arms was adopted on the day of independence and is in the colours of the flag. The three ships are those of Columbus, and the two humming birds represent the two islands. The supporters are a scarlet ibis and a cocrico standing on landscapes representing the two islands.

The flag was adopted the previous June. Its colours are said to stand for the dedication and unity of the people (black), the vitality of the land, and the surrounding sea (white). As with Grenada, the flag is 1:2 for use at sea and 3:5 for use on land.

The President's flag is blue with the arms within a wreath. The naval ensign is white with a red cross throughout and the national flag in the canton, within a narrow white border. The flag of the Prime Minister is white with the national flag in the canton and the arms within a gold wreath in the fly.

Tunisia, Republic of

AL-JUMHURIYA AT-TUNISIYA

Established as a Kingdom 20 March 1956

The Husaynid dynasty took over as Beys, or Viceroys, of Tunis in 1705 but had to accept a French protectorate in 1881. The Kingdom was inaugurated on independence in 1956, but the country became a republic on 25 July 1957.

The flag of Tunisia goes back to about 1835 and is closely patterned on that of the Ottoman Empire. There was formerly a Standard for the Bey and a coat of arms, both very elaborate. The arms were an oval shield charged with a green flag bearing a red sword of Ali, and flanked by flags of Tunisia and of the Bey. Around the shield was the collar of the Order of Glory. The *zûlfaqar*, or split sword of Ali, also appeared on the Bey's standard. Some of the features of the royal arms were carried over into the republican arms. The quarters contain a black lion rampant holding a sword, a balance, and a ship at sea, whose foresail was marked with the emblem of the Phoenician goddess Tanit. This has disappeared in the modern rendering introduced on 30 May 1963, and the lion and balance have changed places. The scroll is now actually on the shield; it bears the motto, 'Order, Freedom, Justice'.

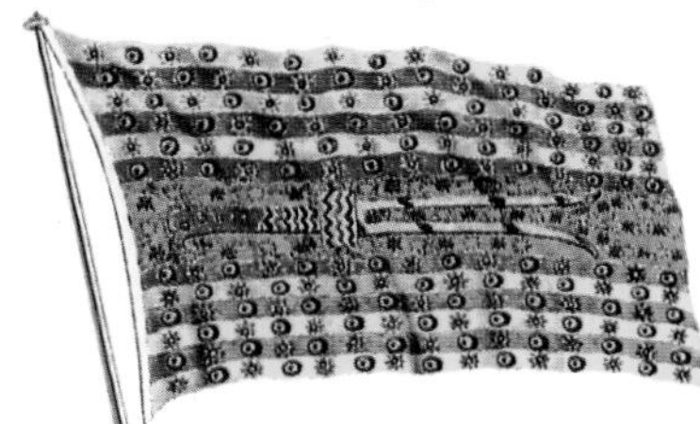

***Above:** The banner of the Bey of Tunis, depicting the zul-faqar.*

***Above and left:** The arms and flag of Tunisia.*

TURKEY, REPUBLIC OF

TÜRKIYE CUMHURIYETI

Established as a Republic 29 October 1923

Below and bottom: The flags of Commander-in-Chief of the Navy and of a Vice-Admiral.

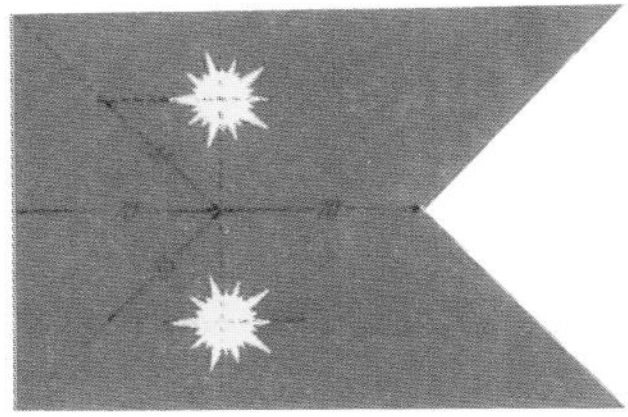

Turkey is all that remains of the once extensive Ottoman Empire founded by Osman about the year 1300. The Turks conquered most of the Middle East and the Balkans and took Constantinople in 1453, thus extinguishing the Byzantine Empire. In the nineteenth century they lost more and more territory, culminating in their defeat in the First World War. Mustafa Kemal emerged as the national leader in the War of Independence. In 1923 the country became a republic under Kemal Atatürk, and the capital was transferred to Ankara. On 3 March 1924 the Caliphate (the religious title held by the Sultans) was abolished.

Although the crescent and star emblem on the flag of Turkey is very well known, its origin is very poorly documented and wide open to speculation. It first appeared in 1793, although of course the crescent as an emblem goes back to the earliest days of civilization. The star that accompanied it on early flags usually had eight points, as in the badge of the Order of the Crescent, instituted in 1801. Red was the colour of the Ottoman dynasty, hence Turkish flags were always of this hue, despite the variations depicted on early flag charts.

Abdul Hamid (1876–1909) was responsible for a Pan-Islamic movement that attempted to counter the nationalist movements in various parts of the empire: one result of this was to popularize the crescent and star as a badge of Islam, especially on a green field (the colour associated with the Prophet).

The national flag did not change with the republic, but was more closely defined by regulations of 5 June 1936. These introduced a flag for the President and a wide range of departmental and rank flags.

Above and left: The emblem and flag of Turkey. Turkey has no official arms.

TUVALU

Established as a Queen's Realm of the Commonwealth 1 October 1978

Above and right: The arms and flag of Tuvalu.

See: The Union Jack

Tuvalu was formerly known as the Ellice Islands, and from 1892 to 1975 was part of the Gilbert and Ellice Islands protectorate. The group consists of nine small islands with a total area of 24 square kilometres (9.6 square miles).

Tuvalu acquired a coat of arms on 3 December 1976. In the centre is a depiction of a *maneapa*, or meeting house, above blue and yellow waves. On the yellow border are eight mitre seashells alternating with banana leaves. The eight shells and leaves represent the name 'Tuvalu', which means 'Eight Islands'. The motto is *Tuvalu mo te Atua* ('Tuvalu for God').

In 1976 these arms were placed on a white disc in the fly of a British Blue Ensign, and this still serves as the ensign for the government's ship.

The national flag was adopted on 1 October 1978 and consists of a light blue ensign with nine yellow stars arranged in the same pattern as the islands themselves lie in the sea. The discrepancy between the nine stars and the eight shells can be explained by the fact that one of the islands is uninhabited.

UGANDA, REPUBLIC OF

Established as a Queen's Realm of the Commonwealth 9 October 1962

Uganda once consisted of several African kingdoms, of which Buganda was the largest. A British protectorate over Buganda was established on 27 August 1894, and later over the other kingdoms. However, these maintained their separate existence until 1967. The Kabaka Mutesa II of Buganda was the first President of Uganda, but he was deposed on 24 May 1966. Uganda became independent in 1963, and a republic on 9 October 1963, and a unitary state on 8 September 1967.

The flags and arms of the African kingdoms had only a marginal influence on the national emblems of Uganda. On the arms adopted on 3 September 1962 the shape of the shield, the crossed spears, and the drum refer back to the arms of Buganda, but the crested crane (the sinister supporter) is the former flag-badge. Underneath the shield is a river, representing the source of the Nile, and at the top of the shield blue and white waves for Lake Victoria.

The flag adopted on independence was of six stripes in the colours of the Congress Party, with the crane on a white disc in the centre. This has remained unchanged since 1962. A flag for the President was adopted on 26 September 1963; it is red with the stripes of the national flag along the lower part and the arms in the centre of the red field.

***Above and above left:** The arms and flag of Uganda.*

UNION OF SOVIET SOCIALIST REPUBLICS

SOYUZ SOVIETSKIKH SOTSIALISTICHESKIKH RESPUBLIK

Established as the USSR 13 January 1924

The USSR is a federation of fifteen Soviet Socialist Republics based on ethnic-linguistic groups or 'nationalities'. Of these the Russian RSFSR is the largest, and contains sixteen smaller Autonomous Soviet Republics. ASSRs also exist in other Soviet Republics and are also based on ethnic-linguistic groups. The latest Constitution was adopted in 1977. In theory all SSRs are entitled to separate foreign relations with other countries: in practice only the Ukrainian and Byellorussian republics do so, by means of separate representation in the United Nations.

The Bolshevik Revolution of 1917 and the subsequent civil war divides the flag history of the country into two distinct parts. Before the establishment of the Soviet State all the flags were based on models – mostly red, white, and blue – introduced by Peter the Great, the modernizing Tsar who founded the navy and introduced many new ideas and techniques from Western Europe. After the creation of the Soviet Union (1918-22) all flags were based on the Red Flag, which emerged from the French Revolution and was taken over by the Marxists, of whom Lenin was the most outstanding leader. The civil war itself, which lasted until 1924, produced flags for many secessionist and rival regimes in different parts of what was once the Russian Empire. Some of these succeeded in preserving their new independence (Finland and the Baltic States) but others (Ukraine, Armenia, etc) were reincorporated into the new Soviet Union.

See: The Red Flag, The Pan-Slav Colours, Suppressed Nations

***Above and left:** The arms and flag of the USSR; the national motto appears in 15 languages on the scroll.*

***Above:** The emblems and flags of some of the Soviet Republics as shown on picture postcards.*

***Above:** A Regimental Colour from the time of Catherine the Great.*

Imperial Russia used a civil ensign of white, blue, and red horizontal stripes from the time of Peter the Great until the Bolshevik Revolution. The colours and the layout were derived from the Dutch Tricolour, the flag of the Netherlands, although the flag was not officially adopted until 1799. The naval ensign was white with a blue saltire and, like the flag of Scotland, was associated with St Andrew. The Imperial standard was very similar to those of Germany and Austria, with a yellow field bearing a double-headed eagle, reflecting the claim of the Tsars to be the successors to the Roman Emperors.

The Imperial arms included a red shield with a representation of St George (the patron saint of Moscow) slaying the dragon. The arms also bore the chain of the order of St Andrew and small shields representing the various parts of the Empire. The eagle grasped an orb and sceptre and wore three crowns. The Imperial standard for use at sea had the eagle grasping maps of the surrounding oceans in place of the orb and sceptre and omitted the smaller shields. In 1915 a version of the Imperial standard was placed in the canton of the national flag, perhaps to emphasize the unity of crown and people. After the Tsar's abdication (15 March 1917) the eagle lost all its trappings, and the plain horizontal tricolour became the national flag.

This flag was used by the 'Whites' in the civil war, in contrast to that of the 'Reds'. The flag used by the Red Army was indeed red with a red, yellow-bordered star containing a hammer and sickle. These emblems emerged early in the Revolution and were incorporated into the arms of the first Soviet republic, the Russian Soviet Federal Socialist Republic, founded on 10 July 1918. They represent the union of industrial and agricultural workers. The star is said to represent the world (with a point for each continent), or perhaps the guiding role of the Communist Party. In practice it was a handy way of expressing the Red Flag as a badge.

The flag of the Soviet Union was adopted on 31 January 1924 as part of the Constitution that united the RSFSR with the then three other republics (Ukraine, Byellorussia, and Transcaucasia). The hammer and sickle were placed in the canton of a red flag under the red, yellow-edged star. The flag, and all other republic flags, then and now, were to be in the proportions 1:2 (unlike the previous Imperial ones, which were always 2:3). Although the details have changed from time to time, this is still the basic flag of the Soviet Union, acting as a government and civil ensign for land and sea.

A naval ensign was introduced on 27 May 1935 and unlike the national flag this does have the old proportions of 2:3. The jack was adopted on 7 July 1932 and is reminiscent of the flag of the Red Army. The arms date from the same time as the national flag, and depict the world overlaid by the hammer and sickle with the red star above and a rising sun below. Around these is a wreath of wheat bound with a red ribbon containing the motto, 'Workers of the World Unite', in the languages of the fifteen republics.

Each republic has a flag of its own and a coat of arms. Each ASSR also has a flag, based on that of the republic in which it is situated. In Estonia, Latvia, and Lithuania the pre-Soviet flags have now been given official recognition and are used as 'national flags' as opposed to the former 'state flags'. In other republics the pre-Soviet flags are often seen, but have no official status as yet.

Estonia The national flag, adopted on 4 July 1920, is a horizontal tricolour of black, blue, and white. It was originally the flag of a students' association and became popular during the struggle for independence.

Latvia The flag is in a dark red supposed to be characteristic of local fabric, with a narrow horizontal white stripe. It was adopted on 18 November 1918.

Lithuania The flag is a horizontal tricolour of yellow, green and red, supposed to be a compendium of the favourite colours of Lithuanian associations. It was adopted on 19 April 1918. The flag and the old arms were readopted by the independent republic declared in March 1990.

***Above:** The arms and flags of Estonia, Latvia and Lithuania on pre-War cigarette cards. These arms and flags are now in use again.*

UNITED ARAB EMIRATES

AL-AMIRAT AL-ARABIYA AL-MUTAHIDA

Established as the United Arab Emirates 2 December 1971

The UAE is a federation of seven emirates on the Persian Gulf previously organized as the Trucial States Council (established 30 March 1968), to which Qatar and Bahrain also belonged for a short time. Except for Fujairah, the emirates are all ones that had a treaty relationship with Great Britain dating from 1820. One of the provisions of this was that they would all use red flags with white borders. Such flags are still used by the individual states in the federation.

See: The Pan-Arab Colours

The national flag was adopted on the day the state was established, and is a variation of the Pan-Arab colours first employed during the Arab Revolt. The arms were adopted at the same time, and depict the falcon (officially described as an eagle) found on the arms of Abu Dhabi, the largest state. The *dhow* is taken from the arms of Dubai. The chain has eight links, one of which is for Qatar, which in the end did not join the federation.

***Above and left:** The arms and flag of the United Arab Emirates. The name on the scroll is that of the state.*

UNITED KINGDOM OF GREAT BRITAIN AND NORTHERN IRELAND

The United Kingdom was founded by the parliamentary union of England and Scotland on 1 May 1707, to which Ireland acceded on 1 January 1801. Following the Treaty of 6 December 1921 what is now the Republic of Ireland withdrew, and the expression 'Northern Ireland' was substituted. The Kingdom does not include the Channel Islands or the Isle of Man, which are separate dependencies of the Crown. Prior to 1707 the English crown had acquired the Principality of Wales in 1301 and the Kingdom of Ireland in 1541. On 24 March 1603 the crown was inherited by the King of Scotland. There was an *interregnum* between the execution of Charles I (30 January 1649) and the accession of Charles II (29 May 1660).

See: The Union Jack, Regional and Civic Flags.

England, Scotland, and Ireland have separate heraldic traditions, which were gradually merged to form the joint emblems of the United Kingdom.

***Above and above right:** The Royal Arms and national flag of the United Kingdom.*

ENGLAND

The royal arms of England are three yellow lions on red, in a posture called *passant guardant* in heraldry. These date from the reign of Richard I, at the dawn of heraldry. During the reign of Edward III (1327-77) the arms of France in their 'ancient' form (blue, powdered with golden lilies) were quartered with those of England. In the reign of Henry V (1399-1413) the quarter for France was modernized to three lilies only. The national flag is the red cross on white of St George, first documented in 1277.

***Above:** The Queen's Personal Flag for use in the Commonwealth.*

Above: *The Saltire, the national flag*

Above: *The former flag of Northern Ireland.*

Above: *The Red Dragon of Wales.*

SCOTLAND

The arms of the King of Scots are a red lion rampant on a yellow field within a frame, or tressure, decorated with fleurs-de-lis. The plain lion dates from the reign of William the Lion (1165-1214) and the tressure from at least 1222. The fleurs-de-lis are said to commemorate the long-standing alliance between Scotland and France.

The national flag is known as the Saltire and is the white diagonal cross on blue of St Andrew, first documented in 1286-92.

IRELAND

Henry VIII, first English King of Ireland, established that the gold harp on blue was the royal arms of Ireland, but it did not appear on the royal arms in his reign. There was no Irish national flag, parallel to those of England and Scotland, although the Cross of St Patrick was often illustrated as being the flag of Ireland. A coat of arms was granted to the government of Northern Ireland in 1924, and in 1953 a banner of the arms was authorized for use by the general public. It became obsolete in 1972, but is still widely used by the Loyalist population. Officially the flag of Northern Ireland is the Union Jack.

WALES

The arms of the Principality of Wales, as used later in the heraldry of the English Princes of Wales, clearly have an English origin, being four lions passant guardant countercharged on quarters of yellow and red. This dates back at least to Dafydd ap Llewelyn in 1240 (his mother was the daughter of King John). The badge of Wales, as used on the flag, is the Red Dragon, which is of very ancient origin. It was first combined with the Tudor colours of green and white in the time of Henry VII.

First Union With the accession of James I & VI in 1603 new royal arms and banners were instituted, as well as a united flag for use at sea. The new royal arms quartered the arms of England, France, Scotland, and Ireland. The flag for use at sea only united the crosses of England and Scotland, and was instituted on 12 April 1606. At first it was for use by all vessels, but on 5 May 1634 it was restricted to ships in the royal navy. Since at least 3 July 1633 it has been referred to as the 'Union Jack'. English civil vessels at this time began to use the Red Ensign: a red flag with the Cross of St George on a white canton. In a similar way Scottish ships used the Red Ensign with a Saltire in the canton. The flags of St George and St Andrew were worn as jacks.

Civil War and Commonwealth There was little change during the period 1649-60, except that a new navy flag was instituted: the Cross of St George combined with the harp of Ireland (this was a banner of the arms of the Commonwealth). With the union with Scotland in 1654 the 1606 Union flag was revived, but with the harp on a shield in the centre. This lasted until the Restoration.

Second Union With the new union with Scotland in 1707 the arms and flags were all revised. The royal arms contained quarters with England and Scotland partly impaled. The Red Ensigns now had the Union flag in the canton: the Union flag was that of 1606. The royal arms were revised again with the dynastic union with Hanover in 1714.

Third Union The union with Ireland had no effect on the royal arms, since the harp was already one whole quarter of the arms. But the Union flag was revised to include the Cross of St Patrick. This was incorporated, rather ingeniously, by counterchanging it with the Saltire, although this is not very evident today since most union flags are made to incorrect specifications. The naval ensigns also had the new Union flag placed in their cantons.

Regulations of 1864 By an Order in Council of 9 July 1864, the present system of flags was instituted. By these the Union flag became the jack for naval vessels and the White Ensign the only ensign for commissioned ships of the Royal Navy (previously the Blue and Red Ensigns had also been used). The Red Ensign was reserved for civil vessels and the Blue Ensign for ships in the government service. In 1865 the Blue Ensign was also allocated to vessels in the service of colonial governments, which is how it came to be the flag used in Australia and New Zealand. From 1864 onward the Admiralty imposed its own interpretation of the Union Jack on to flags for use on land as well as at sea.

The royal standard of today is a banner of the royal arms, which date in terms of their composition from the accession of Queen Victoria (20 June 1837), which brought an end to the union with Hanover. The claim to France had been abandoned, so the present arms represent only England, Scotland, and Ireland. In Scotland the Red Lion occupies the first and fourth quarters. The harp is now said to represent Northern Ireland, although this would be difficult to sustain in heraldic terms. Modern royal standards are often manufactured in the Admiralty proportions of 1:2 and use a very dark, unheraldic red. Each member of the royal family has his or her own coat of arms and in many cases these are used as banners as well. Prince Charles has three banners, two of which are for Scotland and Wales. The Queen has a badge-flag of blue with the crowned royal initial in gold in the centre within a chaplet of roses. This was instituted on 5 December 1960 and is used in Commonwealth countries that are not Queen's Realms. For those that are she has a royal standard for each, consisting of a banner of their arms with the same emblem as in the badge-flag over all in the centre.

There is a very wide range of departmental, specialized, and distinguishing flags. British models for these have often been imitated in other countries, as in the case of naval rank flags. The flag of an Admiral is the cross of St George, which is the reason this flag can no longer be used at sea by civil vessels. The system of distinguishing flags dates from the boat flags used in the eighteenth century. In this system a Vice-Admiral has a red disc in one canton of the flag and a Rear-Admiral two.

BRITISH DEPENDENCIES

The basic flags for a dependency are the Union Jack on land, the Red Ensign for civil vessels, and the Blue Ensign for government vessels. The Governor has a Union Jack with the badge of the dependency in the centre within a garland of laurel leaves.

UNITED STATES OF AMERICA

Established 4 July 1776

Armed conflict between Great Britain and its American subjects broke out in April 1775. The Declaration of Independence of the then thirteen colonies was made in 1776. Their independence was recognized by Britain on 30 November 1782. On 17 September 1787 the present Constitution was adopted, which was ultimately ratified by all the states. From 1795 onward new states were formed and admitted to the Union; the fiftieth state, Hawaii, was admitted on 18 March 1959.

The Stars and Stripes evolved during the War of Independence, although there were earlier patriotic flags, including one of nine red and white stripes that was used in Boston as early as July 1769 and again in 1773 at the time of the Boston Tea Party. The five red stripes on this possibly represented the New England colonies. The 'Liberty' flag hoisted at Taunton, Massachusetts, in 1774 was a British Red Ensign with the inscription 'Liberty and Union' in the red field.

The Grand Union flag, as it is now called, apeared at the end of 1775 and seems to be an adaptation of the Red Ensign, with stripes to represent the united colonies. There is some evidence that it was used on American ships at Philadelphia on 3 December 1775, but a lot more to attest to it being hoisted at Prospect Hill in Cambridge, Massachusetts, where the Continental Army was encamped, on 1 January 1776. It became the general flag for the colonies, along with the Rattlesnake flag with which it was sometimes combined.

The actual Stars and Stripes was created by removing the British flag from the canton and replacing it with a blue panel charged with thirteen white stars. It came into existence by a resolution of Congress on 14 June 1777. There is no evidence that the stars were always five-pointed or that they were placed in a ring. In the first known depiction dated 1778-9 the stars are arranged in rows. Nor is it now known why a 'new constellation' was used to replace the Union Jack. However, this powerful combination of stars and stripes has had an effect all round the world. Before it came into existence practically no flag employed a pattern of stars: since its birth, thousands of flags have done so.

The original flag had thirteen stars, but following the admission of Vermont and Kentucky in 1791/92 the number of stars and stripes was increased to fifteen (1 May 1795). With five other states due to be admitted, it was decided in 1818 to return to the original pattern of stripes and to add a star to the flag for each new state on the 4 July following its admission, and this practice has been followed ever since. Specifications for the design were issued in 1912 and for the colours in 1934. The exact layout of the stars is specified each time new ones are added, and in modern times they have always been in rows.

The President's flag contains the form of the coat of arms or, rather, seal used by the President, within a ring of fifty stars. The present basic design was introduced on 29 May 1946. The Vice-President's flag is white with the same device in the centre, but only four stars, in blue in the corners. This design was restored on 7 October 1975.

Each branch of the Armed Forces has a ceremonial flag, or Color, and the country has a very wide range of departmental, distinguishing, and rank flags. On the other hand, the Stars and Stripes does duty as the naval and civil ensign, as well as being the national flag on land. Each member of the Cabinet has a Color, and his or her deputy has a flag of the same design but with the colours reversed.

Each state of the Union has a flag, a seal, and a state emblem such as a bird, a tree, or a flower. The flags are of various origins and dates, but can be roughly grouped into the following categories:

(i) Flags derived from the Civil War. The Stars and Bars and the Southern Cross have been revived directly or indirectly in the flags of many of the states that were in the Confederacy, including Alabama, Arkansas, Florida, Georgia, Mississippi, North Carolina, and Tennessee. The flag of Virginia also dates from the Civil War.

(ii) Flags derived from Military Colors. These include ones like the Colours of Connecticut, Rhode Island, and Massachusetts, derived directly from flags used in the War of Independence, as well as ones for regiments formed for the Civil War or the wars with Mexico and Spain. Most of the flags with plain blue backgrounds and seals or coats of arms fall into this category, the archetype being the flag of North Dakota, which is an almost unaltered Military Colour.

See: The Heritage of the Stars and Stripes, Flag Competitions

Above and above right: *The arms and flag of the United States.*

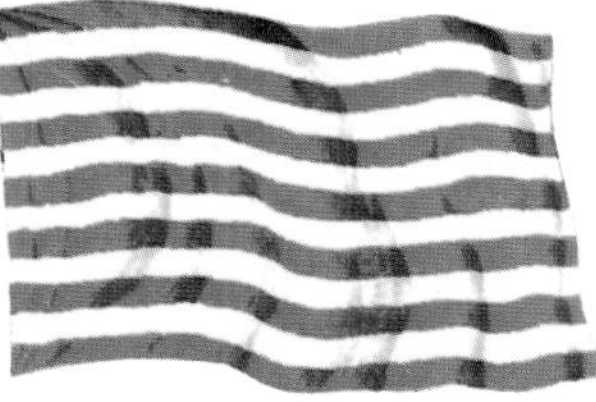

Above: *The flag of the "Liberty Boys", 1769.*

Above: *The Cambridge or Grand Union Flag, 1776.*

Above: *The Stars and Stripes, 1777.*

Above: *The First Confederate Flag, 1861.*

Above: *The "Southern Cross" or "Flag of the South".*

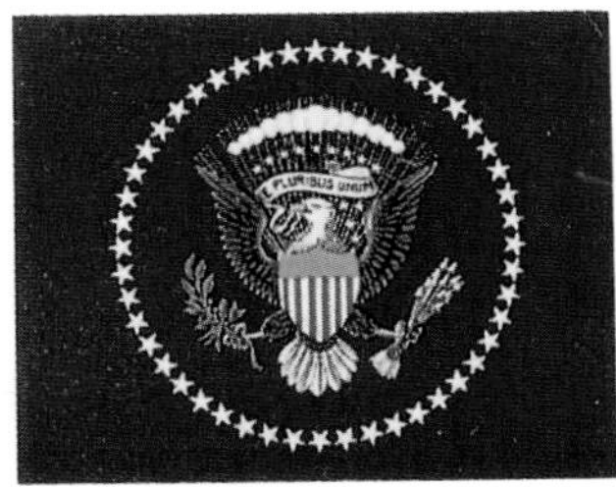

***Above:** The flag of the President.*

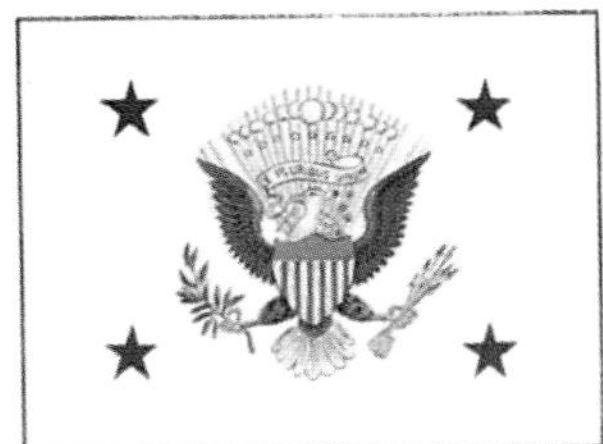

***Above:** The flag of the Vice-President.*

(iii) Flags that refer to former rulers. France and Spain are the countries whose flags are most often used as a source of inspiration. France has inspired the flags of Iowa, Missouri, and Illinois, and Spain those of Arizona, New Mexico, and Colorado, while the flag of Maryland is the banner of the former proprietors, the Crossland-Calverts.
(iv) Flags of formerly independent states. Texas, California, and Hawaii fall into this category.
(v) Flags derived from design competitions or adopted following pressure from the Daughters of American Revolution. The occasion for the adoption of a state flag was in some cases the Centennial of 1876. Competitions were held in Alaska, Indiana, Nevada, Oklahoma, and Wyoming.
(vi) Purely indigenous. This category includes most of the other states, where purely local circumstances and ideas led to the adoption of a particular design. Examples include South Carolina, Louisiana, Washington, West Virginia, and Ohio.

CONFEDERATE STATES OF AMERICA

The first flag of the Confederate States of America was hoisted on 4 March 1861, although some of the states had already adopted their own independence flags. The new flag was known as the Stars and Bars, and is clearly derived from the Stars and Stripes. The seven stars stood for the then seven members of the Confederacy. In September 1861 the Battle Flag was introduced for use in the field. This introduced the idea of the 'Southern Cross', or saltire, which seems to have been an adaptation of the flag used for a while in South Carolina. It was a square flag with a white border all round. The form later used as a jack, more oblong in shape and without the white border, is the flag now known as the Flag of the South. On 26 May 1863 a new national flag was adopted, consisting of a white flag with the Battle Flag in the canton. This was known as the Stainless Banner. The final flag, adopted on 4 March 1865, added a vertical red strip in the fly.

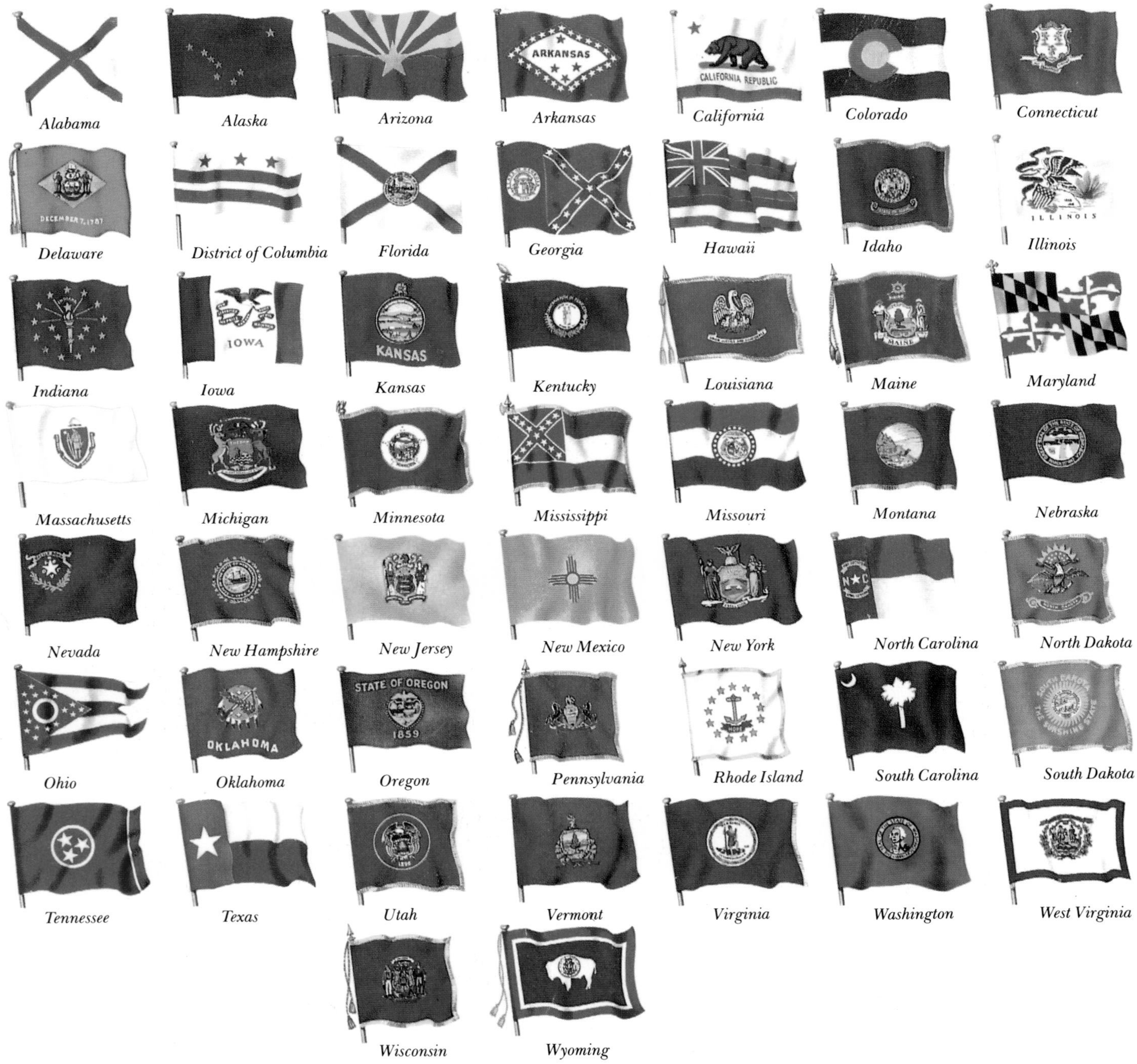
Alabama
Alaska
Arizona
ARKANSAS
Arkansas
CALIFORNIA REPUBLIC
California
Colorado
Connecticut
Delaware
District of Columbia
Florida
Georgia
Hawaii
Idaho
ILLINOIS
Illinois
Indiana
IOWA
Iowa
KANSAS
Kansas
Kentucky
Louisiana
MAINE
Maine
Maryland
Massachusetts
Michigan
Minnesota
Mississippi
Missouri
Montana
Nebraska
Nevada
New Hampshire
New Jersey
New Mexico
New York
N C
North Carolina
North Dakota
Ohio
OKLAHOMA
Oklahoma
STATE OF OREGON
1859
Oregon
Pennsylvania
Rhode Island
South Carolina
South Dakota
Tennessee
Texas
Utah
Vermont
Virginia
Washington
West Virginia
Wisconsin
Wyoming

URUGUAY, REPUBLIC OF

REPÚBLICA ORIENTAL DEL URUGAY

Established 25 August 1825

Uruguay was formerly part of the Spanish Viceroyalty of the River Plate and was involved in the struggle for emancipation in Argentina. The national hero, José Artigas, based in the Argentine province of Entre Rios, organized the *Liga de los Pueblos Libres* in 1813-15 against both Argentina and Brazil. In 1817 the country was occupied by Brazil and incorporated as the Cisplatine Province into the subsequent Brazilian Empire. In 1825 there was a rising led by the 'Thirty-three', which led to the declaration of independence. This was a secured by a treaty with Brazil and Argentina on 27 August 1828.

The flag of Artigas and the League of Free Peoples, which is now used as the jack of the Uruguay Navy and as the basis for the Air Force roundel, was like that of Argentina but with a diagonal red stripe across it. This flag is also the provincial flag of Entre Rios. The flag of the Thirty-three was a horizontal tricolour of blue, white, and red, with the motto, *Libertad o Muerte*, across the central stripe in black. The national flag did not appear until independence had been secured in 1828. The flag then had nine blue stripes, but the present design was instituted on 11 July 1830. The blue and white stripes and the sun are the same as those used in Argentina; here the stripes stand for the then nine provinces of the country.

The flag of the President is white with the national arms in the centre. These date from 1865 but contain elements from earlier national emblems, including the rising sun, the balance, and the fortress of Montevideo. The arms reached their present form in October 1908.

Above and above right: *The emblem and flag of Uruguay.*

See Central and South America

Above: *The arms of Uruguay.*

VANUATU, REPUBLIC OF

RIPABLIK BLANG VANUATU/REPUBLIQUE DE VANUATU

Established 30 July 1980

The New Hebrides group was formed into an Anglo-French condominium by the convention of 27 February 1906. The Vanuaaku Pati led the country to independence under the name of Vanuatu in 1980.

The national flag is in the colours of the Vanuaaku Pati and is based on their party flag. The design originally submitted was without the Y-shaped yellow 'pall', which was added at the last moment. The device in the black triangle is a boar's tooth, symbolic of prosperity. Within this are two crossed leaves of *namele* fern, symbolic of peaceful intentions. The Y-shape is said to symbolize the geographic layout of the archipelago. There is also a coat of arms, rather, an emblem, showing a Melanesian warrior standing in front of a volcano, behind which are the tooth and fern leaves. The motto is *Long God Yumi Stanap*, in the Bislama tongue, meaning 'We stand together with God'.

Above and left: *The arms and flag of Vanuatu; the motto means "We Stand Together with God".*

Far left: *The colonial badge of the New Hebrides.*

VATICAN CITY STATE

STATO DELLA CITTÀ DEL VATICANO

Established 11 February 1929

Above: *The flag of Pope Julius II (1503–1513) as shown on a German cigarette card.*

Right and above right: *The flag and arms of the Vatican.*

The Vatican City state is all that remains of the once extensive temporal domains of the Pope, which included all Rome, Latium, Umbria, the Marches, and Romagna. All except Rome and Latium were incorporated into Italy in 1861 and the remainder in 1870. The state was revived by the treaties of 1929, which recognized the Vatican as a sovereign state.

The modern Vatican colours of white and yellow were adopted in 1808 (they had previously been red and yellow). In the nineteenth century yellow and white flags were in use, including the present design, which was the Papal civil ensign from 1825 to 1870. It was re-established as the flag of the Vatican on 8 June 1929. Although the official model specified a square flag, in practice the flag is usually made 2:3. The emblem on the white panel is the crossed keys of St Peter (by tradition a golden key and a silver key) beneath the triple crown, or *tiara*, of the Pope. This emblem is only a badge, not the arms of the Papacy or of the Pope himself, which are different in several ways.

The Pope's personal flag is in fact similar to the Vatican flag, but has his own coat of arms on the white panel. The Vatican flag can, if necessary, be used at sea, and is also flown at the properties belonging to the state outside the Vatican itself.

The flag of the Sovereign Military Order of St John of Jerusalem, which is based in Rome and which also claims to be an independent sovereign power, is red with a white cross throughout.

VENEZUELA, REPUBLIC OF

REPÚBLICA DE VENEZUELA

Above and right: *The arms and flag of Venezuela. On the state flag the arms appear on the upper hoist.*

See: Central and South America

Venezuela was part of the Spanish Viceroyalty of New Granada, from which it declared its independence on 5 July 1811. On 7 August 1819 it joined with Colombia to form a new federation of Greater Colombia, but seceded on 30 April 1830.

The flag adopted immediately after independence was just like that used by Miranda in his unsuccessful attempt to raise Venezuela in 1806, ie, a horizontal tricolour of yellow, blue, red, but a few days later it was modified to double the width of the yellow strip and to add a panel in the hoist containing an allegorical scene. This went on to become the flag of Greater Colombia in 1819. When Ecuador joined the federation the upper yellow strip contained three blue stars instead of the panel. When Venezuela resumed its independence the stars were omitted and the republic's arms were placed in the centre of the flag. On 20 April 1836 the stripes reverted to their original equal form, and on 25 February 1859 seven stars were added to the canton. The seven stars represented the seven provinces that had joined in the declaration of independence in 1811. On 29 July 1859 the stars were placed in white on the blue stripe, in a circle with one in the centre. The present arrangement, with the stars in an arc, was instituted on 15 July 1930. The stars were omitted altogether in the period 1942-54.

The state flag has the arms in the canton. The present form of the arms dates from 15 April 1953. The dates on the scroll refer to the formation of the Junta of Caracas (19 April 1910) and the adoption of the federal constitution (20 February 1850). The republic currently consists of twenty states, many of which have arms and flags.

VIETNAM, SOCIALIST REPUBLIC OF

CÔNG HÒA XÃ HÔI CHU NGHĨA VIÊT NAM

Established 2 July 1976

Prior to unification Vietnam consisted of two rival regimes: the Republic of Vietnam, based in Saigon (Ho Chi Minh City), and the Democratic Republic, based in Hanoi. The latter had been formed in 1945 and became an autonomous republic within the French-organized Indo-Chinese federation on 6 March 1946. The French had acquired Indo-China piecemeal in the nineteenth century, but lost control to the Japanese during the Second World War; they returned in 1945, but again quitted the country in 1954. The Empire of Annam was another state in their union, and it became independent as Vietnam, including Cochin China, on 13 July 1949, and a republic on 26 October 1955. After a long war the southern government collapsed on 39 March 1975 and the south was united with the north in 1976.

The flag of modern Vietnam is similar to that adopted for the republic of 1945. The present design dates from 30 November 1955. It gave rise to the flag used in the south by the National Liberation Front, or Viet Cong, which was divided equally red over blue with the yellow star in the centre. The flag of the Republic of Vietnam, dating from 14 June 1948, was yellow with three horizontal stripes of red, being an adaptation of the flag of Annam.

The arms of Vietnam are very similar to those of the Democratic Republic, the only difference being in the name on the scroll. The emblem is itself derived from that of China.

See: The Red Flag

Above and left: *The arms and flag of Vietnam*

Above: *The flag of the Emperor of Annam prior to World War II.*

WESTERN SAMOA

SAMOA I SISIFO

Established 1 January 1962

Western Samoa is the part of Samoa that passed under German control by the Tripartite Treaty of 7 November 1899. It consists of the islands of Savai'i, Upolu, Manono, and Apolima, which at one time formed the kingdoms of the Tuiaana and Malietoa monarchs. New Zealand took a mandate on the islands in 1920 and administered them until independence in 1962.

Samoa had several flags before it was taken over by the Germans and the Americans. The basic flag of the Malietoa kingdom, probably inspired by missionaries, was red with a white cross throughout and a white star in the canton. King Tamasese of the Tuiaana line, who favoured the German cause, used flags with black crosses.

A new flag was introduced on 26 May 1948, following the adoption of a new constitution. This was blue with a red canton containing four stars of the Southern Cross, similar to those on the flag of New Zealand. On 24 February 1949 a fifth star was added, so that the Southern Cross now resembles the one on the Australian flag. This flag was retained when independence was resumed in 1962.

Above: *The flag of Samoa prior to 1900.*

Above and left: *The arms and flag of Western Samoa.*

Yemen Arab Republic

AL-JAMAHURIYA AL-ARABIYA AL-YAMANIYA

Established 27 September 1962

See: The Pan-Arab Colours

Above and above right: The arms and flag of the Yemen Arab Republic. On the unification of the two Yemens in May 1990, a flag like the one above but with no star in the middle was adopted by the new state.

The republic was set up by Nasserite officers in 1962 on the death of the hereditary Imam and King, Ahmad bin Yahya. Civil war followed between the Nasserites and supporters of the House of Rassi until the cease-fire of 1967.

The flag of the Mutawakkilite Kingdom was red with a sword and five white stars. These emblems commemorated the ruling family's descent from Ali and Fatima and the Imamate of the Shi'ite Zaydi sect. The flag adopted for the republic was exactly like that of Egypt as it was at the time, but with only one green star. This has remained in use ever since, whereas the royalist flag is now used only in exile. The national emblem contains an eagle bearing a shield. On the shield is a design rather like that on the royalist arms: a representation of a dam with a coffee bush above it. The President's flag is like the national flag, with the arms in the canton.

Above: The flag of the Imam of Yemen.

Yemen People's Democratic Republic

JUMHURIYAH AL-YEMEN AL-DIMUKRATIYAH AL-SHA'ABIYAH

Established 30 November 1967

See: The Pan Arab Colours

Above and right: The arms and flag of the Yemen People's Democratic Republic.

The republic consists of what was formerly the colony of Aden, the Arab states in the Federation of South Arabia, and other Arab states in the area formerly under British control. The Federation was first formed on 11 February 1959 and became the Federation of South Arabia on 4 April 1962. Aden colony became a state within the federation on 18 January 1963. British rule was brought to an end in 1967 by the National Liberation Front, which formed the People's Republic and expelled the traditional rulers.

Nearly all the Arab states in Aden had their own flags, several having quite a wide range of emblems. Aden first of all had the usual British colonial badge system, but on joining the federation acquired a flag of its own. The federal flag was divied horizontally into stripes of black, green, and yellow, with the green fimbriated in yellow and a large white crescent and star over all.

The flag adopted by the People's Republic is like that of Egypt but with a red star, placed on a light blue triangle in the hoist. The coat of arms is also very similar to that of Egypt, differing only in the name on the scroll and the pattern red stripe near the hoist.

Above: The flag of the Qu'aiti Sultan of Mukhalla and Shir.

YUGOSLAVIA, SOCIALIST FEDERAL REPUBLIC OF

SOCIJALISTICKA FEDERATIVNA REPUBLIKA JUGOSLAVIJA
Established 29 November 1945

Yugoslavia is a federation of states with varying histories and origins. Montenegro had remained independent of the Ottoman Empire while Serbia became independent in 1815; Bosnia and Herzegovina were annexed from Turkey by Austria, whereas Croatia was a traditional part of Hungary, and Slovenia of Austria. Macedonia was won from Turkey by Serbia in 1913. The Kingdom of Serbs, Croats, and Slovenes was formed on 1 December 1918 under the King of Serbia, and was renamed Yugoslavia in 1929. During the Second World War the Communist partisans became the effective controllers of the country and set up a republic in 1945; this became the Federal Republic on 31 January 1946.

By the end of the nineteenth century all the component parts of Yugoslavia except Macedonia had acquired flags in the Pan-Slav colours of red, white, and blue, arranged in various patterns. These are still used today, with the addition of the large red, yellow-edged star that was the badge of the Partisans. The flag adopted for the new kingdom in 1918 was of blue, white, red stripes, with the crowned shield set over all near the hoist. By the constitution of 1946 this acquired the Partisan star in the centre and also the new proportions of 1:2 (as did the republic flags). A new coat of arms was adopted, consisting of six torches united to form a common flame, beneath the Partisan star. On the scroll is '29.XI.1943', the date of the formation of the provisional Communist government. The President's flag is like the former royal standard, but has the national emblem in the centre instead of the old royal arms.

As noted, the republics still use their old colours with a red star. In the case of Bosnia the tricolour is placed in the canton of a red flag (to distinguish it from the national flag) and in Macedonia, which never had a flag, the device is a plain red flag with the Partisan star in the canton.

See: The Pan-Slav Colours

Above: *The flag of the last King of Montenegro.*

Above and top: *The arms and flag of Yugoslavia: the scroll on the arms can be either red or blue.*

ZAIRE, REPUBLIC OF

REPUBLIQUE DU ZAÏRE
Established 30 June 1960

The King of the Belgians became head of the Congo Free State in 1885 and the territory was annexed to Belgium on 18 October 1908. It became independent in 1960 but experienced several secessionist movements before it was united in 1967 by the present regime, the *Mouvement Populaire de la Révolution*. The country was renamed in October 1971, as were the towns with Belgian names.

The flag of the Congo Free State, allegedly designed by H.M. Stanley, was blue with a large gold star in the centre. This continued to fly when the country was a Belgian colony, and on independence six small stars were added in a vertical row in the hoist. This flag was superseded on 1 July 1963 by one of darker blue with a single star in the upper hoist and a red, yellow-edged diagonal stripe. This in turn was replaced by the present design on 21 November 1971. This is based on the party flag of the MPR, but also refers to the Pan-African colours of red, yellow, and green.

See: The Pan-African Colours

Above and left: *The arms and flag of Zaire. The motto is "Justice, Unity, Work".*

Zambia, Republic of

Established 24 October 1964

Above and right: *The arms and flag of Zambia.*

The territories of Northeast and Northwest Rhodesia, belonging to the British South Africa Company, were united in 1911 and became a British colony on 1 April 1924. The colony was part of the Federation of Rhodesia and Nysaland from 1953 to 1963, and became independent in 1964. The state includes the kingdom of the Lozi (Barotseland).

The flag of Zambia was designed by a graphic artist on the basis of the colours of the dominant political party, the United National Independence Party, although the yellow was changed to orange to make one of the strips in the fly, where it represents the country's mineral wealth, while the soaring fish eagle is taken from the arms of Northern Rhodesia. In those arms it had a fish in its claws but that is now absent. The arms of Zambia are black and white wavy lines, representing the Victoria Falls.

The President's flag is orange with the whole arms in the centre. The flag of the Litunga of Barotseland is red with a white elephant, rather like the old flag of Siam.

Above: *The colonial arms of Northern Rhodesia, showing the wavy lines for the Victoria Falls and also the fish-eagle.*

Zimbabwe, Republic of

Established 18 April 1980

See: The Pan-African Colours

Rhodesia was part of the domains of the British South Africa Company until 12 September 1923, when it became a crown colony. From 1953 it was part of the Federation of Rhodesia and Nyasaland. The white government made a unilateral declaration of independence on 11 November 1965 and thereafter sustained guerrilla attacks from the nationalist movements. It formally became a republic on 2 March 1970. Legality was restored on 12 December 1979, followed by independence under a government led by the Zimbabwe African National Union in 1980. The name Zimbabwe is derived from the ancient African city near Masvingo.

The country has had several flags in its convoluted history. Rhodesia was granted a coat of arms on 11 August 1924, of which the crest was a representation of one of the 'lightning birds' found at Zimbabwe in 1888. The bird is in a crouching position on what appears to be a capital. The shield of the arms was used as an ensign-badge. On 8 April 1964 a more distinctive flag with a light blue field was adopted, with the Union Jack in the canton and the shield in the fly. This was replaced by one of three vertical strips of green, white, green with the whole arms in the centre on 11 November 1968. On 2 September 1979 yet another design of horizontal stripes of red, white, green with a vertical black strip in the hoist and the Zimbabwe bird in the canton was adopted.

The colours of the present flag are derived from the party flag of ZANU, which consists of concentric panels of red, black, yellow, and green, with the addition of white. The Zimbabwe bird appears on a red star in the white triangle. A new coat of arms was adopted in 1983, with the Zimbabwe bird and red star as a crest. The arms appear in the centre of a green flag to form the President's flag. There is also a white triangle with the star and bird, and two patches of the colours yellow, red, and black in the fly.

Above and above right: *The arms and flag of Zimbabwe; both include the "Zimbabwe Bird".*

Above: *The flag of Rhodesia after UDI with the arms of 1924.*

The Early Origins of Flags
The Ancient World

Flag-like objects have been in use since the dawn of civilization. Vexilloids are solid objects that fulfil the same functions as flags, that is, they identify, they mark the presence of a notable person, they carry information about the nature and attributes of that person or a god. A surprising feature of the very earliest religious vexilloids is that they were graphic symbols, not attempts at realistic or ideographic representation. They achieved their effect by using some attribute or symbolic feature of the god, and there are very many examples dating back five thousand years and more. Innana, the Mesopotamian goddess of agriclture, is symbolized by a shepherd's crook, and later deities had similar 'badges'. This was particularly the case in Egypt, where symbolic representations of the deities were common, such as the hawk of Horus, the jackal of Anubis, and the throne of Isis. The Egyptians were the first to use streamers on flagpoles, but it is thought that they were only for decorative purposes and were found only in the precincts of temples. Egypt also provides an example of the use of standards to mark the presence of a king, on a carved macehead of the pre-Dynastic period, and, in an example from the twelfth century BC, of a standard to mark a division of the army.

Above: *Egyptian vexilloids with a hawk and an ibis, both symbols of ancient gods.*

It is doubtful if anything in the nature of national symbols existed in this early period. All that can be said is that vexilloids of different groups had characteristic forms and followed characteristic themes. The standards of the early Anatolian civilzation were stags, like the famous example from Alaça Hüyük, whereas the Assyrians used standards with bulls and the emblem of Assur, the divine archer of the Sun (a winged disc). In more elaborate form the winged disc became the emblem of the Persians. The Babylonian stele of Ur Nammu, *c.*2100 BC shows very clearly two emblems whose use continued into modern times: the crescent moon and the rayed star of Shamash, the sun-god. Another emblem recently revived is the double-axe, or *labrys*, of Crete. Standards in the form of double-axes once stood in the temple of Knossos.

When trade and warfare took to the seas, emblems did acquire a more 'national' character, but were still normally the devices of the patron god or goddess. The Phoenicians were the first to put flagstaffs on their ships, in the form of poles that could be slotted into the inward-curving prows and sterns of their galleys. These bore the crescent and disc of Astarte, the moon-goddess, and also decorative streamers.

The Romans preferred the sky-god Jupiter as their patron, and so used his emblems, the eagle and the thunderbolt, on their standards. The Romans were the first to systematize the use of standards to mark the units of an army. Each legion had an eagle and each cohort a *signum*. Each detached unit had a *vexillum*, one of the first kinds of vexilloid to use fabric. The auxiliary cavalry used the *draco* standard and the *imago*, the portrait of the Emperor. Roman standards, especially those of the legions and the cohorts, were liberally decorated with honorific awards, and could also have small pieces of fabric hanging from a crossbar.

It is from the Romans that some long-standing ideas about the 'honour' attached to a military symbol are derived. They treated their standards as holy objects, kept them under lock and key, and suffered the utmost disgrace if they were lost to the enemy.

The earliest use of fabric flags dates from about the fourth century BC. The flag painted on a wall at Paestum, a Samnite colony in southern Italy, cannot be said to have a significant design, but its form is very like that of a modern flag, complete with *cravat* (a streamer attached to the flagpole above the flag). The Roman *vexillum* did appear to have a significant design, to judge by the only known example still in existence, which has the image of the goddess of victory painted on it. The Romans also had another fabric flag, called a *flammula*, which consisted of red streamers attached to a spear. It is thought that this was used to mark the presence of the general. This usage appears to derive from the *phoinikis* used in Greek times to mark the commander's ship, a practice copied by the Romans.

The last fabric flag used in Roman times was the *labarum*, which was a development of

Above: *The palette of King Narmer showing standards being carried by the victorious Egyptians.*

Below: *A Babylonian temple with standards above the gateway.*

the vexillum, being a purple cloth with the portraits of the Emperor and his family or colleagues embroidered on it. This dates from Christian times and had the Christian *Chi-Rho* emblem as a finial.

None of these devices was ever flown from flagpoles: all were intended to be carried by hand. So by the time of the collapse of the Roman Empire, the modern flag had still to be invented.

***Above:** Roman military standards with a signum (**top**), and an eagle (**above**), as depicted on German cigarette cards, and an eagle with honorific awards on a staff.*

Vexilloids Known from Early Civilizations – Actual Specimens

*c*2400–2200 BC: standards found at Alaça Hüyük, stag, stag with two bulls, sun disc

*c*2200 BC: Bronze bull standard from Horoztepe

*c*1500 BC: Wooden statuette with standard of Horus

*c*1500 BC: double-axe standard of Crete

1122–221 BC: stag standard from Chou dynasty

*c*900: bronze standard from Luristan

700–600 BC: eagle's head standard from Kuban

450–400 BC: wood and leather standard of elk from Pazyryk graves (Altai)

*c*350 BC: bronze standard from Ein Gedi

206–220 BC: elk standard from Han dynasty

Vexillum found in Egypt

Signum found in Essex;

Horse standard found at Vindolanda

Dragon-head from Niederbieber

Standard of *beneficarius* from Strasbourg

PROTO-HERALDRY

Until the Moslems began to conquer the Middle East, there is very little evidence of *laterally* attached flags, ie, ones secured by one edge only to a vertical staff. It seems as if this practice reached the Mediterranean and the Middle East from China, where such flags were used at an early date.

Nobody knows exactly what flags were used by the conquering armies of Islam, although several emblems have come down to us from that period. These include the 'Hand of Fatima', the split sword of Ali known as the *zûl-faqar*, and various kinds of ornamental finials. The Prophet is said to have used a flag called a *liwa* of black with a white border. The *borda*, or green cloak, of the Prophet was used afterwards by his followers. By tradition red flags with the *zûl-faqar* were used by the Shi'ites, who venerated Ali and Fatima.

On the Christian side, in the Dark Ages the practice grew of bestowing banners that had been blessed by the Pope on his chosen agents. These were called *pallia* and, like Mohammed's cloak, were originally garments. *Pallia* were given to St Augustine, Charlemagne, and William the Conqueror. No exact description or depiction of them remains, unless the flag carried next to William the Conqueror in the Bayeux Tapestry is his *pallium*. Another garment that later became a flag was the cloak or cape of St Martin. The actual cloak survived for a long time, like Mohammed's in Cairo, and became a cult object of the Frankish kings. The word 'chapel' is actually derived from the shrine in which it was kept.

***Above:** A Moslem flag depicting the zul-faqar.*

***Right:** The gonfanon of William the Conqueror as depicted in the Bayeux Tapestry.*

The pagans of Europe clearly had distinguishing signs, as is known from several literary references. The object found in the Sutton Hoo burial, the grave of King Redwald of the East Angles, *c.*AD630, is thought to be a standard, and the device on a penny of the Jarl of york, *c.*AD920, is thought to be a flag. The penny of a later Viking ruler of York depicts the raven, the famous emblem of the Horsemen. The raven standard is mentioned several times in Nordic literature. One was claimed to have been captured from marauding Danes by King Alfred's forces at the Battle of Cynuit (AD878). This is supposed to have been the very flag of Ragnar Hairybreeks whose sons harried England and killed King Edmund of East Anglia. Ragnar's flag was called *Léodbróga* and may well have been named after him. Sven Forkbeard had a similar flag when he conquered England in 1013. Harold Hardrada, who invaded England in 1066, had a banner called *Landeythan*, or the 'Landwaster'.

***Above:** Charlemagne installs Roland as his representative in Spain and presents him with a gonfanon as a sign of authority.*

The English fought at Hastings under the Dragon of Wessex. This is thought to be a vexilloid like the Roman *draco*, made of a hollow tube of fabric attached to a hollow metal head. This they inherited from the British, who in turn probably adapted it from the Romans. A dragon standard was used by the Norman rulers of England, illustrating the practice, employed by the Romans, of incorporating captured insignia into their own panoply.

Sources from the later Byzantine Empire also indicate that flags more like modern ones had come into use by the eleventh century. Their cavalry flags were known as *banda*, and were very similar to the flag of William the Conqueror, with long streamers attached to the flying end. The Byzantine Empire also favoured the double-headed eagle device, now so widely associated with the idea of 'Empire'. In their heraldry it was gold on red, and it became widely used in the time of Andronikos Palaeologos (*c*AD1261). The cross with four letters between its arms is thought to date from the Latin Empire (1204–61), but opinion is divided as to what the letters are. They reappeared later in the arms of Serbia.

***Above:** A gilded vane from Soderala Church, Halsingland, 11th century AD. (Historika Museet, Stockholm).*

Later Islamic flags assumed fantastic shapes and decorative ingenuity. This was due to the Koranic ban on representational art. Instead, and in complete contrast to European heraldry, they relied heavily on calligraphic inscriptions, often religious texts. An example is the banner attributed to the Moorish state of Granada, which was red with the inscription *Wa il ghalib ill'Allah* ('There is no conqueror but God'). This tradition lives on today in the flag of Iran.

Meanwhile, in Asia an even greater power arose, that of the Mongols. The flag of Genghis Khan, and the use made of flags by his hordes (which were in fact divided into regiments known as 'Banners', like the later Chinese Army), has been well described in literature. Unfortunately, no exact description of the nature of the flags has been given. It seems as if standards with horsetail tassels of various colours were used. The standard of the great Khan himself consisted of nine yak-tails depending from a rack of crossbars. Mongol standards often made use of a 'flaming trident', a device like the blades of a trident with flames surrounding them. After the conquest of China, Mongols used laterally attached flags but still with the horsetail ornament and flaming trident.

***Above:** A Persian painting of c1530 shows flags with flaming trident finials.*

***Left:** The flag of the Byzantine emperor Andronikos Palaeologus, as depicted on a German cigarette card.*

THE DAWN OF HERALDRY

Heraldry traditionally began with the Crusades. Two factors were involved: the need to distinguish the Christians with a badge that showed they were on Crusade, with all that that implied, and the need to identify actual individuals when they were wearing armour that covered the face. This problem had already arisen at, for example, the Battle of Hastings, where Duke William was obliged to raise his helmet to show his face, and later helmets were much more anonymous.

The first badge of the Crusaders was of course a cross. With the development of the surcoat, the cross could be worn on the front and back of the warrior, as well as on pennons and flags. By tradition crosses of different colours were agreed upon in 1188 for the Crusaders of different nationalities, but a later development, whereby the different colours became associated either with various patron saints or with military religious orders, became more widespread. It is from this system that the red cross on white of St George, the white cross on red of St Denis, and the black cross on white of the Teutonic Knights emerged. The white cross on red was another Crusader flag used against the pagans in Europe, and hence this became the battle flag of the German Empire.

Personal heraldry was simple to start with, and it is from this period that the most basic heraldic patterns originate, such as the rampant lion, the black spread eagle of Germany, the castle of Castile, and the red and white stripes of Austria. Many of these were in fact 'arms of dominion', ie, they represented not just the king or prince but also the place or area that he ruled.

The next stage in heraldry was to make the devices hereditary, a custom that became established in the early thirteenth century. The laws of heraldry that have grown up since then also dictate that each coat of arms must be unique to its bearer and only be used by him. The laws also included the 'rules of tincture', which are still valid today. By this rule heraldic 'tinctures' are divided into categories, of which the main ones are the 'metals' (gold and silver, or yellow and white) and the 'colours' (red, blue, green, purple). No colour or metal may lie next to another colour or metal unless they are separated by a tincture from the other category. This is what gives rise to the practice of 'fimbriation', eg, the separation of a black stripe from a red field by means of narrow white edging, as on the flag of Trinidad.

A consequence of the 'unique' rule was the invention of badges and livery colours. The great men who wore their own arms often had retainers and armed forces of their own who needed to be distinguished from those of other magnates. The way chosen to do this was to develop a set of colours, known as livery colours, which could be used in their uniforms, and a badge or badges, which could be used on their clothing or on pennons and flags. The livery colours were often the prime 'metal' and prime 'colour' from the great man's arms, but not always. The monarchs of England and

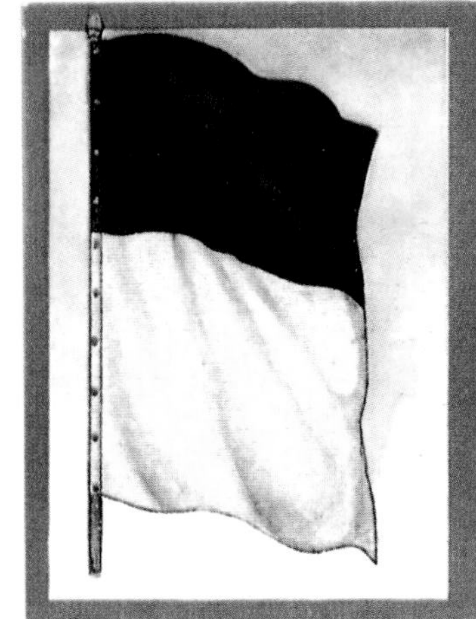

Top right and right: *Flags of the military religious orders of the Templars and the Knights of St John, as shown on a German cigarette card.*

Above: *The cross allocated to the Flemings for the Crusade of 1188. The traditional arms of Spain (**near right**) and France (**far right**) as shown in a manuscript of c1350 AD.*

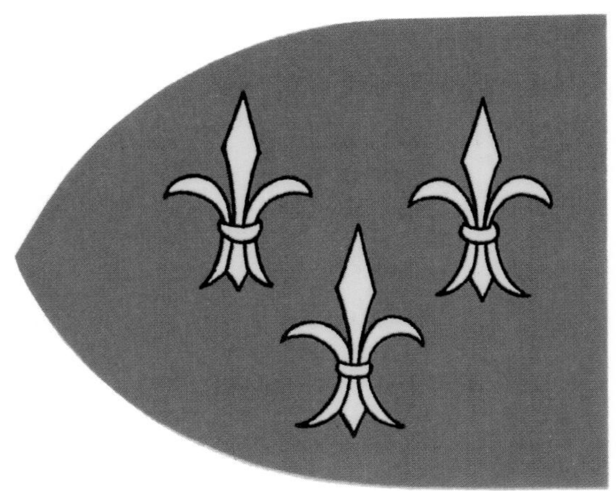

France, for example, often used colours unrelated to their arms, such as the white and green favoured by the Tudor monarchs. Badges were usually quite unrelated to the arms, such as the well-known White Boar of Richard III and the radiant sun of Louis XIV. They were also hereditary and could only be given out by the head of the family.

***Above:** A heraldic badge-flag showing the badges of Richard III, the Sun in Splendour of York and the White Boar of Gloucester, on a field of the Yorkist colours (blue and maroon).*

Flags with crosses seem to derive from the Crusader period, which was in fact a long period (1096–1291) coinciding with the development of both heraldry and modern nation-states. Certainly the cross flags of England, France, and Denmark derive directly from the Crusader cross, and others do so indirectly, such as the cross of Switzerland. Many more flags derive from the 'arms of dominion', either as armorial flags or as flags in the livery colours of these arms. Examples of these are the flags of Austria, Spain, Luxembourg, Poland, Sweden, Hungary, Malta, San Marino, Monaco, Belgium, and the Vatican.

Another development parallel to the heraldry of notable persons was that of Christianity. Christian saints acquired badges or attributes reminiscent of those of the gods mentioned in the section, 'The Ancient World'. Those who had died a martyr's death often had a cross badge, such as the saltire of St Andrew (used in Scotland, Burgundy, and Russia) or else the emblem of their martyrdom, such as the wheel of St Catherine. Others had attributes symbolic of their most oustanding characteristic, such as St George with the dragon, St Michael overcoming the devil, St Martin's cape, and the scallop shell of St James, which later became the universal badge of Christian pilgrims. The badges of the four apostles also had an effect on heraldry, the most famous example being the lion of St Mark, used by the Republic of Venice. The eagle of St John was used by the Spanish monarchs, but the attributes of Matthew (the angel) and the Luke (the ox) are less common. The keys of St Peter became the badge of the papacy at an early date, and other religious emblems, such as the badge of the Trinity and of the Holy Ghost, were in widespread use.

***Above:** The arms and standards of Sir Bryan Stapleton and Henry Stafford as shown in the Wriothesley manuscript of the early 16th century. (British Library Board).*

***Below:** The badge of Louis XIV ("The Sun King") on a military flag; the motto means "Equal to Any".*

***Left:** Images of the Count of Aragon **(above)** and the King of Castile **(below)** with their arms blazoned over their entire equipment.*

Flags at Sea
FLAGS FOR USE AT SEA

The use of flags at sea was the beginning of flags as they are known today, since they were made to be actually flown from masts and staffs rather than merely held in the hand. The period also saw the development of heraldic sails, ie, ones painted with armorial devices all over. Several examples of these are shown on corporation seals from the period.

The earliest sea flags of the Middle Ages were the banners and pennons of the warriors who used ships for transport and conflict, but it was also during this period that devices symbolic of nationality began to emerge. The first of these were the 'arms of dominion', such as the three lions of England, and the fleurs-de-lis of France, but gradually the right to use these arms became restricted to the monarch and his appointed agents. Eventually, in England, only the Admiral, or commander-in-chief of the fleet, was to enjoy this privilege. This meant that lesser flags, such as the Cross of St George, had to be used to denote nationality. During the pre-Reformation period many such flags were of a pictorial nature, carrying depictions of the saint in a characteristic pose.

In the thirteenth century the development of the arms of the Cinque Ports and its component towns provided another form of distinctive banner. The Cinque Ports arms are a combination of the Royal Arms of England with three ship hulls, signifying their duty to provide ships for the King. A similar development took place in the Hanseatic League, which united trading cities in northern Europe.

After the Reformation the banners with religious figures tended to be confined to Portugal and Spain, and simpler flags became prevalent in England and adjacent countries.

The next development in sea flags was the creation of 'house flags' for trading companies. Both England and the Netherlands had such companies, whose object was to establish trading links with places beyond Europe. The Guinea Company used a flag based on that of St George, while the flags of the Muscovy Company and the Cathay Company were combinations of the royal arms and the Cross of St George. The flags of the Dutch companies were based on the *Prinsenvlag*, the tricolour used during the long struggle for independence against the Spaniards. 'Logos' in the forms of interlaced initials were placed in the centre of this flag. These flags were all licensed by their national authorities.

As commercial shipping became more frequent, unofficial flags for use by merchant vessels also became widespread. In France flags of blue and white and in the Hansa cities flags of red and white were in use, and in England flags with stripes, such as the green and white of the Tudors, with the national cross in the canton, developed in the time of Queen Elizabeth. The final development of this period was the invention of the canton: a system for placing one flag in the upper hoist quarter of another.

As at sea the flags used by fighting units on land were at first those of the territorial magnates. These employed banners and standards for themselves and pennons for their followers. Their personal standards were often very elaborate, making use of their whole range of badges and mottoes, as in those used in Eng-

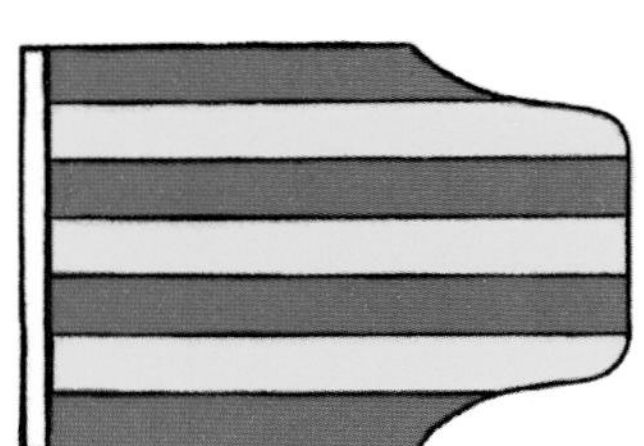

Above, top to bottom: *Naval flags of Spain from a flag chart; Castile, Aragon, the flag of Christopher Columbus and the cross of Burgundy (the "saltire raguly").*

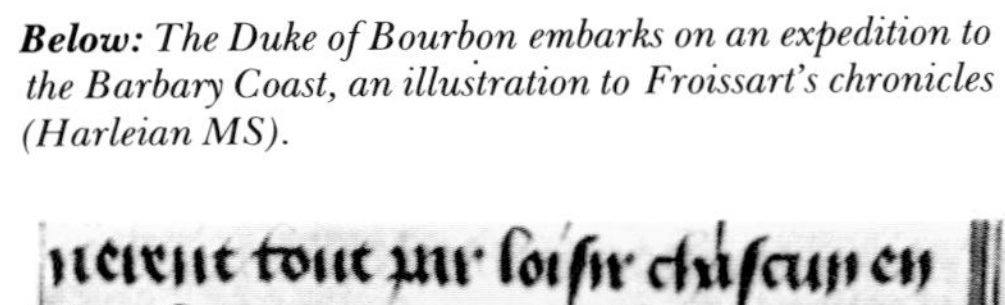

Below: *The Duke of Bourbon embarks on an expedition to the Barbary Coast, an illustration to Froissart's chronicles (Harleian MS).*

Left: *The Mary Rose, "the flower I trow of all ships that ever sailed", as depicted in the Anthony Roll. The Mary Rose was a principal vessel in the fleet of Henry VIII. (By permission of the Masters and Fellows of Magdalene College, Cambridge).*

Below: *The Defeat of the Spanish Armada: the English ships with the Cross of St George and the Spanish with red and yellow flags. (National Maritime Museum).*

land in the Wars of the Roses, in which the blue and white of Lancaster was opposed to the blue and maroon of York. During the Hundred Years' War, which involved England, France, and Burgundy, many elaborate flags and banners were employed, including the white flag of Joan of Arc. Toward the end of the sixteenth century, military manuals began to include sections on how to set up systems of flags for the various divisions of an army, but these mostly assumed that the troops were raised and commanded by a magnate and would wear his colours. During the seventeenth-century Civil Wars in England, adaptations of these systems were in fact used on the parliamentary side but not by the royalists.

The end of the sixteenth century saw the development on land of more ad hoc flag systems, rather than ones based on coats of arms, and a move began toward allegorical scenes and figures rather than ones that followed the rules of medieval heraldry.

THE AGE OF DISCOVERY

Early vessels made their voyages by coasting, but by the Middle Ages the art of navigating from point to point using a compass was understood. For this purpose a route map was needed which was supplied from about 1250 onward by annotated maps depicting the coasts of the Mediterranean and adjacent seas. These maps are known as *portolanos* and were first prepared by Genoese navigators. Of interest to vexillologists is the fact that they were very often decorated with flags. The oldest such chart in existence dates from 1306, and others were made in the same form up to the mid-sixteenth century. The flags depicted are not just 'arms of dominion' but also town flags of places with local rights. The charts are not always very valuable sources of information, but the later ones give us clues as to the flags in use at a particular time in history, and also the actual shapes of the flags.

In about 1350 an unknown Spanish friar wrote the first guidebook to the world illustrated with flags. These were usually depicted as shield-shapes and, like the ones in the *portolanos*, included many fanciful and fantastic entries, so that even the entries for well-known places have to be treated with caution. However, the temptation to make up designs for places about which nothing is known for certain was not confined to the fourteenth century.

The Portuguese were the first to sail round the world, and to discover the routes to Africa and India. They reached Madeira in 1416, the Azores in 1427, and Cape Verde in 1460. These voyages of exploration were inspired by Henry the Navigator, who was Grand Master of the Order of Christ and who, with the Order's help, founded a navigation college. The flag of the Order was used extensively by Portuguese ships and in a somewhat different form is still

Above: *The flags of the Portuguese explorers as depicted on a Brazilian postage stamp, including the armillary sphere and the cross of the Order of Christ.*

the flag of a colonial governor. It was in memory of Henry the Navigator that the *armilla*, or armillary sphere, was used in later Portuguese flags. This was a device that aided navigation by providing an analogue of the earth in relation to the zodiac.

The Spaniards reached America in 1492. The day 12 October 1492, when Christopher Columbus landed on an island in the Bahamas, is still commemorated as the Day of the (Hispanic) Race, because it marked the start of Spanish expansion into the Caribbean and Central and South America. Columbus is credited with two flags: the banner of Castile (Castile quartered with León) and a special flag carrying the ciphers of the Catholic monarchs, Ferdinand and Isabella. The *conquistadores* Cortés and Pizarro, who later conquered Mexico and Peru, also had flags with them. These were their own personal flags, since their expeditions did not have the same royal warrant that Columbus's had.

EARLY FLAG CHARTS AND ALBUMS

The earlier section, 'Flags for Use at Sea', made mention of early illustrations of flags on the *portolanos* and in the manuscript of the Spanish Friar. It was to be a long time before systematic attempts to illustrate flags were undertaken in any serious way. In England one of the earliest such manuscripts is the album composed by Jonathan Turmile to illustrate the cavalry standards used by the Parliamentary troops in the Civil War. The album was kept up during the war, since the author added pictures of the flags captured from the royalists at Edge Hill and Naseby. Several other contemporaries composed similar albums but none was quite so well presented as Turmile's.

In the Netherlands a famous early tract is the De Görtter manuscript, from abut 1600. This depicts the flags used in the armies fighting in the Netherlands at that time, and tells not only their designs but also their size and how they were displayed. This valuable document is now in the Royal Library in Brussels.

Collections of flags for use at sea appeared in the Netherlands in 1667 in the form of a manuscript now in the Library of the United States Naval Academy in Annapolis, Maryland, and in a manuscript of 1669, edited in replica form in 1966. Both of these are anonymous. A manuscript ascribed to J. Moutton from France is dated 1670 and is very similar to the previous one, with finely painted pictures of flags, some of which are almost identical to the Dutch manuscript. Further collections were produced in England. Downman's manuscript of 1685, now in the National Maritime Museum, Greenwich, is the first English collection of sea-flag pictures. It was followed in 1686 by Gradon's *Insignia Navalis*, commissioned by Samuel Pepys and now in the Pepys Library in Cambridge. Neither of these documents is up to the standards set by their Dutch and French precursors, although both contain some intriguing illustrations. A further collection appeared in the manuscript of Captain van der Dussen in 1690.

The late seventeenth century saw a sudden increase in the amount of flag information being published. A book by Desroches on naval terminology (1687) was the first to include drawings of actual flags, followed by the key work by Carl Allard (1694), which had a large number of flag drawings. These were all in line but they were often recycled in the eighteenth century in forms that could be coloured by hand. Some of Allard's flags have survived into flag books in quite recent times. His work was pirated and repirated by publishers throughout the century, with little regard as to whether the flags were accurate or out of date.

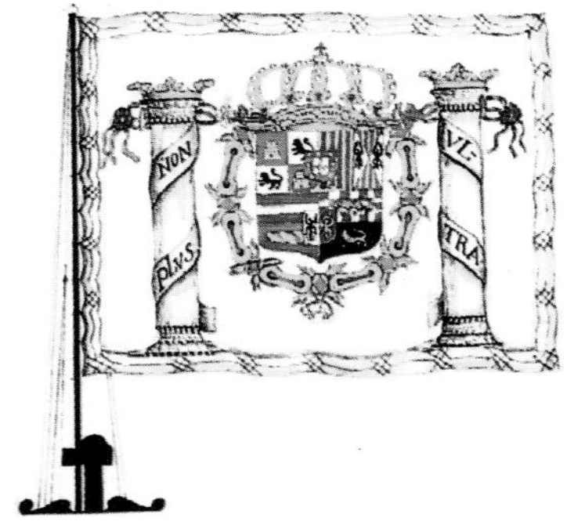

Above: *The Royal Arms of Spain on a flag from a 17th-century manuscript.*

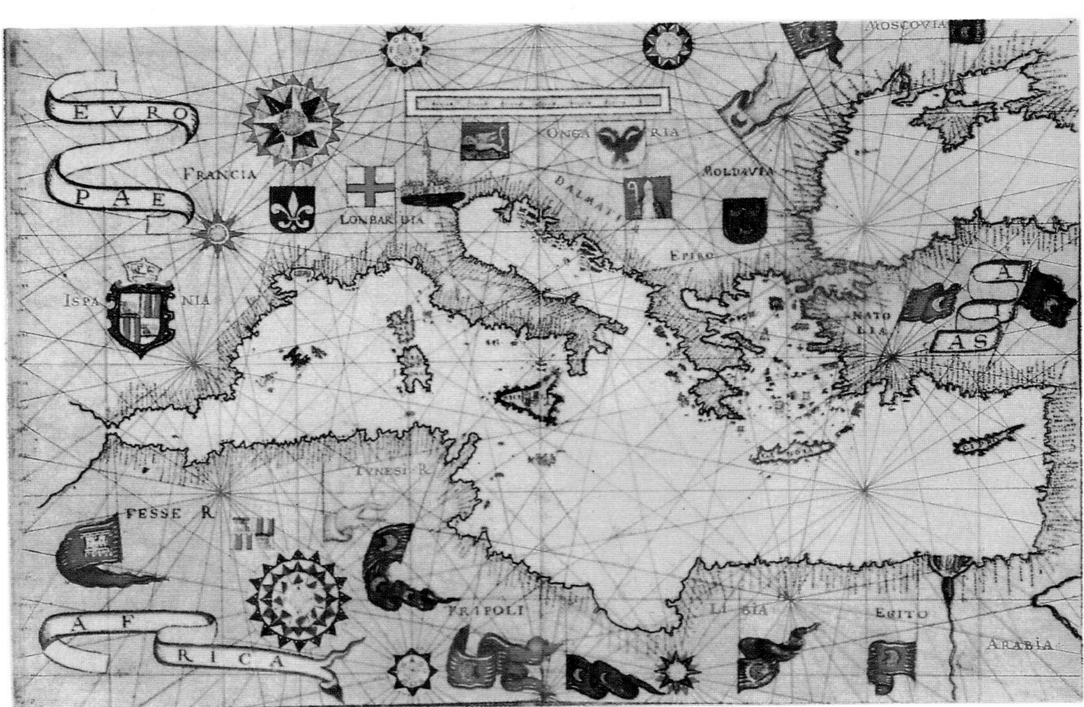

Right: *A Venetian portolano map of the Mediterranean, depicting the flags of the countries bordering the sea, c1586.*

FLAGS CHARTS AND ALBUMS

The publication of flag charts began in the eighteenth century, and many of these are available today in replica or facsimile form. They often copied from each other (and carried on the same mistakes), as well as using pure fantasy for the flags of exotic places such as China and the Barbary States. By Napoleonic times, when the navies of Europe were greatly expanded, the 'Flags of All Nations' theme was carried over into scarves and handkerchiefs, used as gifts for sailors.

Flag charts of this period were often printed on clothbacked paper, and could also be folded into handbooks. These were published for the convenience of ship's officers, although their many inaccuracies must have made them somewhat unreliable.

The best of these handbooks appeared under the imprint of J. W. Norie (1819) and later Norie and Hobbs (1848), with subsequent editions. In the days before colour-printing became general, such books and charts were often hand-painted.

The first official album (ie, a handbook of illustrations with minimal text) appeared in France in 1858. This was the *Album des Pavillons, Guidons, Flammes, de toutes les Puissances Maritimes* by Captain Le Gras, published by the Secretary of State for the French Imperial Navy and very well printed in colour. In 1868 the American Bureau of Navigation began the publication of *Flags of Maritime Nations from the Most Authentic Sources*, reprints and revisions of which continued until very recently. In Great Britain George Hounsell produced *Flags and Signals of All Nations* in 1874, with the approval of the Admiralty, and the next year the Admiralty took over the work itself and began to produce its *Drawings of the Flags in Use at the Present Time by Various Nations*. Neither of these was as good as the Le Gras album, but the Admiralty did produce amendments between editions in the form of paste-in slips. Later editions were produced in 1889, 1907, 1915, 1930, and 1955/58.

The German Admiralty also produced a flag-album in 1905, with later editions in 1926 and 1939, the latter being the best flag-album ever produced. Germany also saw the production of Ruhl's *Flaggen aller Staaten der Erde* from 1880 onward. Ruhl's albums worthy of note are H. V. Steenbergen's *Vlaggen van alle Natien*, published in the Netherlands in 1865, with captions in Dutch, French, and English, and the French *Album des Pavillons Nationaux et des marques distinctives des Marines de Guerre et de Commerce*, published from 1923 onward.

Flag information has also been retailed to the amateur collector, and in former times a favourite way of doing this was by means of cigarette cards and silks. In Great Britain, Players produced a series of 50 *Flags of the League of Nations* (*c*1928) and 50 *National Flags and Arms* (*c*1936). Their 50 *Flags of the World* produced in the 1900s was particularly good and seems to rely heavily on Ruhl's albums. Most of these collections included albums in which the cards were to be inserted.

Cigarette card collections produced in Germany include Bulgaria Cigarettes' *Flaggen der Welt* in two volumes (*c*1930), Massary Cigarettes' *Wer nennt die Länder, kennt die Fahnen?* in several series (also *c*1930)), and *Die Welt in Bildern* series, edited by Dr Neubecker, the famous German vexillologist. He also produced a series for Nork Cigarettes entitled *Länder, Wappen und Nationalfarben* (*c*1930).

Flag publishers have also produced albums and charts of commercial flags. The most famous of these are the series of charts of the flags of the shipping lines of the world produced by the Liverpool *Journal of Commerce*. These were published regularly until the Second World War and may still be obtained in replica form. Lloyd's Register of Yachts also published a handbook of flags of yacht clubs and yacht owners, but unfortunately no longer does so. There continues to be an interest in flag charts, although few satisfactory ones are currently available.

Left: *A late 16th-century map of the Baltic Sea and the German Ocean, now the North Sea.*

Flags as Early Political Symbols

The American Revolution

There was no flag for the American colonies as such prior to the outbreak of hostilities with the motherland. The home government had appointed a special jack for vessels in the service of colonial governments in 1701, but there is little evidence of it being used. There had also been a flag for New England at one time. The Gradon Manuscript illustrates a Cross of St George with a tree in the canton, and later collections show this flag as a canton to both the Red and Blue Ensigns. The tree is sometimes shown as a terrestrial globe on a stand, probably a misapprehension. It is possible, therefore, that colonial civil ships had their own version of the jack and ensign for merchant vessels before 1707 (when the Union Jack was placed in the canton of the ensigns).

A Red Ensign with the motto 'Libery and Union' was hoisted at Taunton, Masssachusetts, in October 1774 as one of the first acts of defiance. The erection of Liberty Trees was another such act, and a flag of red and white stripes had been used in Boston as early as July 1769. The pine tree emblem evolved in New England at a very early date, and may later have come to be identified with the idea of the Liberty Tree. Another emblem popular at the time was the rattlesnake, with its associated motto 'Don't Tread on Me'. The snake was particularly American, and was later shown with a rattle of thirteen segments.

No special flag was available on the American side at the first engagements at Lexington and Concord, although the 'Bedford Flag',

Above: *The rattlesnake flag popular during the American Revolution.*

Right: *A selection of Liberty (**top right and top left**) and Union flags dating from the 1770s.*

which seems to have been an old English civil-war cavalry standard, was brought out on this occasion. The use of the Red Ensign with a motto in the fly, of the old Red Ensign with the Pine Tree flag in the canton, or of a plain Pine Tree flag seems to have been among the resources open to the Americans. It seems likely, therefore, that the colonial flag evolved from these sources during 1775. The notion of the striped fly for a modern Red Ensign may have come from the 1769 Liberty flag of Boston, but with the nine stripes increased to thirteen.

Another project was for a rattlesnake flag, proposed by Colonel Gadsden of South Carolina. This was plain yellow with the snake and motto. A Pennsylvania regiment raised in 1775 used a Red Ensign with a rattlesnake badge in the fly (Protector's Independent Battalion, Westmoreland County). A flag of stripes with a rattlesnake was used by the South Carolina Navy. The ships commissioned by Washington to cruise in Massachusetts Bay used the Pine Tree flag from September 1775. The flag bore the motto 'Appeal to Heaven'.

The flag hoisted at Propect Hill, outside Cambridge, Massachusetts, on 1 January 1776 had previously been flown on the *Alfred* at Philadelphia, where it was described as 'English Colours but more Striped', in other words, as the British Red Ensign with white stripes across the field. It seems as if it is just a coincidence that this flag was the same as that used by the East India Company. This is the flag known to history as the 'Continental Colors' or the 'Grand Union Flag'.

The flag lasted in this form until 14 July 1777, when the Stars and Stripes was created. That flag was used in many different forms by the armies and ships of the new United States during the remainder of the War of Independence.

Alongside the Americans fought the French. They were organized into traditional regiments, each of which had two colours. One of the two colours was the Regimental flag, which bore their livery colours in the cantons between the arms of the white cross. The Colonel's Colour was white with a white cross (outlined in silver thread) and decorated with fleurs-de-lis.

The Germans in the British service had a variety of regimental colours, of which four are now held in American museums. They did not come in pairs like the British and French colours but were often two-sided, ie, with a differing design on either side.

In addition to this wealth of symbols, each state had its own regimental colours and there were very many standards and flags of irregular units. Some states, such as Connecticut, Massachusetts, and South Carolina also had distinctive naval ensigns.

The flags of the United States, 1776-7 ***(top)*** *and 1777-9* ***(above)***.

Above: *The Pine Tree Flag, another popular emblem during the Revolution.*

Left: *Brunswickian soldiers of the British Army with their colours.*

THE FRENCH REVOLUTION

The flags of the Bourbon dynasty that ruled France before the Revolution were mainly white, but there was no national flag as such. In fact in many ways the idea of a flag to represent the whole population as well as the government, and for use as a naval ensign as well, was one of the major contributions of the Stars and Stripes. The French naval ensign at this period was plain white. The royal standard was also white, powdered with golden fleurs-de-lis and with the whole royal arms over all in the centre.

The Revolution began for all practical purposes with the attack on the royal fortress of the Bastille on 14 July 1789. The day before, the Paris militia were issued with blue and red cockades, the livery colours of the city. Three days after the fall of the Bastille the King was presented with one of these cockades and placed it on his hat. Lafayette, who had been a commander of French troops in America, proposed that there should be a national cockade of red, white, and blue, which was agreed to on 4 October. At the same time colours were adopted for the sixty divisions of the National Guard; these were usually in red, white, and blue.

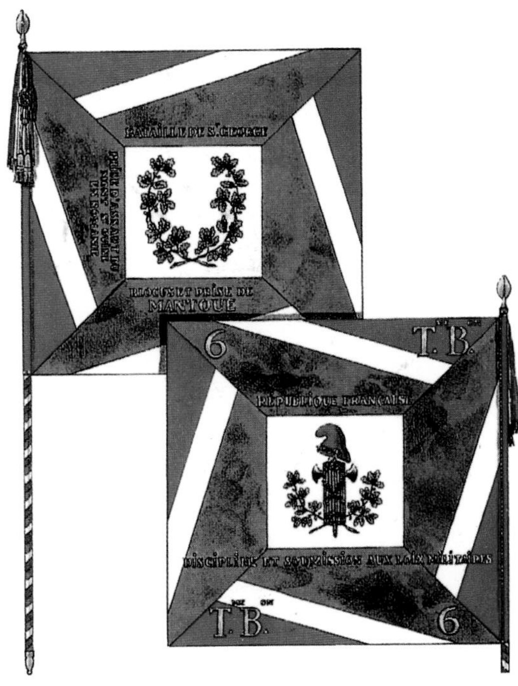

Right: *A demi-brigade flag of the 3rd battalion of the Army of Italy, 1797, showing the obverse* (**above**) *and the reverse* (**below**).

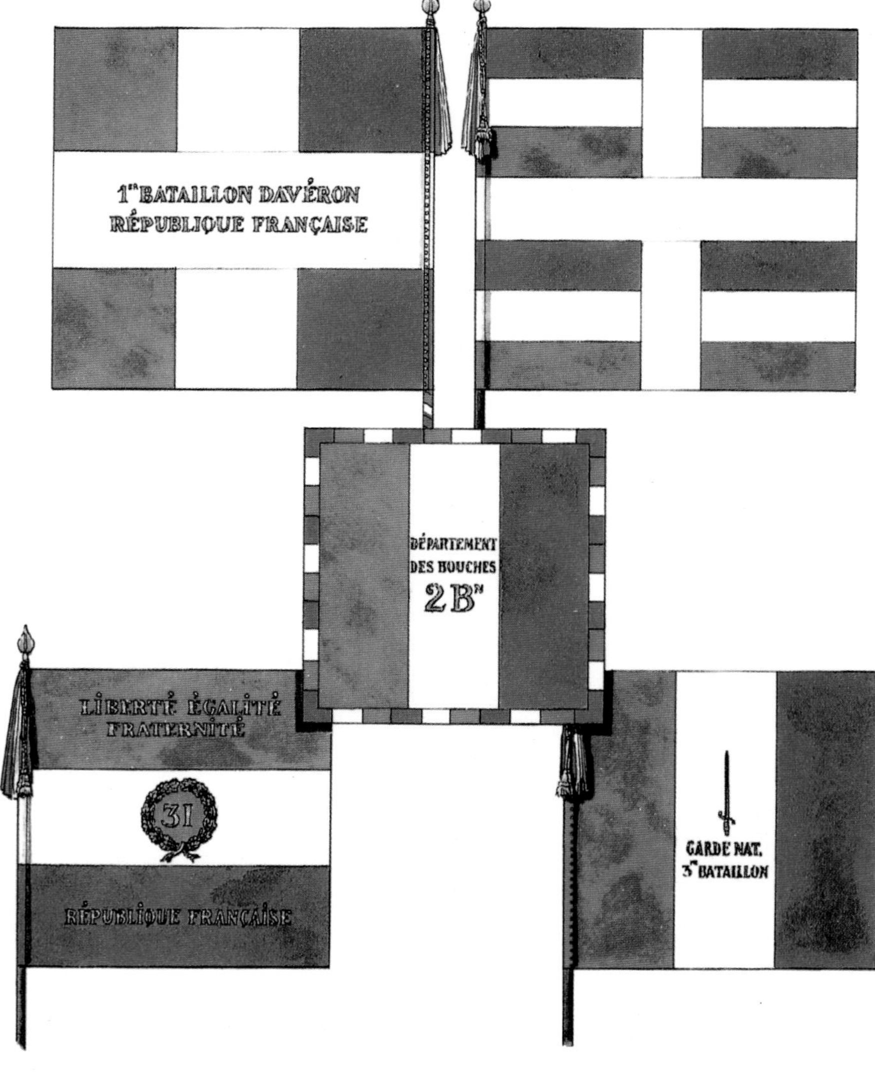

Above: *Flags of the Volunteer battalions, 1791-3.*

On 22 October 1790 the white cravat on military colours was replaced by a tricolour one, and on 30 June 1791 a new system of army colours was devised, using the new national colours. At the same time the naval flags were revised. By a resolution of 24 October 1790 the new naval jack would be a vertical tricolour of red, white, blue with a white inner border and an outer border half red and half blue. The new civil and naval ensign would be white with this jack in the canton.

Following the declaration of the Republic, 21 September 1791, further changes were made with a view to eliminating the Bourbon white

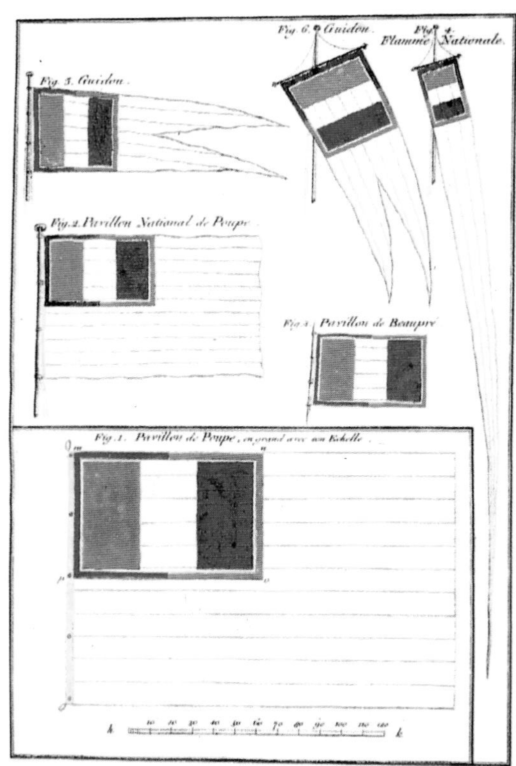

Right: *The official specifications for the first Tricolour flag, 1790.*

from the national flags. By a decree of 15 February 1794 the modern Tricolour, or *Tricolore* as it is called in French, was substituted for the previous jack and ensign. So far as the French Army was concerned, new colours followed the reorganization into 'demibrigades' on 8 January 1794, an arrangement that lasted until further reorganization was undertaken by Napoleon in 1803. It was thus under the new demibrigade colours that the French fought the campaigns in Italy, Belgium, and Egypt. One of these colours found its way to Ireland in support of the Rising of 1798 and is now in a British Army museum.

One of the interesting features of these colours is that they were all in different patterns of red, white, and blue. Because of the necessity to make so many different patterns the shapes and designs were very ingenious, some bringing to mind Op Art motifs of the 1960s.

REVOLUTIONARY TRICOLOURS

One of the first actions of the French revolutionaries was to export their ideas and their system to neighbouring countries. This happened first in Italy, where a revolution took place in Reggio in August 1796. On 6 November 1796 Napoleon gave out colours to the new Lombard Legion in Milan in the colours green, white, and red, arranged vertically in an obvious variation on the *Tricolore*. The Cispadane Federation was formed, which became the Cispadane Republic on 28 December 1976. In January it adopted its emblem, a quiver with four arrows, and on 21 January its new standard of green, white, and red with the same device in the centre. The first flag was displayed on 12 February 1797 and is now claimed as the true precursor of the modern Italian tricolour.

*Two flags of Lucca, as a republic, 1803-1805 (**top**) and as a principality 1805-1814 (**above**).*

The next state to be formed was the Cisalpine Republic (17 July 1797). This definitely used the tricolour in its modern form, as from 11 May 1798. In January 1802 there was a further transformation into the Italian Republic, which adopted a flag on 20 August of that year. The new design had a red field with a white lozenge throughout containing a green rectangle. When the state ultimately became the Kingdom of Italy in March 1805, the new royal arms were added to the centre. These arms were far from revolutionary, as those of the Cispandane Republic had been, but were a compendium of the arms of dominion of the component parts of Napoleon's Italian realm.

Some other flags are known from the Napoleonic period in Italy. The flag of Lucca (18035) was white with a red lozenge throughout and a blue border all round, and that of the Principality of Piombino and Lucca (1805-9) was a plain horizontal tricolour of blue, white, red. During Npoleon's occupation of Rome, the republic had a tricolour of black, white, and red, and the republican regime in Ancona, then detached from the Papal States, was blue, yellow, and red horizontally with the name 'REPUBBLICA ANCONITANA' on the yellow part in black. Piedmont, on the other hand, used a horizontal tricolour of red, blue, yellow. The vassal kingdom of Etruria (1801-7) had a flag of five blue and white stripes with the royal arms over all in the centre. The flag for civil use was a horizontal triband of blue, white, blue. The flag of the Parthenopean Republic was a vertical tricolour of blue, yellow, and red, but that of the Kingdom of Naples was blue with a border of white and aramanth checks all round.

Napoleon was also active in Switzerland, where he formed the Helvetian Republic in 1798. This had a horizontal tricolour of green, yellow, and red, with the title on the yellow stripe. During this period new cantons were formed, several of which derived their heraldry from French models.

__Below:__ Austrians flee from Brussels under cover of the Belgian colours, 1789. (Heeresgeschichtliches Museum, Vienna).

In 1795 the French created the Batavian republic out of the old Dutch state. They altered its flags by adding a 'canton of Liberty', a white panel with an allegorical scene. This was placed at the hoist end of the red stripe. The flag of Admiral de Winter, captured at Camperdown, was blue with the Canton of Liberty in the upper hoist. This flag is now in the National Maritime Museum, Greenwich. The canton was removed when the Kingdom of Holland was formed.

The Belgian revolution of December 1789 gave birth to another tricolour, of horizontal stripes of red, yellow, and black, the colours of Brabant. These colours were taken up again in 1830, but were subsequently arranged vertically. The tricolours that marked revolutionary states in the early days gave way to modified flags redolent of imperialism.

THE YEAR OF REVOLUTIONS

The Year of Revolutions is the name given to the period 1848-9, when risings against traditional and authoritarian rulers took place in many European states. As with the events of 1830 the inspiration for many of the risings came from revolutions in France. In many of these risings, new tricolours appeared, since by now the tricolour form had become the mark of revolution in itself.

In Germany, however, the native tricolour dated from the rising against France in the War of Liberation (1813-14). The colours of black, red, and gold were derived from uniforms of the Lützow Freikorps, which led the German resistance. The colours were later taken up by the students and were used at the great patriotic rallies at Warburg Castle (1817) and Hambach (1830). In 1848 they were assumed by the new all-German parliament in Frankfurt.

Above: *The German Tricolour.*

Other places where new tricolours came to the fore were Romania, Hungary, Slovakia, Schleswig-Holstein, and Ireland. In some cases the colours of the tricolour flags were derived from the traditional heraldry of the country. This was so in Romania, where the flag united the red and yellow of Wallachia with the blue and red of Moldavia, and in Hungary, where the colours derive from the red and white stripes on the national shield and the green mound on which the patriarchal cross is standing. The red, white, and blue of Schleswig-Holstein also derives from the shields of the two provinces, whereas that of Slovakia imitates the Russian colours.

Above: *The Hungarian Tricolour.*

Above: *The Irish Tricolour.*

In Ireland it was the tricolour form of flag that provided the inspiration. The colours were home-grown: the traditional green of Ireland and the orange of the supporters of King William, with white added to express peace and unity. Irish delegates to the French Assembly saw the *Tricolore* used to great effect in Paris and decided to take the idea home with them.

In Italy, the Napoleonic tricolour was brought out again. As the revolutionaries gained ground, they produced changes in the flags of their states. In Parma the tricolour replaced the traditional flag; in Venice the tricolour was adopted with a traditional flag in the canton; in Naples a tricolour border was added to the white flag of the Bourbons. In Savoy-Sardinia it was decided as early as 23 March 1848 to adopt the tricolour with the addition of a Savoy shield. A quite large shield was used, with a blue border round it to separate the red of the shield from the red of the flag. Later the shield was shrunk in size to occupy only the white part. Nevertheless the blue border remained, and this was the form of

Above: *The Italian Tricolour.*

the flag adopted for Italy at unification.

Of the flags hoisted in the Year of Revolutions, many were lowered in 1849. That of Germany was not adopted again until 1919. that of Hungary until 1867, and that of Ireland until 1921. That of Slovakia was only ever used as a national flag when it was a Nazi puppet state, but in general the flags first used to symbolize the 'people power' of 1848 are as powerful today as they were then.

CENTRAL AND SOUTH AMERICA

At one time all Central and South America was ruled either by Spain or by Portugal. The Portuguese domain, Brazil, broke away in 1822 and the Spanish dominions also achieved independence in the first two decades of the nineteenth century.

Much of the credit for the liberation of Latin America from Spanish rule must go to a few active enthusiasts, inspired by the ideas of the American and French revolutions, and also by the fall of the Spanish monarchy in 1808. When Napoleon took over in Spain, some local governments declared for the Bourbon king, but others took the opportunity to separate from the motherland. Several names stand out as the liberators of South America, including José de San Martín, Simón Bolívar, Francisco de Miranda, and General Belgrano.

Even before Miranda began to organize an expedition to Venezuela in 1806, there had been a Rising organized by Gual and España in 1797. These used a flag with a large radiant sun, and four stripes of yellow, red, white, and blue in the fly. Beneath the sun was a blue band with four white stars.

***Above:** Francisco de Miranda's flag.*

Miranda experimented with several flags before settling on the tricolour of yellow, blue, and red. This was hoisted for the first time on Colombian soil on 4 August 1806. These colours were later explained as signifying the sea that lay between the patriots and the 'tyrants' of Spain. In 1811 Miranda returned to Venezuela and saw his colours adopted as those of the new state. Colombia and Ecuador retained these colours when they separated from Venezuela.

Venezuela, Colombia, Peru, and Bolivia were liberated with the help of General Simón Bolívar, who was credited with a flag that also had a radiant sun in the centre on a blue field with a red border all round. However, this did not become the basis of any national flag.

General Belgrano used the colours adopted in Buenos Aires on 25 May 1810, and turned them into a flag that he hoisted at Rosario on 27 February 1812. In 1813 the colours were taken up by San Martín to make a flag for the Army of the Andes, in 1814 by Artigas and his League of Free Peoples, and in 1816 by Louis Aury, who led a maritime expedition to Central America. The Argentine government accepted the flag and adopted it on 25 July 1816. The state flag was created on 25 February 1818 by placing the 'Sun of May' in the centre. The flag of the Army of the Andes was in the Belgrano colours, with an emblem over all which later became the arms of Argentina.

***Above:** General Belgrano's flag.*

The flag of Artigas, the national hero of Uruguay, was adapted from the Belgrano flag by adding a diagonal red stripe. This flag is now the naval jack of Uruguay and the flag of the province of Entre Rios in Argentina.

Following the declaration of the independence of Argentina and the victory of the Army of the Andes, a tricolour of blue, white, and red was adopted in Chile on 24 May 1817. This is the flag of the *Patria Nueva*, the second attempt at independence. Later that year the colours were rearranged into the present pattern.

San Martín went on to Peru in September 1820 and landed a liberation Army. He set up the Peruvian Legion and endowed them with a flag on 20 October. The emblem showed the sun rising over the mountains and was on a background of red and white, colours associated with the Incas, as was the sun emblem.

The blue and white colours were also adopted in Central America. The first flag is said to have been created by Colonel Arce on 20 February 1822 and presented to a unit from El Salvador going off to fight the Mexicans, who had annexed the central provinces. When the United Provinces of Central America were set up, the same flag was adopted on 21 August 1823. The state flag had the emblem in the centre, and the civil ensign the motto, *Dios Unión Libertad*. The emblem was a Masonic triangle (symbolic of equality) containing five volcanoes and a cap of Liberty (cf Army of the Andes) and a rainbow. Around the triangle was the name *Provincias Unidas del Centro de America*. Flags like this were subsequently used in Nicaragua, El Salvador, Honduras, Costa Rica, and Guatemala.

***Above:** Simon Bolivar's flag.*

***Above:** Artigas's flag.*

***Above:** The flag of the Andes Army, 1817–1818.*

***Above:** Jose de San Martin's flag.*

PORTUGAL AND BRAZIL

In 1807 the royal family of Portugal removed to Brazil to escape the depredations of Napoleon. Portugal and Brazil were constitutionally united on 16 December 1815 as the United Kingdom of Portugal, Brazil and the Algarve. A coat of arms was assigned to Brazil, consisting of a crowned armilla (see section, 'The Age of Discovery'). A flag was devised for the new Kingdom on 13 May 1816, of white with the *armilla* supporting the crowned shield of Portugal. On 22 April 1821 Dom Pedro was appointed Regent of Brazil by his father, King João VI, who was obliged to return to Portugal. On 7 September 1822 Dom Pedro proclaimed the independence of Brazil at Ypiranga, near São Paulo.

Top left and right: *Flags commemorating The independence of Pernambuco, 1645, the congress of 1798 (Minas);* ***middle left and right:*** *the 1817 and 1823 revolutions;* ***above left and right:*** *the flag and the arms of the republic of Rio Grand (1835).*

Right: *Flags of Brazil, 1500-1649* ***(near right)****, 1649-1808* ***(far right)****, 1808-1816* ***(below near right)****, 1816-22* ***(below far right)****.*

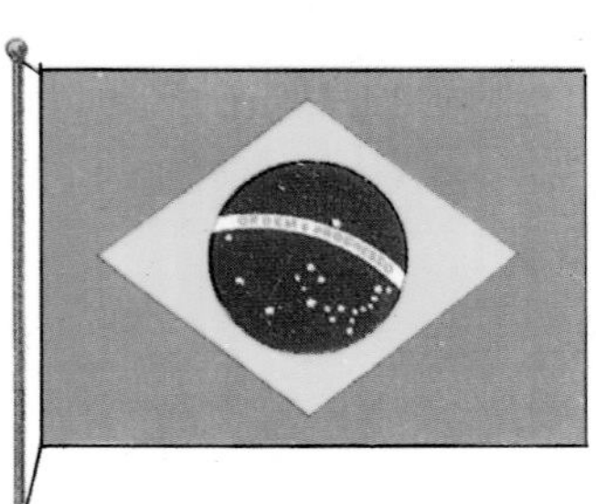

Above: *Flags of Brazil, as an Empire 1822-1889, and a Republic, from 1889.*

The colours of Portugal before these new arrangements were red and blue, as on the military flags of the period, but on 23 August 1821 they were changed to blue and white, the ancient colours seen in the *quinas*, the five shields, each bearing five white discs, which were the oldest arms of Portugal. At Ypiranga Dom Pedro took off his cockade in these colours and put on one of green and yellow, which were henceforth to be the colours of Brazil. On 19 June 1823 the King of Portugal reverted to the previous red and blue cockade, but no change was made to the flag. In 1826 João VI died and his two sons, Pedro and Miguel, began to dispute the succession. Pedro's claim was passed on to his infant daughter Maria. At first her party only occupied the Azores, and it was at Terceira on 18 October 1830 that the blue and white flag was established in opposition to the old flag still used by King Miguel. For use on land the flag had equal parts of blue and white, but at sea the blue was only one third of the field. In either case the crowned shield was centred on the dividing line. The flag was first hoisted on the mainland in July 1832 and remained in use until the revolution of 1910.

Meanwhile, in Brazil Dom Pedro had been crowned Emperor on 1 December 1822 and had adopted an Imperial standard of green and yellow. The ordinary flag was green with a yellow lozenge and the arms in the centre, a design that seems to have been inspired by the flag of Napoleon's Kingdom of Italy, while the arms continued to use the *armilla*. In 1828 Uruguay was lost and in 1889 republican fervour broke out. At first the republicans intended to use a flag similar to the Stars and Stripes with thirteen green and yellow stripes and a blue canton with 21 stars (one for each state), but at the last moment the present design was adopted.

Each state has a flag and arms of its own. Some of the flags go back to earlier days and some of them (the ones in green and yellow stripes) are flags intended for the republic. One of the federal territories only, Amapá, has a flag of its own.

Top to bottom, left to right: *Brazilian postage stamps showing flags of the states of Brazil, Algoas, Bahia, the Federal District, Pernambuco and Sergipe.*

THE RED FLAG

The people's flag is deepest red, it shrouded oft our martyred dead, and ere their limbs grew stiff and cold, their life's blood stained its every fold.

Such is the poetic description of the origin of the Red Flag, and it is true that it is the colour of blood, the oldest and most powerful of symbols. As a flag it was often used as a 'Flag of Defiance', as in the flag used in the siege of Ostend (1601-4), when that city held out for three years against the Spaniards, and in the flag hoisted on pirate ships to intimidate their victims.

During the French Revolution it was hoisted as a sign that martial law had been declared, as when Bailly, the Mayor of Paris, had it displayed in the Champs de Mars on 17 July 1791. As a consequence when he was later taken to the guillotine the mob taunted him by turning a Red Flag, and thereafter used the Red Flag themselves as a sign of defiance. The Red Flag was brought out again in the Revolutions of 1830 and 1848 and was proposed as the national flag at that time. In fact the *Tricolore* did have a red cravat attached to it for a while. It was used again in the Commune of 1870 and hence became associated with the 'Communists'.

Above: *The flag of the Revolutionary Party of Benin.*

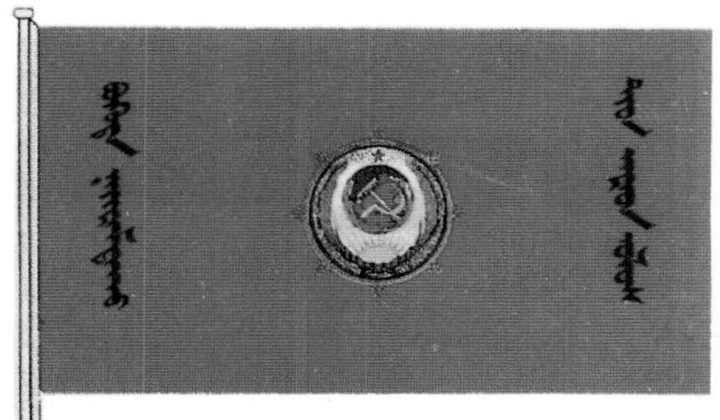

Above: *The flag of Tannu Tuva.*

In Russia the Red Flag was used in the Revolution of 1905 and again in 1917. The Bolshevik flags were all red, with white or yellow inscriptions, and the flag chosen for the Russian republic in July 1918 was also red, with gold initials. This in turn led to the flags of the other Soviet republics and to the flag of the Soviet Union, adopted in 1924.

The Red Flag was used for a while by Communist revolutionaries in Germany and Hungary at the end of the First World War and later in Mexico, but it was only in the former Chinese empire that it became the flag of effective governments. These were set up in Tuva (now in the USSR), Mongolia, and Jianxi. The Red Flag was formally adopted for the Chinese Soviet Republic on 7 November 1931 and by the Chinese People's Liberation

Below: *A Soviet poster for a war loan showing red flags with inscriptions (Imperial War Museum).*

Right: *Red flags, one of them showing Karl Marx, in a procession celebrating the Russian revolution.*

Above: *The flag of FRELIMO, the governing party of Mozambique.*

Army on 1 August 1927. The PLA flag is now the army and navy ensign of China. The flag of the Chinese People's Republic was adopted on 1 October 1949.

Outside China the Red Flag had also been adopted by the Vietnamese revolutionaries under Ho Chi Minh and was used for the republic set up there in August 1945. This flag, adopted on 29 September 1945, was the forerunner of the flag of the National Liberation Front, or Viet Cong, and the present flag of Vietnam. A flag with a red field was also adopted by the Khmer Rouge movement, which seized control of Cambodia in 1976.

In Africa red flags have also been used, in some cases by movements that have become governments, such as in the Congo People's Republic (1 January 1970) and Benin. In the latter country the party flag is red with a green star, but the national flag has the colours reversed. In Mozambique the party flag of FRELIMO is also red with yellow emblems similar to those that appear on the national flag. The flags of Marxist parties are generally red with yellow emblems, although several variations are possible. The star used is usually yellow, or red edged with yellow, like that used in the Soviet Union. Sometimes hammers and sickles are used, but very often tools with local relevance are preferred, like the hoe and machete.

Below and bottom: *The flags of the Congo People's Republic and the Chinese People's Republic.*

Some Marxist flags are red and black, like those of the MPLA in Angola, the FSLN in Nicaragua, and the 26 July Movement in Cuba. There are often special reasons for this, not connected with Marxism.

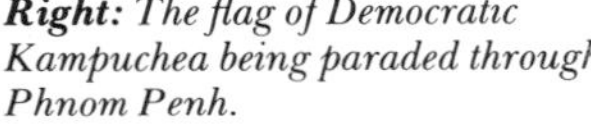

Right: *The flag of Democratic Kampuchea being paraded through Phnom Penh.*

FLAG GENEALOGY
THE DUTCH TRICOLOUR

The early Dutch Tricolour, with an orange upper stripe, is the one that gave rise to the flags of orange, white, and blue used in the United States and South Africa. In each case the flag is claimed to have been brough to these places by early Dutch colonizers: Henry Hudson, who came to New Amsterdam in 1625, and van Riebeeck, who settled at the Cape of Good Hope in 1652. These pioneers are said to have flown the flags of the Dutch East and West India Companies, which were the Tricolour with their ciphers in the centre. These two companies were founded in 1602 and 1621 respectively, and their ciphers contained their initials 'VOC' and 'GWC'. In fact, by the time they were operational the orange of the Dutch flag had changed to red, but that has not prevented later pseudo-historians from assuming that the upper colour was still orange.

***Above:** The Prinsenvlag.*

The flags of New York City and of the Union of South Africa were not created until the twentieth century, but the South African one drew on the flags of the Boer republics set up after the Great Trek (1836): the Orange Free State, the Transvaal, Natal, the New Republic and others.

The modern Dutch Tricolour was the one that inspired Peter the Great, who spent some time in the Netherlands studying shipbuilding and other modern sciences in 1697. He learned the art of distinguishing the flags of warships from civil ships, and the uses of ensigns, jacks and pennants. From the arms and flags of Amsterdam he derived the saltire cross of St Andrew and applied it to Russian flags. This story carries on in the section, 'The Pan-Slav Colours', with the Russian models in turn being adopted in Eastern Europe.

British possession of Cape Colony was confirmed in 1815, and was not welcomed by the Dutch settlers who were still loyal to the Dutch Tricolour, which had been used by the Republic of Swellendam in 1795. The Great Trek itself in 1836 is said to have used a flag of blue with a red saltire, known as the *kruisvlag*. This is also said to be the flag of Zoutspanberg.

The first new republic the settlers established was in Natal. From 1839-1843 this state flew an adaptation of the Dutch Tricolour. This later formed the inspiration for the flag of the President of South Africa. The Orange Free State was formed in 1854 and adopted a flag in

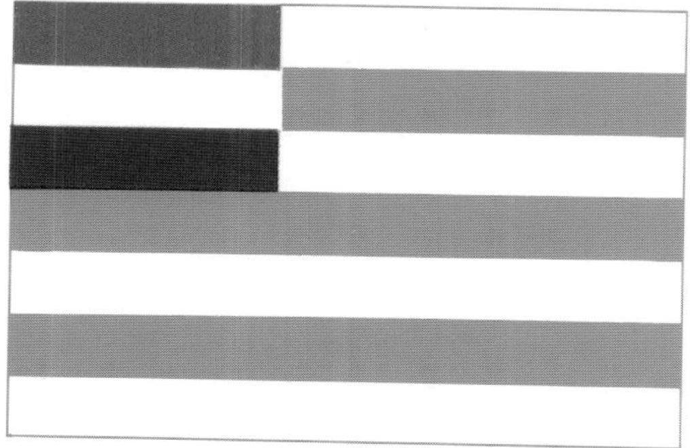

***Above:** The flag of the Orange Free State.*

1856. The design was actually sought from and granted by the King of the Netherlands and has the Dutch tricolour in the canton.

Transvaal, or the South African Republic, was formed in 1850 and adopted a flag in 1857. This is the Dutch Tricolour with a green stripe (for hope and youthfulness) in the hoist. It is known as the *Vierkleur.*

Smaller, less permanent states also adopted flags, including Lydenburg (the plain Dutch Tricolour), Goshen (in this case the German Tricolour with a green strip in the hoist), Stellaland, and the New Republic (like that of Transvaal with the blue and green tranposed). These smaller states were eventually incorporated into the Transvaal or Natal.

In 1927 all these traditions were revived in the debate over the new flag for the Union of South Africa, and as can be seen this is based on the original Dutch Tricolour with the flags of Great Britain, the Orange Free State, and the Transvaal in the centre.

The flag of Henry Hudson was used in New York City and New York State to form the basis of flags for local use. A flag for the City of New York was introduced on 1 May 1915 to commemorate the city's 250th anniversary. In the centre is the city seal. The date on this was altered from 1664 to 1625 in 1975. The flag of the Mayor has an arc of five blue stars over the seal, one for each borough.

The Borough of Bronx has a flag adopted in 1915, with the arms within a laurel wreath in the centre of the *Prinsenvlag.*

Brooklyn has a white flag with its seal, which contains the Dutch motto, *Eendraght maakt Magt*, and the figure of Liberty.

Manhattan has the same flag as the City of New York, except for the band around the sea. In place of the laurel wreath is a circular band with the legend 'President of the Borough of Manhattan NYC'. In place of the date are two blue stars.

The Borough of Queens has a flag dating from 1912, which uses the colours of the arms of the first Dutch governor and a tulip to recall its Dutch origins. The flowers lie within a ring of wampum.

Richmond, or Staten Island, has a flag of blue containing its seal, which is depicted in orange. The 'S' stands for *Staten*, the Dutch name for the legislature. The flag was adopted in 1848.

Albany, the capital of New York State, also uses the *Prinsenvlag* with its arms in the centre, which dates from 1789.

***Above:** The flag of The Transvaal.*

***Above:** The flag of Goshen, 1882–85.*

***Above:** The flag of New York City.*

THE UNION JACK

In 1603 the English throne was inherited by the King of Scots who thus came to rule all the British Isles. He called his new realm 'Great Britain', but the 'great' was merely to distinguish it from Lesser Britain, or Britanny. A new coat of arms was devised, and a commemorative gold coin, called a 'Union', was issued.

But confusion arose over the flags to be flown by both naval and merchant vessels. Before the union of the crowns, Scots and English (and Irish) ships had flown the crosses of St Andrew and St George, respectively, often in the canton of striped or plain ensigns. King James wanted there to be a 'Union' flag as well, and heralds and shipmasters sat down to devise one. The Scots came up with several ideas, which mostly gave prominence to the Scottish saltire. The English likewise favoured a quartered flag, with St George in the first quarter. In 1606 the King plumped for a design that placed the Cross of St George on top of the saltire, much to the chagrin of the Scots, many of whom continued to use designs with St Andrew on top. This was the first Union Jack, authorized on 12 April 1606.

***Below:** Scottish drafts for a proposed Union Jack, 1606 (National Library of Scotland).*

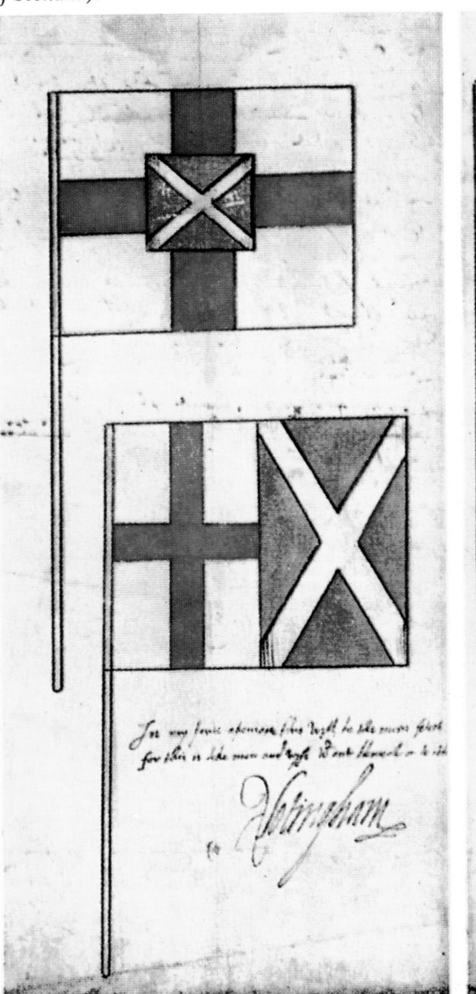

However, there was clearly resistance to the idea of the flag, which had to be flown in addition to the national flags of England and Scotland, and on 5 May 1634 the use of it was restricted to ships of the Royal Navy, with civil ships continuing as before 1606.

With the execution of Charles I the 'Union' flag became obsolete, but Parliament soon decided on a new one, which reflected England's domination of Ireland. The second Union Jack, of 5 March 1649, combined St George with the Irish harp. However, after the new union with Scotland (12 April 1654), a third Union Flag was instituted, to reincorporate the saltire. This flag, of 18 May 1658, was the 1606 pattern but with the Harp over all in the centre. This design lasted until May 1660, when the 1634 system was readopted.

***Above:** The third form of the Union Jack, 1658.*

In the following years the distinction between navy and merchant ships became more conspicuous and legislation decreed that the civil ships must restrict themselves to the national cross and ensign (usually a Red Ensign) and not use the Union Jack at all.

With the parliamentary union with Scotland (1 May 1707), the Union flag, however, was added to the cantons of the ensigns. White, Red, and Blue Ensigns had been in use by the Royal Navy since the early seventeenth century to distinguish the various squadrons, a system that continued until 1864. Merchant ships could continue to use their national crosses as jacks.

On 1 January 1801 the fourth Union Jack

***Top and above:** The original Red Ensign with the flag of England only in the canton and the modern Red Ensign.*

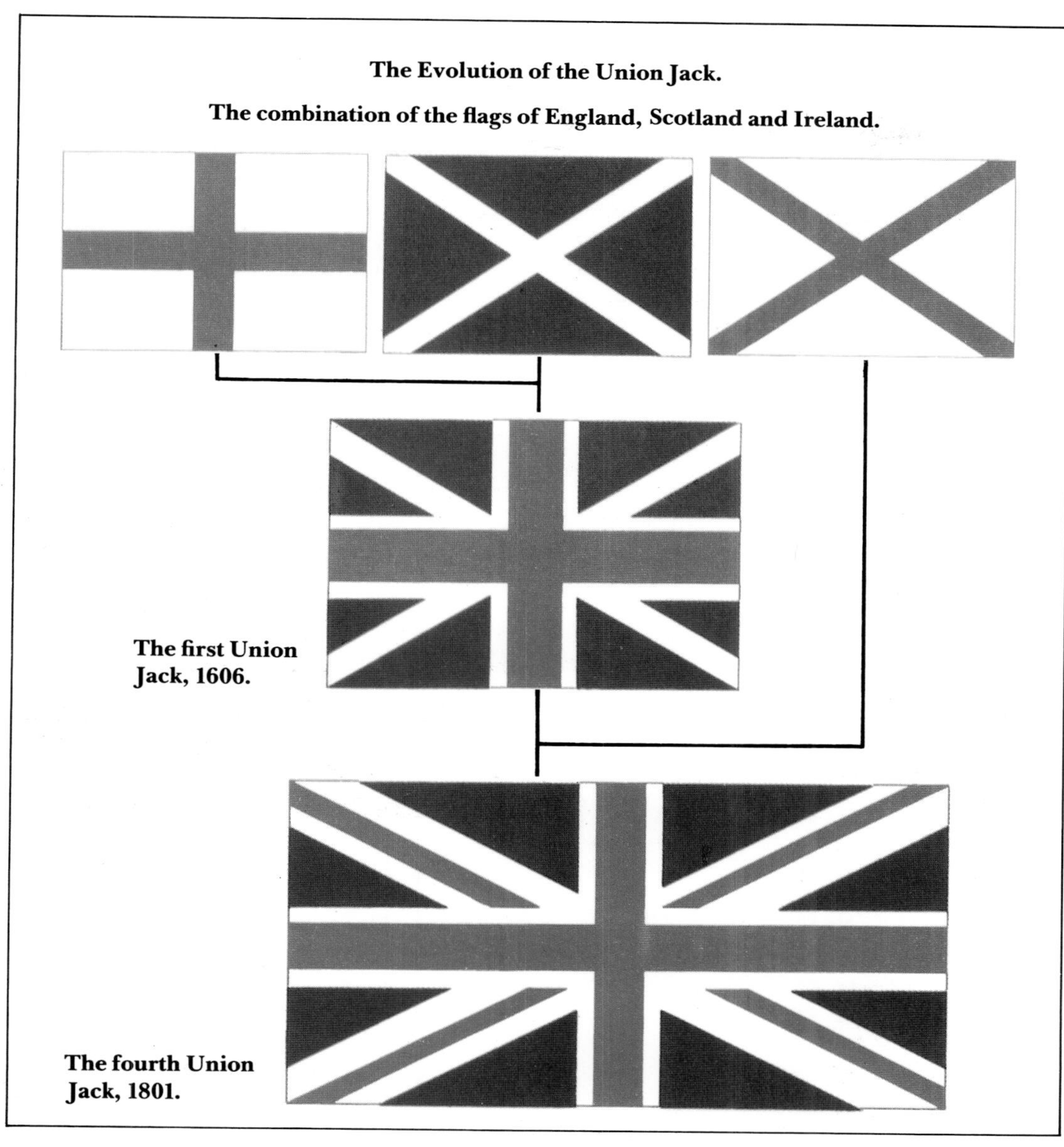

came into effect, which included a red saltire to represent Ireland. The design was the work of the then Garter King of Arms, Sir Isaac Heard, and rather ingeniously combined the three crosses. Today only military colours are made according to the rules.

The regulations of 1864 set up the flag system in use today, whereby Royal Navy ships fly a White Ensign and Union Jack, government ships fly a Blue Ensign and Jack, and civil vessels fly the Red Ensign. It has recently been made clear that civil vessels can also fly the old Pilot Jack (a Union Jack with a white border).

From 1865 vessels in the service of colonial governments were allowed to use the Blue Ensign with a badge in the fly, and these governments were required to design badges for the purpose. From 1869 governors of colonies were allowed Union Jacks with their badges in the centre, within a laurel wreath. Civil vessels could only fly a Red Ensign with a badge if they obtained a warrant from the Admiralty. These were issued to Canada (1892), New Zealand (1899), and Australia (1903), as well as to some other countries which are now independent. This has given rise to the tradition that Commonwealth countries have flags with the Union Jack in the canton. Today, apart from Australia and New Zealand, only Fiji and Tuvalu carry on this practice.

Today only Bermuda, Guernsey, and the Isle of Man have British Red Ensigns with

badges, but the ensign system has lived on in some other countries that were once British. Thus Sri Lanka, India, Pakistan, Bangladesh, Mauritius, Fiji, Ghana, Malaysia, and the Solomon Islands have their own Red Ensigns with their respective national flags in the canton, while the Bahamas, Malta, and Singapore have civil ensigns of more distinctive designs.

Sri Lanka, India, Ghana, Jamaica, Malaysia, Nigeria, Papua New Guinea, Kenya, Grenada, and Fiji have White Ensigns. In several cases the original Cross of St George throughout has been removed and replaced by a distinctive emblem or just a white field.

*Derivatives of the Union Jack in the flags of Australia and New Zealand (**left**), Fiji (**top**) and Tuvalu (**above**).*

THE HERITAGE OF THE STARS AND STRIPES

The flag of the United States was the first to use stars and the first to use the stars to represent its component parts. This idea very quickly became widespread and flags with stars are now among the most common.

***Right:** The modern Stars and Stripes.*

The Kempner flag hoisted in West Florida in 1804 was probably the first to employ these ideas. It had stripes of blue and white, a red canton, and two white stars, and was part of an attempt to detach the area from Florida. Similarly, the Republic of West Florida flag of 1810 had a single white star on a blue field. This is the Bonnie Blue Flag later used elsewhere. A similar attempt to detach Texas from Mexico was made in 1819 under a flag like the Stars and Stripes but with only one star.

The first national flag to be based directly on that of the United States was the Chilean flag of October 1817. Opinion is divided about who was responsible for the design of this flag, and it could have been an American engineer in the patriot army. The colours were already in use but the five-pointed star was an innovation.

A further flag was created for Texas in 1836, which was like that of 1819. This was used as a naval ensign. The well-known flag of Texas as used today was adopted on 25 January 1839.

Other state flags that are based on the Stars and Stripes include Florida (flag of 4 July 1846–3 July 1847), Illinois (9 March 1901–3 July 1908), Louisiana (February 1861), New Mexico (19 March 1915–15 March 1925), Ohio (9 May 1902–present), Utah (1847–60), and Vermont (1 May 1804–1 June 1923).

The flags of the Confederate States of America, adopted in 1861, were derived directly from the Stars and Stripes. Although they did not use the stripes to represent the component parts, they did use the stars. After the Civil War a number of states adopted flags based on those of the Confederacy. These were Alabama, Arkansas, Florida, Georgia, Mississippi, North Carolina, and Tennessee. The flag adopted for South Carolina in 1860 was more in the nature of a forerunner of the Confederate Battle Flag, but did not last long as the state flag.

***Above:** The flag of Texas.*

***Right:** Four versions of the Confederate flag used during the Civil War: two variants of the "Stainless Banner" (**top left and right**), The Stars and Bars (**bottom left**), the "Southern Cross", and the flag of the state of Alabama in the middle.*

Arkansas

Georgia

Mississippi

North Carolina

Ohio

Tennessee

Above: *Six state flags related to the Stars and Stripes or the Confederate Flags.*

The flags of Cuba and Puerto Rico have a common origin. The flag of Cuba was designed by Narciso López in 1848. The general design and the single star express the idea of unity with the United States. *La Estrella Solitária* (cf the 'Lone Star' of Texas) was to be added to the 'splendid North American constellation'. A flag like that of Chile, but with the blue and red reversed, was used in the Rising of 1868–78, and is now the naval jack of Cuba. The Puerto Rican flag was adopted on 22 December 1895 and symbolized the same idea of emancipation with the aid of the USA.

Above: *The flag of Puerto Rico.*

Above: *The flag of Cuba.*

The flag of Liberia was first used on 9 April 1827. At that time it had thirteen stripes but had a couped cross in place of the stars. The general design represented affiliation with the USA, and the cross the Christian ideals of the founders of the state.

On 28 April 1865 El Salvador decided to adopt a flag based on that of the United States but with stripes in the Central American col-

Above left and left: *The flags of Liberia, and El Salvador, 1875-1912.*

ours. There were nine stripes, representing the departments, and a red canton with nine (later fourteen) stars. On the state flag the arms were placed in the canton instead of the stars. These flags were in use until 17 May 1912, when the original design was reverted to.

In 1903 the politicians who were trying to detach Panama from Colombia designed a new flag. The first idea of Bunau-Varilla was for a flag of seven red and yellow stripes with a blue canton containing two linked hemispheres, symbolic of the canal that would be built there. However in November 1903 he, his wife, and Guerrero created the present flag of red, white, and blue with stars, which was smuggled into Panama in time for the declaration of independence.

Other flags that borrow from the Stars and Stripes include the flags of Uruguay, Greece, and Malaysia. In the case of both Uruguay and Malaysia, the stripes stand for the component parts, whereas in Greece they represent the national motto. Some Brazilian state flags are based on the Stars and Stripes, as was the provisional flag of the republic of 1889.

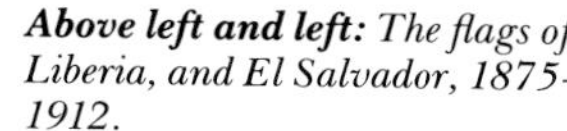

Above: *The flag of Greece.*

Above: *The flag of Malaysia, 1963, based on an earlier version.*

Above: *The flag of Uruguay, 1830.*

THE PAN-SLAV COLOURS

The section on the Dutch Tricolour traces the development of that flag and its influence around the world. One of those influences was on the formation of the flags of Russia under Peter the Great (1672-1725). He was anxious to build up the Russian Navy as a means of securing his borders and relied heavily on foreign experts. As 'Peter Mikhailov' he travelled more or less incognito to Western Europe in 1697, spending some time in Amsterdam and Leiden, and on his return began to impose Western notions on the Russians. He instituted the national order, the Order of St Andrew, in 1699, and a flag bearing the saltire of St Andrew (like that of Scotland but with the colours reversed) became the ensign of his new navy. The flag for civil vessels was to be like that of the Netherlands, but with the stripes in the order white, blue, red (this was only officially adopted in 1799). The jack was to be a combination of the Cross of St George (red with a white cross) and the saltire of St Andrew, making it very like the British Union Jack with the colours reversed.

Top and above: *The Russian Tricolour, and the version combined with the Imperial arms used during the Great War.*

Right: *The Russian Imperial standard for use on land.*

The arms of Russia included the black double-headed eagle inherited from Byzantium, the shield of St George slaying the dragon (St George was the patron saint of Moscow), and lesser shields with the arms of the provinces. The earliest imperial standard was the tricolour with the eagle in gold in the centre, with the blue stripe widened to accommodate it.

Pan-Slavism was a movement that began among the Slavic people of Eastern Europe in the eighteenth century, especially involving the Czechs, Slovaks, and Croats. The first Pan-Slav Congress was held during the Year of Revolutions in Prague and demanded home rule for the Slav provinces of the Austrian Empire. They did not propose to exchange Austrian domination for Russian, but did find that Russia offered a necessary counterbalance. A further congress was held in Moscow in 1867, and the movement gained impetus after the Russian Revolution of 1905.

Serbia was the first Slav state to adopt the Russian colours, in about 1835. The Serbian flag was the same as the Russian one but inverted. The Slav provinces of Austria adopted similar tricolours at the time of the 1848 Congress, each placing the colours in a different order: Slovakia: white, blue, red (just like Russia); Slovenia: white, blue red; Croatia: red, white, blue (like the Netherlands); and Bosnia: blue, white, red. These were, of course, the colours used by the nationalists, not the official ones dictated by the government.

Montenegro only adopted the Pan-Slav colours toward the end of the century, when a flag like that of Serbia was introduced. Serbia and Montenegro had different arms on their flags.

The Sorbs, a Slavic community in what is now East Germany, also adopted a tricolour in 1848, of blue, red, white. There is no Sorb state as such but the flag is still in use.

Below: *The arms and flag of Serbia on a British cigarette card; (the arms are erroneous).*

Above: *The flag of Croatia.*

Above: *The flag of the Sorbs.*

Above, far left: The flag of the Kingdom of the Serbs, Croatia and the Slovenes (Yugoslavia), 1920.

Above left: The flag of Slovakia, 1848.

Left: The flag of the protectorate of Bohemia-Moravia established by the Germans, 1939.

The flag of Bulgaria is also a Pan-Slav flag, adopted in 1878. In its case green was substituted for blue, not just for the sake of distinction in a flag that would otherwise have been identical with that of Russia, but also to symbolize hope and youthfulness.

After the First World War the southern Slav states united as Yugoslavia, with a flag of blue, white, red, and Czechoslovakia was formed with a flag of white over red (the Czech colours) with a blue triangle based on the hoist.

During the Second World War four artificial Slav states were set up by the Germans: Bohemia-Moravia, Slovakia, Croatia, and Serbia. Bohemia-Moravia was endowed with a tricolour of white, red, blue, although the Czechs had never adopted the Slav colours. Slovakia used the 1848 flag, with its arms in the centre. Serbia reverted to the pre-1918 flag, as did Croatia, also with its arms in the centre. Slovakia and Croatia both had a range of distinguishing and rank flags.

After the Second World War a red, yellow-edged star was added to the flag of Yugoslavia and to the flags of its component states.

THE PAN-ARAB COLOURS

Before the First World War there was a move toward 'Pan-Arabanism' by Arabs who wanted emancipation from the Turkish Empire. In 1914 the Young Arab Society decided on a flag of green, white, and black. Together with red these colours had already been given poetic interpretations by Arab nationalists, and it was also claimed that they represented the main dynasties of Caliphs.

This tricolour was adapted by Sherif Husein of Mecca in 1917 for his forces. In his flag the colours were arranged black over green over white, with a red triangle based on the hoist (the first example of this kind of flag design – but achieved simply by adding the red Hashemite pennant to the tricolour). The red triangle was for his own dynasty, which it was intended would provide the future kings of Arabia.

This flag was in fact used for the short-lived Kingdom of Syria set up in March 1920, and for Husein's own kingdom of the Hejaz. It was adopted for Transjordan in March 1921. At about this time the order of the stripes was changed to black, white, green, to restore them to the form invented by the Young Arabs. When Husein's son Faisal became King of Iraq, the flag was varied by making the triangle into a trapezium and adding two white stars to it. A single white star had been used on the flag of Syria, and was later added to the flag of Transjordan. The seven points of these stars stood originally for the seven parts of the Greater Syria. The Republic of Syria created by the French adopted a flag in the four colours on 1 January 1932.

Left: The flag of the Arab revolt, 1917. Later the white was placed in the middle.

Above: The modern flag of Kuwait.

Above: The modern flag of the United Arab Emirates.

Above, left to right, top to bottom: *Flags making use of the Pan-Arab colours, South Yemen, Iraq, Syria, Jordan, Sudan and North Yemen.*

Right: *The arms of the Federation of Arab Republics, 1972.*

The Arab Revolt flag lived on to become the flag of Arab Palestine, and variant forms were used later in Kuwait and the United Arab Emirates.

In 1952 the young officers' coup took place in Egypt, which ultimately created a republic and brought Gamal Abdul Nasser to power. The colours popularized by this movement were red, white, and black, and the favoured emblem wa the eagle of Saladin. When the United Arab Republic was formed on 22 February 1958, a flag in these colours replaced the green national flag, with two green stars for the two component states. As a result of this initiative, similar flags were later adopted in other Arab states: Syria (22 February 1958-28 September 1961; 8 March 1963-present); Yemen Arab Republic (27 September 1962-present); Iraq (31 July 1963-present); Libya (1 September 1969-March 1977); Yemen People's Democratic Republic (30 November 1967-present); and Sudan (20 May 1970-present).

During the period of the Federation of Arab Republics (1 January 1972-March 1977) Egypt, Syria, and Libya had a common flag and a common emblem in the centre of it. The emblem was based on the arms of Syria and was the golden hawk of the Quraish tribe (the tribe of the Prophet, and therefore the badge of the Hashemites). The scroll bore the title of the state and underneath was the name of the component state. Syria still uses the arms in this form, as does Libya, but Egypt has reverted to the eagle of Saladin.

Above: *The flag of the Liberation Rally, Egypt 1952.*

THE PAN-AFRICAN COLOURS

The Pan-African colours derive from two sources of inspiration. The first is the flag created in 1917 by Marcus Garvey for the United Negro Improvement Association, of red, black, and green stripes. He was a proponent of the 'Back to Africa' movement and saw these colours as those of a new Negro state which would arise in Africa. The colours became well known as those of the Black Power movement in the USA and the Caribbean, and were taken up by many other black activists.

The second source is the colours of Ethiopia. The coronation of Ras Tafari as the Emperor of Ethiopia in 1930 had a profound effect on Afro-Americans, especially in Jamaica, where the Rastafarian movement was born. In the course of time the Ethiopian red, yellow, and green merged with the Garvey black, red, and green to form the familiar combination.

Above: *The colours of Ethiopia.*

At the end of the Second World War, a number of prominent African politicians became influenced by both the Garvey and the Rastafarian movements. Jomo Kenyatta and

Hastings Banda adopted the Garvey colours for their own developing political movements, as did Forbes Burnham in Guyana. Kwame Nkrumah adopted the Rasta colours for Ghana, the former Gold Coast, when it became independent in 1957. He also used Garvey's symbol of a Black Star, first used on the flag of the Black Star Line in 1919.

Nkrumah was anxious to spread African nationalism to other countries, and also to try to form the sort of United States of Africa which had also been envisaged by Garvey. His ideas did spread and the Ghanaian colours were adopted very quickly throughout West Africa. Three states also used black stars on their flags, and a flag was envisaged for the United States of Africa like that of Ghana but with more black stars.

The Rasta colours have also been employed in the flags of West Indian states, although it is not known if this was done deliberately. As in most cases the official explanations given for the colours used in flags have very little bearing on reality.

Left and above left: *Flags using the Pan-African colours: Guinea and Cameroon.*

Left and far left: *Pan-African colour flags with black stars: Ghana and Cape Verde.*

Below left and far left: *The flags of Kenya and Malawi, derived from the Garvey colours.*

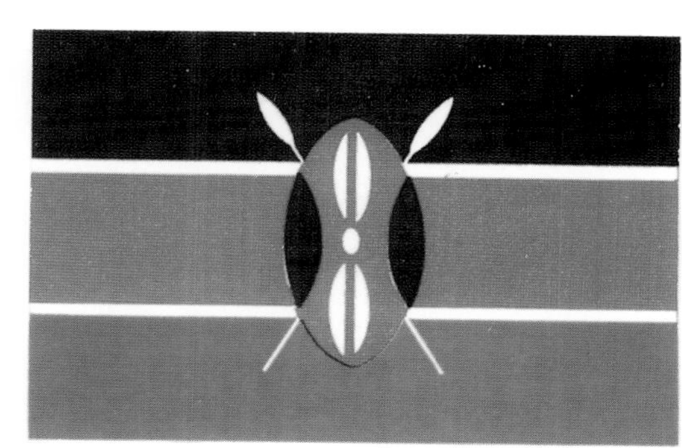

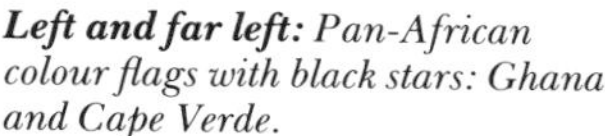

Above: *The Lion of Judah on the flag of Ethiopia.*

Above: *The flag of the African National Congress.*

List of flags using Pan-African colours

Ghana:* 10 October 1956
Cameroon: 29 October 1957
Guinea: October/November 1958
Central African Republic: 1 December 1958
Mali Federation:* 4 April 1959
Congo: 18 August 1959
Dahomey (now Bénin): 16 November 1959
Togo: 27 April 1960
Senegal: 20 August 1960
Rwanda:* September 1961
Guyana:* January 1966
Zaïre: 21 November 1971
Guinea-Bissau:* 24 November 1973
Grenada: 7 February 1974
São Tomé and Príncipe:* 26 November 1974
Cape Verde:* 30 December 1974
Zimbabwe:* 18 April 1980
St Christopher-Nevis:* 19 September 1983
Burkina Faso: 4 August 1984

The Garvey colours in their original form were used from 1952 onward by the Kenya African National Union, and they formed the basis of the design for the flag of Kenya, adopted on 12 December 1963.

*also with black stars or other black features.

Modern Political Symbols
Aspirant and Colonial States

Aspirant states are ones that are seeking to secede from the nation in which they find themselves in order to set up an independent government of their own. Several of the independent countries of today were once in this category, such as Poland, Czechoslovakia, Finland, Greece, Bangladesh, and Singapore. Secessionism represents the extreme position taken by those who for one reason or another believe that they would be better off with independence. Their motivation is often that they are of a different linguistic, ethnic, or religious group from the majority, and in fact they may once have been an independent entity. In some cases the secessionists speak for all their fellow-countrymen, but there are cases where they have adopted a more extreme position than other parties have.

Arab Palestine is an example of linguistic, ethnic, and religious and cultural differentiation from the state in which the Arabs find themselves. The Arabs were assigned a large section of Palestine by the United Nations in 1948, but it is all now occupied by Israel. They aim to set up an independent state based on the 'West Bank' and Gaza Strip areas. Their flag is that of the Arab Revolt, as revised in 1921.

Kurdistan is an area that straddles the borders of Turkey, Iran, and Iraq. A Kurd state was envisaged by the Treaty of Versailles but was never put into effect. However, Kurds continue to fight for its establishment. The flag is a traditional one.

Western Sahara, or the Sahrawi Arab Republic, is the aspirant state of the inhabitants of the former Western Sahara, now occupied by Morocco. The Sahrawi government is based in Algeria, and it is thought that the flag of Algeria is the inspiration for the crescent and star on the Arab flag.

Eritrea. The Eritrean People's Liberation Front now occupies most of the former Italian colony of Eritrea, which was ceded to Ethiopia after the Second World War.

Tigre. The Tigre Liberation Front is fighting a similar battle in the Ethiopian province of Tigre, and is one of the more successful of several such secessionist groups in Ethiopia.

Burma is the most divided country in the world, with no less than ten liberation armies striving to set up states of their own and in some cases succeeding. The Shans and Karens are the most successful, although they are divided among themselves.

West Irian. The Free Papua Movement aims at expelling the Indonesians from western Papua, which was ceded to them in 1963. They use the flag designed for the transitional state of 1961-3, administered by the Dutch, whose tricolour must have provided some of the inspiration for the design.

Khalistan. The more radical Sikhs are trying to establish a Sikh state in the Punjab, but have not yet won any territory. The Khalistan movement makes use of the traditional Sikh flag known as the *Nisan Sahib*.

Kanaky. The Kanaks of New Caledonia are hoping for independence from France and widespread use is made of the flag of the Kanak

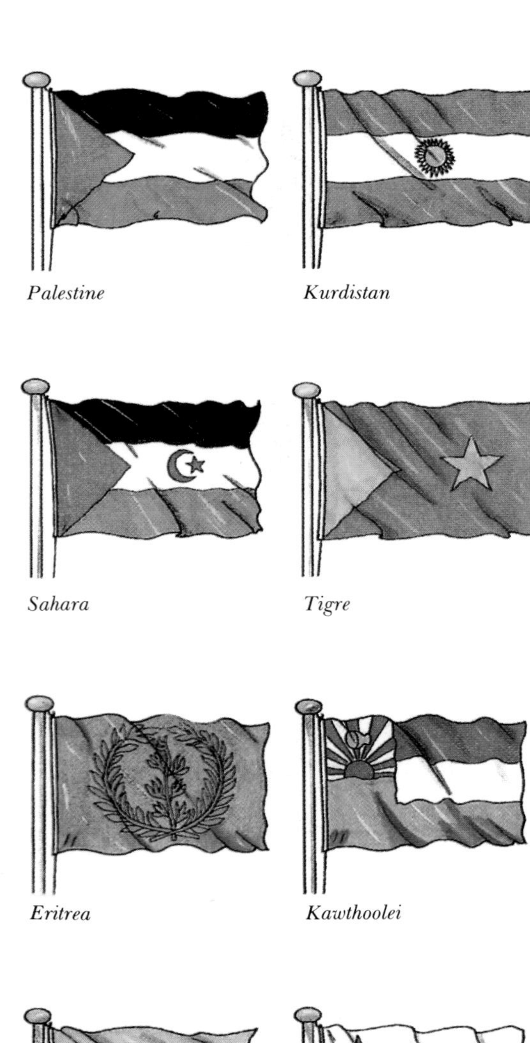

Palestine *Kurdistan*

Sahara *Tigre*

Eritrea *Kawthoolei*

Shanland *Arakan*

West Irian *Kanaky*

North Cyprus *Tamil Eelam*

Socialist National Liberation Front. The device is the carved finial at the end of a roof-beam of the type found on the traditional house.

North Cyprus broke away from the Republic of Cyprus in 1975 to form a separate Turkish state. Its flag dates from 13 March 1984 and was the winning entry in a competition.

Tamil Eelam is the state that the Tamils wish to establish in their part of Sri Lanka. Autonomy has already been granted to Tamil districts, but an armed struggle continues.

SUPPRESSED NATIONS

A special category of aspirant nations are those that once enjoyed a period of independence, or at any rate distinct existence, and are seeking to reassert it. Several of these states are to be found in the Soviet Union, where *perestroika* is giving them a chance to re-establish their identity.

Armenia was independent from 28 May 1918 to 2 April 1921. The flag emerged from several projects in the late nineteenth century. The lower stripe is often described as orange but is in fact a deep yellow.

Azerbaijan became independent on 10 June 1918. The flag used today was adopted on 24 September, but flew only until 20 April 1920, when the Soviet Republic was established.

Byelorussia declared itself independent on 25 March 1918, but was incorporated into the Soviet system on 1 January 1919. The flag appeared immediately after the Tsar's abdication (March 1917) and is derived from the White Knight of Lithuania.

Estonia became independent on 24 February 1918, but entered the Soviet Union on 6 August 1940. The flag dates from 1881 and was formally adopted on 4 July 1920. It was restored as the national flag on 25 June 1988.

Georgia, previously an independent kingdom, became a Social Democratic Republic on 26 May 1918 and remained so until 18 March 1921, when the Red Army took over. The flag was introduced in 1917. It has not yet been officially recognized again.

Latvia became independent on 18 April 1918 and entered the Soviet Union on 5 August 1940. The flag was adopted on 15 February 1922. It was again recognized as the national flag in October 1988.

Lithuania became independent on 16 February 1918 and entered the Soviet Union on 3 August 1940. The flag was officially adopted on 1 August 1922 and re-established in October 1988.

Moldavia declared its independence on 23 December 1917, but attached itself to Romania on 9 April 1918. The part of it that returned to the Soviet Union on 27 June 1940 is now seeking separation once more. Its flag was blue over red horizontally.

Ukraine. The Ukraine declared itself independent on 22 January 1918 and adopted the traditional flag on 22 March. The colours of the flag, first used in 1848, are derived from the colours of the arms of Galicia. The republic was suppressed on 21 November 1920, but in the meantime it had developed a very wide range of flags, many of which included the traditional trident emblem of St Volodimyr.

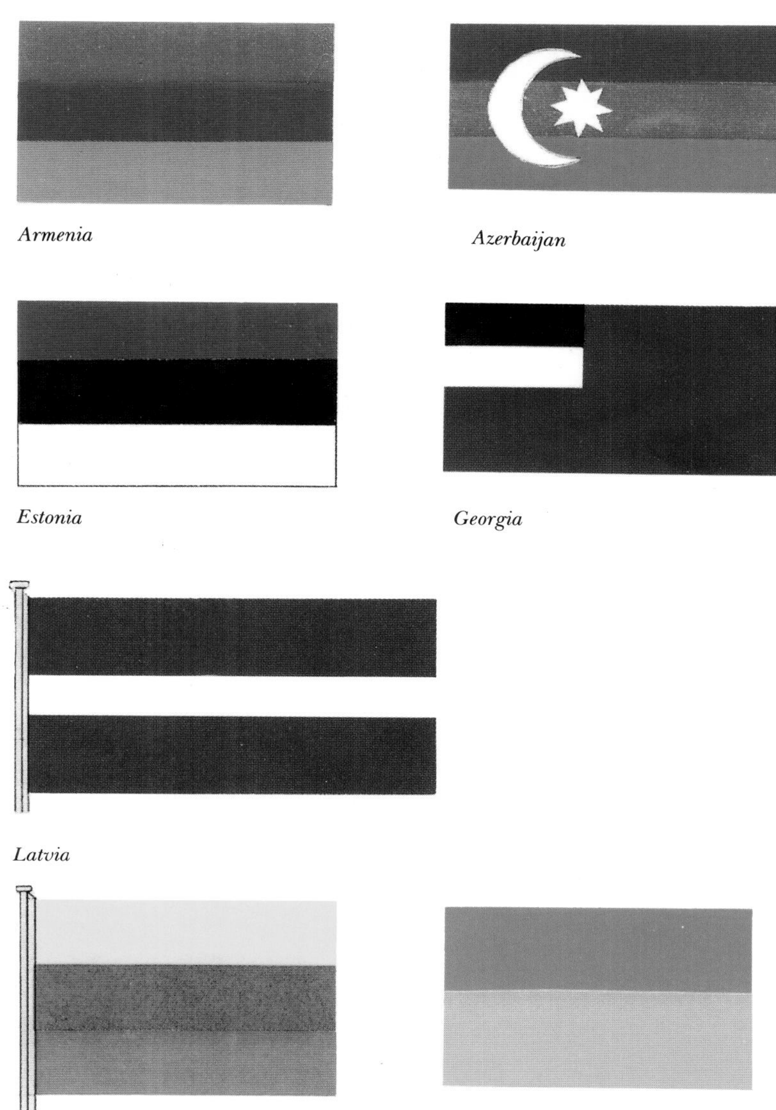

Armenia *Azerbaijan* *Estonia* *Georgia* *Latvia* *Lithuania* *Ukraine*

FLAG CONFLICTS

There are several instances where it is not just inadvisable to fly the flag of one of the aspirant or suppressed states or of any dissident movement, but also positively illegal. This is the case with the flag of Arab Palestine and, until recently, with the flag of the African National Congress in South Africa. In Northern Ireland it is still illegal to display the flag of the Republic of Ireland, and although no official action has been taken for some years against those who do so, it does sometimes provoke sectarian comment and conflict.

Before the fall of Franco it was illegal to display the flag of the Basque State that he had suppressed. The flag was often provocatively put out by the separatists, sometimes with a booby trap to blow up the police trying to remove it. Failing that, they would ostentatiously grow window boxes of red and white flowers with green leaves in order to display the colours. The flag of Catalonia was also suppressed, and to get round the ban its partisans used instead the flag of Barcelona football club, which had red and blue (as opposed to red and yellow) stripes.

***Right:** The flag of the Pays Basques, northern Spain.*

But the greatest conflicts are those where it is a question of changing the national flag. The main areas where flag strife has been prevalent in this respect are Germany after 1918, South Africa in the 1920s, Canada in the 1960s, and contemporary Australia.

In Germany the struggle was between those who wanted to introduce a particularly republican flag, the tricolour of 1848, and those who wanted to keep the Bismarck tricolour of 1867. The issue divided the nation into those who were sympathetic to the republic and those who hankered for the glorious days of the German Empire. The republic was never able to wholly adopt the black, red, gold flag for all purposes, being obliged to compromise with the black, white, red partisans. Conflict over this issue came to a head in 1926, when the Chancellor was obliged to resign because he unduly favoured the black, white, red. Hitler solved the issue at a stroke in 1933 by declaring black, white, red the national colours.

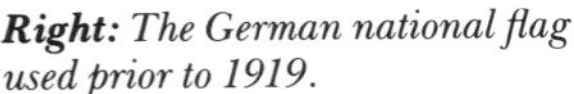

***Right:** The German national flag used prior to 1919.*

In South Africa the issue was the continued use of the Union Jack versus the importation of elements from the heraldry of the Boer republics. Many various compromise designs were considered, which ultimately led to the adoption of the present flag in 1928. Originally the design in the centre was to have been a quartered shield, but the present, more ingenious pattern prevailed. The compromise was that the flag must always be flown alongside a Union Jack, but in 1957, with the National Party securely in power, this provision was abandoned.

In Canada the Union Jack was also desired by a significant section of the population, and just as vehemently resisted by another. When the issue was revived in 1963, the government was once again bombarded with proposals, most of which tried to find a flag of unity. Originally the government favoured a red, white, and blue flag with no Union Jack, but eventually plumped for one that was neither distinctively British nor French-Canadian, but wholly Canadian. Parliament took weeks to debate the proposal, which was eventually adopted on 15 December 1964.

***Above and top:** Two Australian flags, the national flag and the proposed 'Ausflag'.*

The Union Jack is already present in the flag of Australia (and the Blue Ensign version has officially been adopted as the national flag), and the issue is whether it should continue to be there. Australians are not divided on purely political, linguistic, or ethnic lines, as was the case in the earlier flag conflicts, but it is clear that, like the Canadians, they are not all of British extraction. However, the present design still has power as a symbol of attachment to the Commonwealth. Prior to the 1988 Bicentennial celebrations, the Ausflag organization promoted an alternative design, using the same colours and the Southern Cross but omitting the Union Jack. Since then the issue has become less intense, and affection has been transferred to a jokey flag called the Boxing

Kangaroo. This is in the gold and green now recognized as the Australian national colours. A similar flag called the Fighting Kiwi has become popular in New Zealand, another country where the continued use of the Union Jack is also in question. Neither of these animal flags, however, is a serious contender to replace the present national flags.

Left: *The Fighting Kiwi flag.*

SOME FAMOUS FLAG INCIDENTS

The number of critical incidents involving flags is very large, due to their power to symbolize heartfelt emotions, and also to provoke violent reactions. Among those which will certainly go down in history are the following.

Hungary 1956. During the Revolution of October 1956, the Hungarians protesting against the authoritarian Communist regime tore the state emblem out of the tricolour, and left the hole where it had been as a symbol in itself. After the suppression of the Rising, the new government had the grace not to add any new emblem to the national flag.

Romania 1989. A repetition of the above incident took place in Romania in December 1989, where a similar emblem was torn out of the national tricolour. Thereafter the national flag was left without any central emblem.

The Eureka Stockade. In 1854 the miners of Ballarat in Victoria took up arms against the state police and raised a flag of their own at the Eureka Stockade just outside the town. On 3 December the stockade was overrun and the miners dispersed. The flag was torn down and trampled on and then smuggled away by the police. However, it was not forgotten, and the design of the flag became a symbol of protest, particularly among the labour movement. Years later the flag turned up again, and now has an honoured place in the City Art Gallery.

France 1871. After the fall of the Emperor Napoleon III and the Paris Commune, there was a move to restore the Bourbon monarchy. The pretender to the throne was the Count de Chambord, who was offered the throne on condition that he would allow the French people to continue to use the *Tricolore*. This he refused to do because of its associations with republicanism. Consequently, the offer was withdrawn and the government decided to form a republic instead.

Germany 1923. In 1923 Hitler organized his famous *putsch* or attempt to overthrow the government of Bavaria. It was unsuccessful and fourteen Nazis were shot down in the street. The flag they carried with them was damaged and stained with their blood and was thereafter treated as a sacred relic by the Nazis, with its own shrine and bodyguard, and became known as the *Blutfahne*. It was subsequently used to impart virtue to all the other Nazi flags – it was used to touch them during Nazi rallies. It disappeared at the end of the war, but if it could be found today this flag would cause considerable trouble.

South Africa 1879. A body of British troops were overwhelmed by Zulu warriors at Isandhlwana in January 1879, and two officers of the South Wales Borderers tried to escape and save the Queen's Colour of the Regiment. They got away from the battle but were later killed. Both officers won the VC for this, and the incident resulted in a decision to leave ceremonial colours behind in future. The Regiment received the unusual battle honour of a silver wreath to hang on the colour stave.

Roman Empire, 9AD. The eagles of three legions of the Roman Army were lost when the expedition led by Varus into Germany was destroyed in the Teutoberger Wald. Afterward this was made into a famous incident in German history and a massive memorial was erected on the spot. However, for the Romans it was a great setback, which had to be put right by recovering the eagles. Two were found soon afterward, but it was over thirty years later that the Emperor Claudius discovered that the shrine where the Germans were guarding the third eagle was in Bremen, and sent a flying column to retrieve it.

Baltimore 1814. During the War of 1812 the British attacked Fort McHenry in Baltimore (13 September 1814). Francis Scott Key was on board a British ship and observed the action. It looked as if the fort would fall, but next morning he saw the Stars and Stripes still flying above it. It was this incident that impelled him to write the verses 'Oh say can you see by the dawn's early light what so proudly we hailed at the twilight's last gleaming?', which when set to music became the national anthem of the United States on 3 March 1931.

Below: *Hitler is seen here using the* Blutfahne *to touch and thereby impart virtue to another Nazi standard. The* Blutfahne *became a sacred object for the Nazis.*

SOME FAMOUS FLAGS

Wars have often thrown up famous personalities, and some of these had distinguishing flags that are still remembered today.

General de Gaulle

When he became leader of the Free French it was necessary to distinguish the *Tricolore* used by his forces from the plain flag used by the Vichy government. Consequently he added a red cross, known as the Cross of Lorraine, to the white strip. The Cross of Lorraine remained his emblem after the war and became his party symbol. He placed it in the centre of the *Tricolore* again when he became President in 1958.

Above: *The emblem of General de Gaulle, the double-armed cross of Lorraine, was used to distinguish the Tricolore of the Free French forces.*

Field Marshal Montgomery

As Commander of the Eighth Army, which defeated the Germans in North Africa, Montgomery flew the flag of an Army, which in the British system is a horizontal triband of red, black, red. In the centre was the formation sign: a blue square containing a white shield with a yellow cross, symbolic of the Crusaders.

Above: *Montgomery, Commander of the Eighth Army in North Africa, with the Eighth Army shield and flag on his jeep.*

Joan of Arc

The standard used by Joan of Arc was described during her trial in 1431 and has been depicted in many representations of France's national heroine. It was a white streamer with the arms of France on one side and on the other a picture of God and two angels, with lilies and the legend *Jhesus Maria*. After her death the standard was carried at the coronation of Charles VII in Rheims cathedral.

Above: *The standard of Joan of Arc and contemporary heraldic shields.*

Mussolini

The Italian Fascists took their name from the *fasces*, a bundle of rods tied round an axe, which was the symbol of justice in ancient Rome. As *Il Duce*, Mussolini used this badge in gold on a blue flag, within a gold frame.

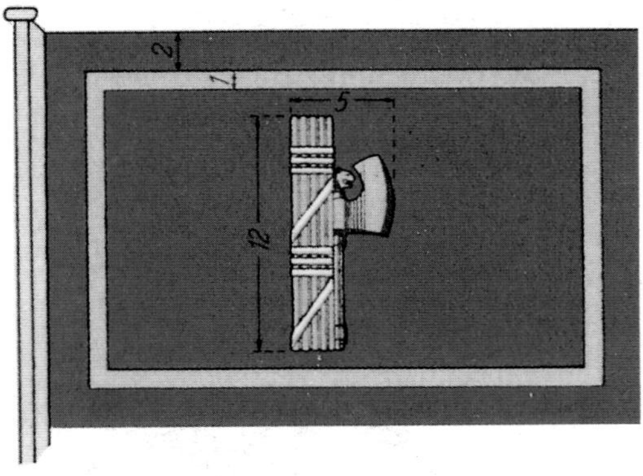

Above: *Mussolini's personal flag with its construction details.*

George Washington

During the winter of 1777–8, when Washington was encamped at Valley Forge, he is credited with using a flag of blue with thirteen six-pointed stars, which seemed to be a canton (or 'Union') cut from a Stars and Stripes. The original flag can now be seen at the Valley Forge Historical Centre.

Above: *The flag used by Washington at his Valley Forge headquarters, with its thirteen six-pointed white stars.*

Left: *William of Orange's standard, asserting his intention to hold to and defend the Protestant religion in England.*

William of Orange

When the Prince of Orange landed at Torbay in 1688, he bore a flag of white with his arms in the centre. These combined his own arms with the Stuart arms of Great Britain to which he was laying claim, together with the British lion and unicorn. On the flag was the legend, 'For the Protestant Religion and the Liberty of England', and his own motto, *Je Maintiendrai.* Above the flag was a streamer that combined the flags of England and the Netherlands. William went on to defeat King James in battles in Ireland, and ever since he was king himself his memory has been kept alive by the 'Orangemen' of Northern Ireland.

Haile Selassie

As Emperor of Ethiopia (1930–74), Haile Selassie used an elaborate standard symbolic of his role and his descent. The field was the Ethiopian colours and in the centre was the Lion of Judah, surrounded by the Collar of the Order of the Seal of Solomon. In each corner were further Solomon's seals in gold, very similar to the *Magen David* used in Israel. On the reverse the collar contained a representation of St George and the Dragon. The House of Shoa, to which Haile Selassie belonged, claimed descent from Solomon via Makeda, the 'Queen of Sheba'.

Francisco Franco

Franco, who became *Caudillo* of Spain in 1939, was not, of course, entitled to use the royal arms, and so devised a personal standard for himself. This was of crimson, with a yellow diagonal stripe at each end of which was the head of a 'wolf-dragon'. On either side of the stripe were the Pillars of Hercules, each with part of the Spanish motto, *Plus Ultra.* The whole thing was in the form of a cavalry guidon, with a gold fringe.

Left: *The Royal banner of Charles I of Spain, the basis for Franco's personal flag.*

Left: *The Emperor Haile Selassie in 1965. The Collar of the Order of the Seal of Solomon is just visible in the middle of the standard.*

FLAGS IN THE THIRD REICH

The Nazis were great users of flags, and unpleasant as the period is, it was a very colourful and dramatic one in terms of flags.

Hitler chose to use the colours invented by Bismarck for the North German Confederation of 1867 (and also used by the Empire of 1870-1918). The parties of the right had always resented the switch by the Weimar Republic to the tricolour of 1848 (see 'The Year of Revolutions') and the Bismarck colours continued to be used by opponents of the Weimar system.

The swastika was derived from ones used by pre-war anti-Semitic organizations and by the *Freikorps*, who carried on the Great War after the Armistice. Hitler's contribution was to combine the swastika with the Bismarck colours. The red field of his flag represented the socialist element in his programme, while the swastika represented the advance of Aryan man.

This was the basic party flag, but it was capable of infinite variations. Before the party came to power, flags and standards were invented for the street army, the *Sturm Abteilung*, or SA and the Protection Squad *Schutz Staffel*, or SS. SA standards were of the *vexillum* type, with a metal vexilloid at the top in the form of an eagle on a wreath containing the swastika. The legend on the flag was *Deutschland Erwache* ('Germany Awake'). The SS used black flags. The flag of Himmler, as chief of the SS, was divided diagonally into black and white triangles with the party badge in gold over all. On SS flags and material the initials were always spelt with the *sig* runes.

The flag of the Hitler Youth was red with a narrow white stripe across it, and the swastika on a white diamond over all. There were many different flags for the various parts of the youth movement.

One of the strangest flags in use at this time was the *Blutfahne*. This was the party flag that had been carried in the *putsch* in Munich in 1923 and was allegedly stained with the blood of the Nazis who fell at that time. The flag was carefully preserved and treated with great honour, and a party rallies it would be presented to Hitler, who in turn would touch each new standard and flag with it, thus passing on some of its magic to them.

One of Hitler's first acts on becoming Chancellor in 1933 was to restore the Bismarck colours as the national flag, effectively abolishing the 1848 tricolour. However the black, white, red tricolour did not last long as the national flag, since in 1935, once he had become Head of State, he made the party flag into the national flag (15 September 1935). New versions of the government flags were introduced. The *Reichskriegsflagge* (army and navy ensign) became the one familiar to us from war films. The service flag (for government offices) was a more elaborate form of the swastika flag.

Hitler himself had a flag. This contained a

***Above:** The front of the SA 'Feldhernnhalle' standard.*

***Right:** The National War flag (the* 'Reichskriegsflagge'*).*

Left: *Adolf Hitler's personal standard, signifying his position as chancellor of Germany.*

Far left and left: *The left and right sides of the personal standard (first pattern) of Reichsmarschall Hermann Göring.*

large swastika of the cotised and upright variety within a golden wreath. In the cantons were the national emblem and the Army badge. The national and party badge was a spread eagle in the Art Deco style, with a head pointing to the dexter when used for the state and to the sinister when used for the party, and grasping a wreath containing a swastika. The army badge had a more Roman-style eagle and no wreath. Other national leaders also had elaborate standards, including Göring who had several, according to his various titles. The Nazis reintroduced the idea of accompanying notables on foot with standard-bearers carrying their official flags.

Military flags were also reorganized and made use of the swastika, the Iron Cross, and the Army eagle. They had different coloured fields according to the arm of the service they represented (infantry, artillery, engineers, etc).

The flags of this period were generally very well made and visually effective. Albert Speer is credited with much of the success of Nazi visual imagery, which was certainly of a very high order.

At the end of the war the Russians ritually dishonoured all the flags and standards they had taken and the Allied Control Commission formally banned all Nazi insignia from Germany.

Flags for Special Purposes
Flags of Heads of State

The first flags of heads of state were the feudal banners and 'arms of dominion' used by territorial magnates, princes, and kings in earlier times. The purest heraldic form of such arms were armorial banners, ie the arms from the shield in the form of a flag. The 'Royal Standard' of the United Kingdom is an armorial banner, although not in the traditional squarish shape that heralds prefer. Elongated banners of the arms with the Queen's badge in the centre are also used for several of the Queen's Realms (Commonwealth countries of which she is Head of State).

Other kinds of armorial flags have also been adopted. One type is the standard as used by the King of Spain, which has a plain field and the whole royal arms in the centre. A variation of this is the royal standard of Belgium, which also has a plain field, but on the shield of arms, and the royal cipher in the cantons. Yet another variation is the ensign-standard used in Scandinavia, where the whole royal arms are placed on a panel in the centre of the cross on the naval ensign. These clearly date, like the British royal standard, from a period when the flag was principally, or only, used at sea. The royal standards of the Netherlands are different again, using part of the arms on flags of distinctive design.

In terms of republican states, several design trends have developed over the years. The United States was the first country to have a Presidential standard, which was very similar to the military colours of the time, ie a blue field with the national arms in the centre. This pattern was made official on 9 August 1882 but had already been in use for about forty years before that. The arms placed on a blue field are or were also used in the Philippines, Cuba, Liberia, Ghana, Trinidad, Malta, and for a while in South Africa.

A variation on this is to place the arms on a field of another colour, usually one of the

Above: *The Royal standard of the United Kingdom.*

Right: *The Royal standard of Alfonso XII of Spain.*

colours of the national flag, as in Dominica, Argentina, Uruguay, Brazil, Israel, Tanzania, Zimbabwe, and Zambia. Some Marxist states have provided their Presidents with red flags with arms, as in East Germany, Mozambique, and Romania.

A further trend is the embellishment of the national flag. One way of doing this, very common in Francophone countries, is to use a square silk version of the national flag, with a heavy gold fringe. This occurs in The Ivory Coast,Chad, Togo, and elsewhere. Another is to add the national arms, either over all in the centre, or in the canton. Centrally placed arms occur in Austria, Chile, Colombia, Ethiopia, Gabon, the Seychelles, Sudan, and Gambia, and arms are added to the canton in the flags of Egypt, the Yemen Arab Republic, and the Yemen People's Republic. On the flag of the President of Pakistan the device is a simplified version of the national arms. On the flag of Saudi Arabia the arms are placed in the lower hoist.

Another trend is to devise a quite distinct flag, which is not in the colours of the flag nor uses the arms. An example is the flag of the President of Indonesia, which is yellow (the colour of royalty), with a golden star. In France the custom has grown up of adding a personal emblem to the centre of the national flag. The current President uses a golden badge consisting of a combined olive and oak tree. In Kenya part of the national arms is used, together with the cockerel emblem of KANU. The flag of the President of India looks like an armorial banner, but in fact is not: its quarters carry diverse emblems, only one of which is the national arms. In South Africa the President's flag is somewhat like the national flag with the whole arms on the white part, and the traditional initials 'S.P.' (for 'State President'). The Presidential flags of Ghana and Nigeria also had inscriptions, but are no longer in use. The President of Zaïre has four flags, corresponding to his various titles.

Finally there is a large class of nations that have no flag at all for their heads of state, a group that includes China and the Soviet Union.

***Above:** The Royal standard of the Sultan of Brunei.*

***Left:** The last Shah of Iran, Shahanshah Mohammed Raze Pahlavi, taking the salute under his flag.*

***Above:** The presidential flags (**clockwise from the top left**) of Brazil, Chile, Surinam, and Uruguay.*

REGIONAL AND CIVIC FLAGS

City flags have been used since at least the dawn of heraldry, largely because Europe contained a number of city-states that jealously maintained their independence over the centuries. Examples include Venice, Geneva, Hamburg, and Bremen; in modern times Danzig, Memel, and Tangier have enjoyed this status. But independent or not, many cities of Europe developed flags for local use, often but not always related to their arms. The Hansa cities of Hamburg, Bremen, Lübeck, Danzig, and others used their flags at sea, and often had well-developed flag systems. The same is true of the Italian city-states that flourished before being incorporated into princely states.

Regional flags spring from several different sources: the most usual is that they were once

***Right and below right:** The arms and flag of Alkmaar in the Netherlands.*

***Far right:** The flag of the ancient republic of Pisa, atop the city's famous leaning tower.*

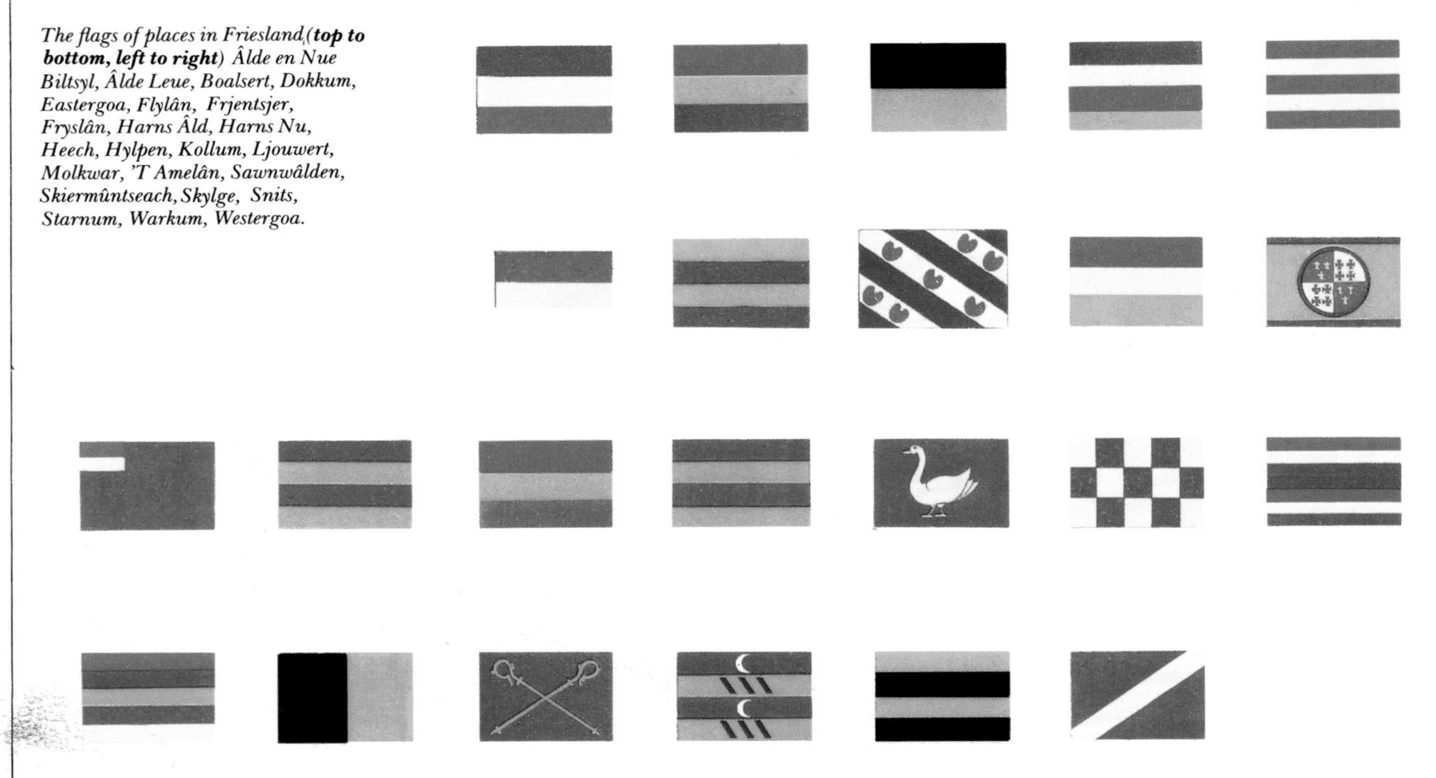

*The flags of places in Friesland,(**top to bottom, left to right**) Âlde en Nue Biltsyl, Âlde Leue, Boalsert, Dokkum, Eastergoa, Flylân, Frjentsjer, Fryslân, Harns Âld, Harns Nu, Heech, Hylpen, Kollum, Ljouwert, Molkwar, 'T Amelân, Sawnwâlden, Skiermûntseach, Skylge, Snits, Starnum, Warkum, Westergoa.*

the flags of independent states (such as Bavaria, Hawaii, Serbia, Estonia, Scotland, Britanny, and the Transvaal), which have been incorporated into larger ones. Another source is modern regionalism, the desire to set up a local identity, often in the hope of improving local economic circumstances. Examples of this are the re-creation of the traditional regions of France and the development of entities such as East Anglia, Cornwall, and Zetland. Sometimes the regions are based on linguistic or ethnic differences, as in the linguistic communities of Belgium. Sometimes this can lead to full-flown secessionism, as in Burma and West Irian (referred to more fully in 'Aspirant and Colonial States').

Regional flags are most frequent in states with federal constitutions, but this does not prevent them from emerging in centralized states. In fact overcentralization is often a stimulus to their development.

Above: *The cross of St Piran, the patron saint of Cornish tinners. The black symbolizes unrefined ore and the white refined metal.*

Above: *The flag of East Anglia.*

*Three flags from Sandaun (**top**), East Sepik (**above middle**) and Enga (**above**), Papua New Guinea.*

Below: *A display of Catalonian flags in a narrow street emphasizes the strength of local nationalist feeling.*

COMMERCIAL FLAGS

The first commercial flags were the house flags of the English trading companies that set out to explore and form trading links with the world outside Europe. They were closely followed by the Dutch and later other companies in Spain, France, and Flanders. The flag of the Cathay Company was used as early as 1577 by Martin Frobisher in the search for the Northwest Passage. The Levant Company flag dates from 1581, the Guinea Company from 1588, and the East India Company from 1599. The first Dutch company, the Far Trading Company, also dates from 1599. The Dutch East India Company was formed in 1602 and was later renamed the United East India Company.

The flags of both English and Dutch companies reflected their nationality: the English by the use of the Cross of St George and the royal arms, and the Dutch by the use of the *Prinsenvlag* with their initials. 'Chambers' of the Dutch companies based in various ports also used the flags of those ports, with their initials.

Modern house flags began as signal flags, to indicate the ownership of a vessel and give other information. Some say that they began in the late eighteenth century with the signal

Above: *The arms of the Levant Company. The Company dominated the current business with Turkey.*

Right: *The flag of the Cathay Company with the Cross of St George and the royal arms.*

Right: *The arms of the Dutch colony of Surinam with a sailing ship and the motto "Justice, Piety, Faith".*

Right: *An early flag of Surinam with the arms of the Dutch colony of Surinam. The small flags (**top to bottom, left to right**) are those of the General East Indies Company and its local branches in Rotterdam, Hoorn, Enkhuizen, Amsterdam, Delft, Middelburg and the chartered West Indies Company.*

station on Bidston Hill, opposite Liverpool where a row of flagpoles carried the flags of Liverpool shipping owners. From Bidston Hill ships could be espied approaching the harbour and the news could be flashed to Liverpool by means of the signal flags. With the general increase in shipping, some means of distinguishing one 'line' from another was an obvious necessity, and 'house flags' of the kind portrayed in the *Journal of Commerce* flag charts became widespread.

In the twentieth century house flags began to be used by companies with land-based interests as well as maritime ones, principally the major oil companies. Shell is a case in point: a company with oil wells, refineries and filling stations on land, and a fleet of tankers for transport. The tanker fleet flags came to be used on land, over the offices and other premises. Other examples include ICI, BP, Exxon, Mobil, Texaco, and ELF.

Commercial companies tend to change their flags more frequently than nation-states do, and they also allow more local variations; a Volkswagen flag might have a blue logo on white, or a white logo on blue. But like those of countries they can have *related* flags ie the flags of an associated or subsidiary company can be related in design to those of the main or parent company (for example, in the flag of Shell Mex-BP, which is in the same colours as the BP house flag but in a different design).

More and more house flags are common for use on land only. But many of these have now fallen prey to a design sickness known as *trenditis* ie the desire to have a design that is not so much effective and successful as trendy and stylish. The old parameters of sea flags – simple colours, simple design, distinctive features, easy memorability – have been abandoned in the face of pressure from corporate identity specialists to employ fashionable typefaces, logos, colours, shadings, elaborations, and inscriptions. It is a melancholy fact, therefore, that modern house flags would be totally unsuited for use at sea, or indeed for most outdoor conditions. It is also salutary that one of the most famous house flags of all time, that of the P & O Line, now does service as a logo in itself. The colours of the flag of the old Peninsular and Oriental Line were those of Spain and Portugal as they were in the nineteenth century, and became familiar to all seafarers. Now they are used more on land, because the simplicity and effectiveness of the design have proved superior to any modern gimmick.

Above left: *The Shell flag, one of the best known of all houseflags and two versions of the livery 1963–72 (**top**), and post-1972 (**above**).*

Below: *A range of company flags and funnel designs from a variety of merchant fleets.*

Cawood Containers Ltd., Belfast

Central Electricity Generating Board, London

Ceylon Shipping Corporation Colombo

Channel Coasters Ltd., (Spillers Ltd.),

Charrington Fuel Oils Ltd., London

Chevron Tankship (U.K.) Ltd., London

Cory Ship Towage Ltd., Cory Tank Craft Ltd., London

Costain Blankevoort (U.K.) Dredging Ltd., London

C. Crawley Ltd., London

Crescent Shipping Ltd., London & Rochester Trading Co. Ltd., Rochester

W. G. S. Crouch Ltd., Greenhithe

Cunard Brocklebank Ltd., (Camel Line & Dry Cargo Vessels) London

Eggar, Forrester Ltd., London

Elder Dempster Lines Ltd., Liverpool

Ellerman City Liners London

Esso Petroleum Co. Ltd., London

F. T. Everard & Sons Ltd., London

Falmouth Towage Co. Ltd., Falmouth

Geest Industries Ltd., Spalding

Gearbulk Ltd., London

Gem Line Ltd., (William Robertson Shipowners Ltd.), Glasgow

General Freight Co. Ltd., London

G. T. Gillie & Blair Ltd., Newcastle

Glenlight Shipping Ltd., Glasgow

Hethking S.S. Pty. Ltd., Sydney, N.S.W.

Holm & Co. Ltd., New Zealand

Holyhead Towing Co. Ltd., Holyhead

Houlder Brothers & Co. Ltd., London

Hoveringham Group Ltd., Nottingham

Humber Tugs Ltd., Hull and Grimsby

PRIVATE FLAGS

Apart from national flags several other kinds of flags are encountered at sea. Commercial house flags have been referred to in an earlier section, so the concern here is with the private flags of yacht clubs and yacht owners.

Private vessels over a certain size, unless they are fishing boats, must naturally display their country's national colours in the form of a civil ensign. But some countries allow yachts to fly either a special ensign or a yacht club flag in addition. Examples of the special ensigns are:

USA. The Yacht Ensign, which is like the national flag but has in the canton a white foul anchor within a ring of thirteen stars, in place of the normal stars. The Power Boat Squadron Ensign has thirteen vertical stripes of blue and white, and the same canton as the Yacht Ensign, but white on red. This can only be used by members of the Squadron.

__Above:__ The flags of the Royal Norwegian Yacht Club (__top__), the Royal Netherlands Yacht Club (__middle__) and the Cruising Club of Switzerland (__above__).

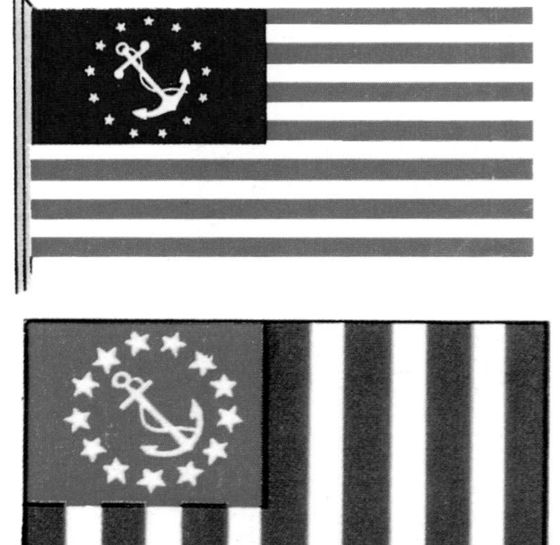

__Right and below right:__ The USA Yacht Ensign and the Power Boat Squadron Ensign.

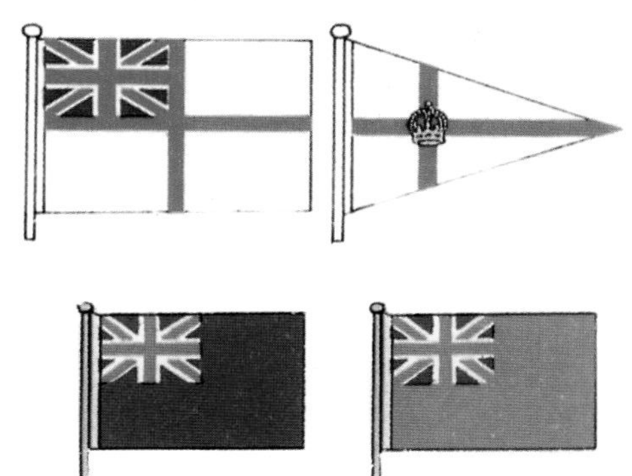

__Above:__ The White Ensign and the UK Royal Yacht Squadron club burgee, the Blue Ensign and the Red Ensign.

Finland. The Yacht Ensign is like the national flag but has a narrow white cross over the blue one. In the canton is placed the yacht club badge. Yacht club officers' flags are based on this design.

Switzerland. Yachts belonging to the Cruising Club of Switzerland add the club badge to the canton of the civil ensign.

Spain. The Yacht Ensign has a gold coronet in the centre of the civil ensign.

Norway. The ensign of the Royal Norwegian Sailing Club is like the naval ensign with the royal monogram in gold on a white square in the centre of the cross.

Netherlands. The Ensign of the Royal Netherlands Yacht Club is the civil ensign with the club badge in the centre (a crowned 'W' in gold on a blue diamond).

United Kingdom. In Great Britain certain clubs have the right to use ensigns, normally the Blue, or sometimes the Red, Ensign, with the club badge in the fly. The owner of a yacht can obtain a warrant to use this ensign instead of the normal Red Ensign. One club, the Royal Yacht Squadron, has the right to use the White Ensign. This does not have any added badge.

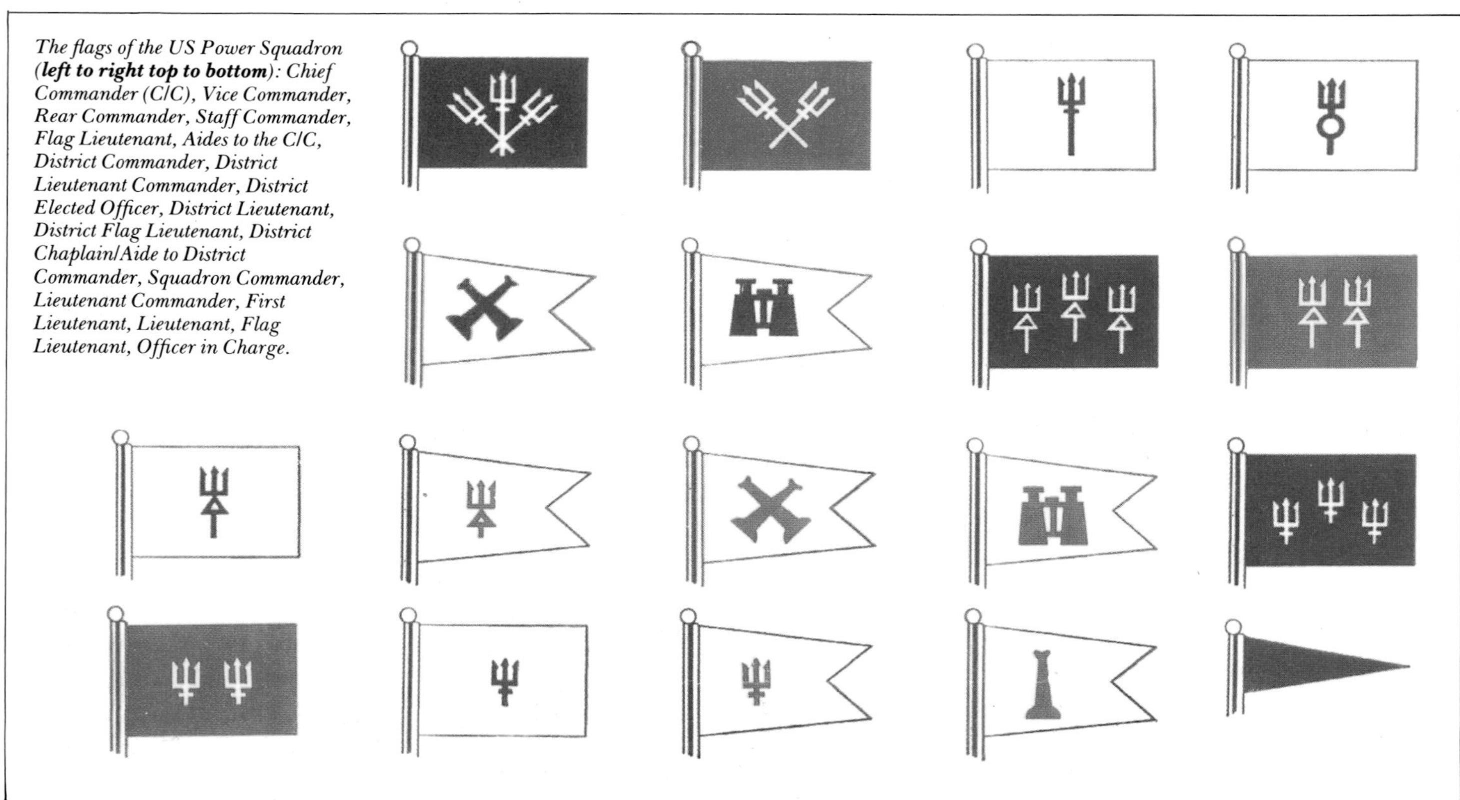

The flags of the US Power Squadron (__left to right top to bottom__): Chief Commander (C/C), Vice Commander, Rear Commander, Staff Commander, Flag Lieutenant, Aides to the C/C, District Commander, District Lieutenant Commander, District Elected Officer, District Lieutenant, District Flag Lieutenant, District Chaplain/Aide to District Commander, Squadron Commander, Lieutenant Commander, First Lieutenant, Lieutenant, Flag Lieutenant, Officer in Charge.

In addition to these substitutes for the national colours, most yacht club members also fly a *burgee*, which is in effect the club flag. The flag can be a normal rectangle, triangular, or swallow-tailed. Most of these flags make some reference to the country or the locality in which they are based, so that the Canadian Boating Federation pennant bears a red maple leaf, the Motor Boat Club of Sweden uses three gold crowns, and the yacht Club of Chile has a white star. In addition to this, many yacht clubs have distinguishing flags for their officers. The Commodore of an American yacht club flies a flag that is the canton of the Yacht Ensign, the Vice-Commodore the same but white on red, etc. The Commander of the Power Squadron has a blue flag with three white tridents, the Vice-Commander a red flag with two tridents. The Squadron has no less than eighteen distinguishing flags.

Finally, over and above the club flags are the owner's, or 'racing' flags. These are the personal pennants of the owner and usually make some reference to his or her personal predilections. If the person has a coat of arms, then they may reflect his colours, badge, or some other feature of the arms. Together with the yacht club burgees, all the various personal flags used to be recorded in the *Lloyd's Register of Yachts*; unfortunately, this is no longer published.

To end on a lighter note: an American practice that provides some fun is the use of the private signal flag for yachtsmen. When hoisted these signals convey such welcome (or unwelcome) messages as 'Cocktail Time', 'Wife on Board' (image of ball and chain), 'We caught a fish' (the flag shows what kind), and so on. Flags such as the Jolly Roger, the Confederate Flag, and regional flags can also be flown.

Morlaix Y.C. France · *Puerto Rico Y.C. USA* · *Carolina (S.C.) Y.C. USA*
Circolo Nautico Posillipo, Italy · *Boston Y.C. USA* · *Corpus Christi Y.C. USA*
Aldenham S.C. UK · *Atlanta Y.C. USA* · *Card Sound Sailing Club USA*
Mombasa Y.C. Kenya · *Royal Bermuda Y.C.* · *Canadian Boating Federation*
Adriatic Yacht Club, Italy · *Riverside (Conn.) Y.C. USA* · *Cannes Y.C. France*

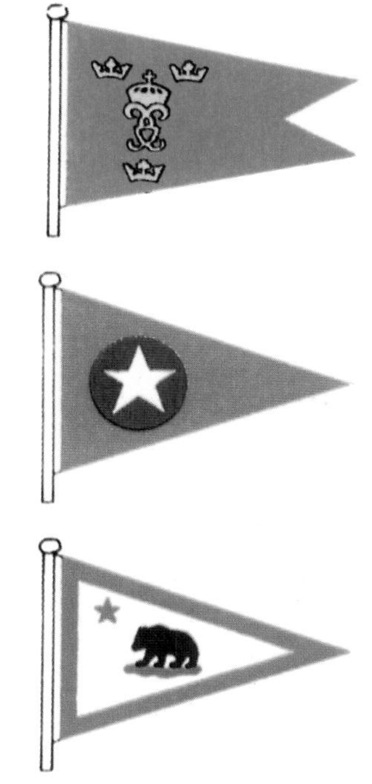

*The burgees of the Royal Motor Boat Club, Sweden (**top**), the Yacht Club of Chile (**middle**) and Monterey Peninsula Y.C., USA (**above**).*

***Above left:** A selection of 15 yacht club burgees.*

***Below:** A selection of club burgees.*

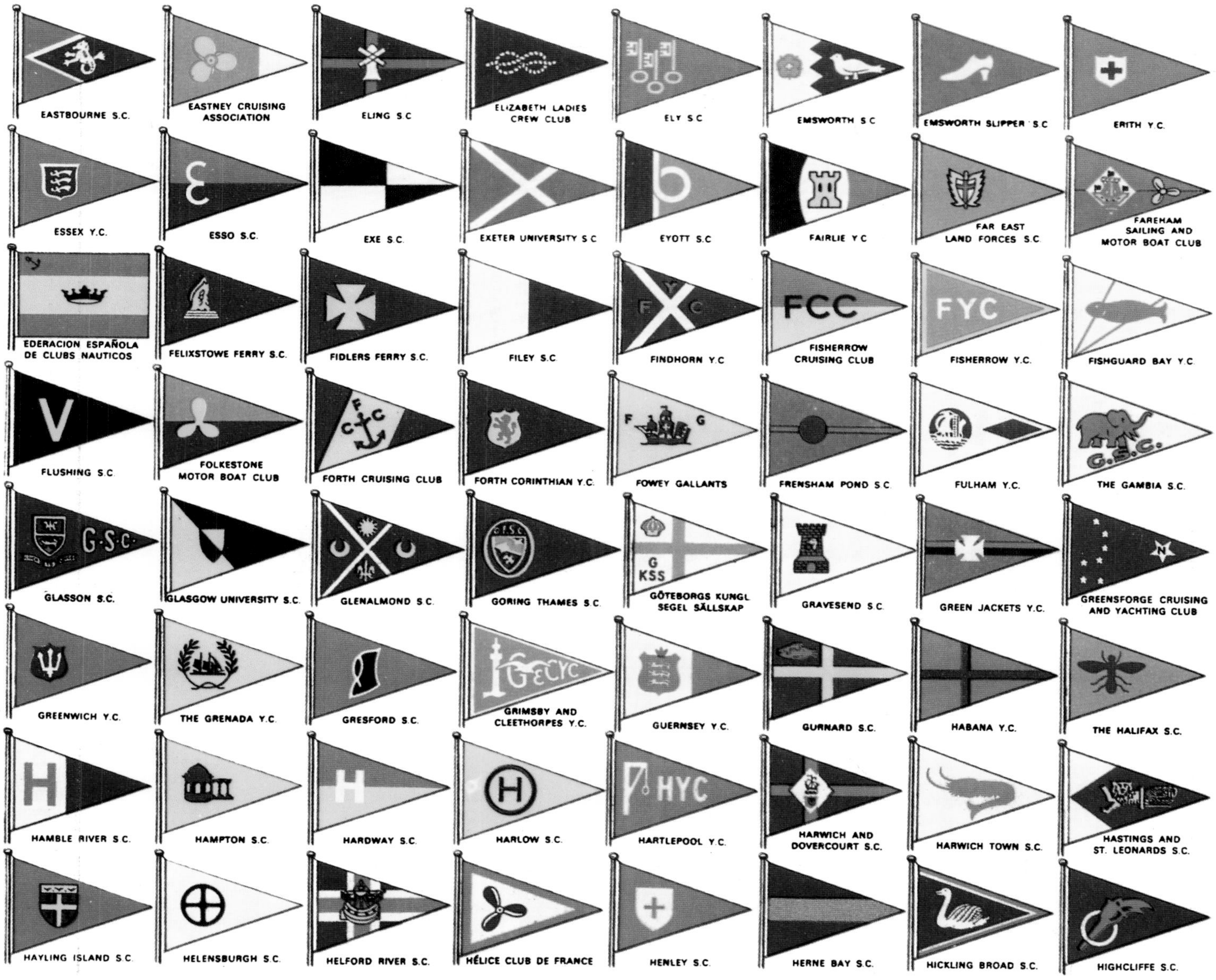

EASTBOURNE S.C. · EASTNEY CRUISING ASSOCIATION · ELING S.C. · ELIZABETH LADIES CREW CLUB · ELY S.C. · EMSWORTH S.C. · EMSWORTH SLIPPER S.C. · ERITH Y.C.
ESSEX Y.C. · ESSO S.C. · EXE S.C. · EXETER UNIVERSITY S.C. · EYOTT S.C. · FAIRLIE Y.C. · FAR EAST LAND FORCES S.C. · FAREHAM SAILING AND MOTOR BOAT CLUB
EDERACION ESPAÑOLA DE CLUBS NAUTICOS · FELIXSTOWE FERRY S.C. · FIDLERS FERRY S.C. · FILEY S.C. · FINDHORN Y.C. · FISHERROW CRUISING CLUB · FISHERROW Y.C. · FISHGUARD BAY Y.C.
FLUSHING S.C. · FOLKESTONE MOTOR BOAT CLUB · FORTH CRUISING CLUB · FORTH CORINTHIAN Y.C. · FOWEY GALLANTS · FRENSHAM POND S.C. · FULHAM Y.C. · THE GAMBIA S.C.
GLASSON S.C. · GLASGOW UNIVERSITY S.C. · GLENALMOND S.C. · GORING THAMES S.C. · GÖTEBORGS KUNGL SEGEL SÄLLSKAP · GRAVESEND S.C. · GREEN JACKETS Y.C. · GREENSFORGE CRUISING AND YACHTING CLUB
GREENWICH Y.C. · THE GRENADA Y.C. · GRESFORD S.C. · GRIMSBY AND CLEETHORPES Y.C. · GUERNSEY Y.C. · GURNARD S.C. · HABANA Y.C. · THE HALIFAX S.C.
HAMBLE RIVER S.C. · HAMPTON S.C. · HARDWAY S.C. · HARLOW S.C. · HARTLEPOOL Y.C. · HARWICH AND DOVERCOURT S.C. · HARWICH TOWN S.C. · HASTINGS AND ST. LEONARDS S.C.
HAYLING ISLAND S.C. · HELENSBURGH S.C. · HELFORD RIVER S.C. · HÉLICE CLUB DE FRANCE · HENLEY S.C. · HERNE BAY S.C. · HICKLING BROAD S.C. · HIGHCLIFFE S.C.

Flags Without End
Flags as Sport

A sport that is growing fast is that of flag-tossing. The art of playing with flags grew up in Italy and is particularly associated with the annual tournaments between the wards of Siena and Florence. In Siena the competition is a bareback horse race around the central square. Before the race, the representatives of the wards parade around the square displaying their flags. These are made of silk and mounted on short weighted staffs, and can be tossed and thrown and waved in graceful movements. The prize for the winner of the race is the *Palio*, or banner of the Virgin Mary, so the whole race has come to be called the *Palio*, and now the art of flag-tossing is known as Palio. Similar displays take palce in other Italian cities, and teams are learning this art all round the world, designing and making their own flags.

***Right:** Flag tossing at St Just in Volterra, Italy.*

Siena is composed of seventeen wards, but only ten at a time take part in the race, which is held twice a year on the feasts of the Virgin Mary (2 July and 16 August). Each ward has a badge, symbolic of its name. The flag is in the traditional colours of the ward, and always includes the badge. The actual design of the flag is not fixed, however, and they change from time to time, always using the same themes. Most of the designs are very striking. The ward's supporters wear scarves of the same design, and during the Palio Siena is a sea of colour.

***Below and below right:** Two historical contrade from Siena, Italy. Colours such as these are displayed in the Palio.*

Precision drilling with flags is popular in the USA and some other countries. The exercises are based on the drills from early military manuals and part of the objective is to demonstrate the correct ways of displaying the national flag, especially in conjunction with other flags. Among the exercises are Posting, Posting and Retrieving, Passing in Review, Presenting the Color, and Saluting. There are also exercises for Color Guards, including Receiving and Dismissing the Colors, Casing and Uncasing, and Movements in various groups. In addition flag-spinning, which comes very close to the Palio sport, is practised.

***Right:** Flags on display in Volterra, Italy.*

FLAG COMPETITIONS

The idea of selecting a national flag by means of public competition is not a new one. Strictly speaking, the first such competition, held in Australia in 1901, was only semiofficial, having been organized by a Melbourne journal, but the result was accepted by the government and ultimately approved by the King.

In that competition there were 32,823 entries. The judges spent six days whittling them down, using criteria they had decided on in advance: the flag must include a Union Jack, it must include the Southern Cross, and it must express the idea of Federation. Only 150 measured up to this, and only one did so successfully, although this same idea had been submitted by five different competitors. The winning design was made up and flown from the immensely tall flagpole of the Exhibition Building in Melbourne on 3 September 1901.

At least five American state flags emerged from design competitions, including Indiana and Wyoming (1916), Oklahoma (1925), Alaska (1926), and Nevada (1929). Here again the competitions were semiofficial, with the legislature's approval being won after the event.

Since the Second World War there have been many such competitions, and nowadays they often precede the independence of the country in question (rather than following it, as in the case of Australia). Canadian journals often ran features inviting their readers to send in designs for a new flag, which they were not slow to do. As soon as the real possibility of a new flag was raised in 1963, designs flooded in.

A similar situation had occured in South Africa in the 1920s, when Dr Malan raised the possibility of a distinctive flag. A formal competition was held in 1925, but even after that people continued to send in suggestions.

Both Canada and South Africa were faced with a problem that did not occur in Australia, namely that *none* of the proposals met the necessary criteria. This has occurred again and again in subsequent flag competitions. What happens in cases like this is that the organizers take the main themes present in the designs and try to fit these into something that will be suitable. This occurred, for example, in the Bahamas, Fiji, Surinam, Trinidad, and the Solomon Islands. There are only a few cases where there was an outright winner ie a design that required no adjustment. These include Greenland, Marshall Islands, Antigua, St Lucia, St Christopher-Nevis, Sudan, Papua New Guinea, and Kiribati.

Another case is where the winning design is adjusted to meet further considerations. This happened with the flag of Nigeria (which originally had a red sun on the white stripe), Guyana (the red and green were originally reversed), St Vincent (fimbriations were added), and Guernsey (the design originally had blue discs between the arms of the cross). Sometimes more than one competition is necessary because of a failure to agree, as happened on the island of Yap.

Finally, there are competitions that have no outcome. The most recent example is that of Hong Kong in 1989, when many thousands of entries were received, but because of the judges' inability to agree it was decided to accept none of them. They had been asked to send the winning design to Beijing for approval, but instead sent a blank sheet of paper.

*The flags of Wyoming (**top left**), Alaska (**above left**) and Indiana (**above**) were the results of flag competitions.*

***Left:** A selection of the public submissions for a design competition organized for the design of a new South African flag, before the present design was accepted in 1927.*

FLAG CEREMONIES AND CUSTOMS

A ceremony familiar to many tourists in London is the Trooping of the Colour. The original purpose of this exercise was to parade the company flag in front of the soldiers so that they could recognize it. In the early days of the English (later British) Army there was a flag for each company in a regiment, a practice that still prevails in the Guards. Undoubtedly the seventeenth-century colours were easier to recognize and remember than modern ones, and so the exercise today is almost entirely ceremonial.

Above: *A flagpole and yardarm decorated with a variety of flags.*

Nailing the Colours to the Mast

In former times, when new colours were made for a military unit, there was often quite a ceremony over placing the nails that fixed the sleeve of the flag to the stave. The nails were not really necessary to keep the flag in place, but joining in the act of hammering them in was a valued privilege.

Flags as Rent

The Dukes of Marlborough and of Wellington pay rent for their homes by means of a replica flag. In the case of Blenheim Palace, given to the first Duke of Marlborough by a grateful nation, the rent is a replica French Royal Standard of the type taken at the Battle of Blenheim (1704). This replica flag is presented to the Queen annually and laid up at Windsor. In the case of the Duke of Wellington, the rent is for Stratfield Saye House and is a replica French military colour of the type taken at the Battle of Waterloo (1815); it is likewise presented annually to the Sovereign on the anniversary of the battle.

Above: *The Duke of Marlborough pays rent by presenting this standard every 13 August, the anniversary of the battle of Blenheim.*

Swearing on the Flag

Many military units require the recruit to swear his oath of allegiance while touching the flag, which is either the national flag or the unit colour. If the recruit is not actually touching the flag he must be in its presence (sometimes one will touch the flag on behalf of all). The idea is that the flag, like a holy book, adds importance and power to the oath. Compare this with the *Blutfahne* ceremony, described in 'Flags in the Third Reich'.

Above: *Swiss guards in the Vatican City swearing allegiance on the flag.*

Illuminated Flags

National flags are not normally left flying in darkness, and so in modern times some important flags have been artificially illuminated so that they never have to be lowered. In the USA four national sites have been approved for this purpose: Fort McHenry and Flag House Square in Baltimore, the Marine Corps Memorial in Arlington, Virginia, and Lexington Common. There are several other unofficial but traditional sites. In Scotland the Saltire now flies at night at Athelstaneford, the place where, it is alleged, the 'vision' of the Cross of St Andrew took place. The Union Jack on the Palace of Westminster is illuminated at night when Parliament is sitting.

Bare Flagpoles

In Scandinavia and the Netherlands it is considered wrong to leave a flagpole without a flag on it. This implies that the building is empty or that the occupants have 'surrendered' in some way. To avoid this, long narrow streamers are hoisted instead. These can be in any design, but are usually versions of the national flag. In Finland streamers in the colours of one's home country are hoisted on the flagpole found outside nearly every summer residence.

Flags at the Olympic Games

There is a flag called the Olympic Standard, a unique flag of white with the five coloured rings. This is handed on from one Games to the next, and flies while the Games are in progress and the participants are under oath. A new one was made for the Games at Seoul in 1988.

When the national teams enter the opening ceremony, they are led by the flag of Greece, with the rear brought up by the flag of the host country. The teams each carry their own national flag. When medals are presented the flags of the winners are raised and their national anthems are played.

Right: *The flag of the Olympic Games.*

Bibliography

Banderas y Escudos del Mundo (Editorial America, Virginia Gardens, Florida, USA, 1986)

Charrié, Pierre, *Drapeaux et Etendards de la Révolution*, (Copernic, Paris, 1982)

Crux Australis, journal of the Flag Society of Australia

Crampton, William, *The Complete Guide to Flags* (Kingfisher Books, 1989)

Crampton, William, *Eyewitness Guides: Flag* (Dorling Kindersley, 1989)

Crampton, William, *The Observer's Book of Flags*, (Frederick Warne, 1988)

Davis, Brian Leigh, *Flags and Standards of the Third Reich* (Macdonald's and Janes, 1975)

Die Welt in Bildern: Album 8: Historische Fahnen

Doublet, Luc, *L'Aventure des Drapeaux* (Cherche Midi, Paris, 1987)

Emblèmes et Pavillons, journal of the Société Française de Vexillologie

The Flag Bulletin, journal of the Flag Research Center, Winchester, Mass, USA

Flagmaster, journal of the Flag Institute, Chester, England

Flagscan, journal of the Canadian Flag Association

Info-Bulletin from the Vlaggen Dokumentatie Centrum Nederland

Lloyd's Register of Shipping, *Register of Yachts*, various dates (Lloyd's of London)

Loughran, J L, *A Survey of Mercantile House Flags* (Waine Research, Wolverhampton, 1979)

Mastai, B & M D'Otrange, *The Stars and Stripes* (Alfred Knopf, New York, 1973)

Neubecker, Ottfried, *Heraldry, Sources, Symbols and Meaning* (Macdonald's and Janes, 1977)

Oberkommando der Kriegsmarine, *Flaggenbuch* (Berlin, 1939)

Pedersen, Christian Fogd, *Alverdens Flag i Farver*, (Politikens Forlag, Copenhagen, 1979)

Smith, Whitney, *Flags Through the Ages and Across the World* (McGraw-Hill, Maidenhead, 1975)

Vexillinfo, bulletin of the Societas Vexillologica Belgica

Visser, Derkwillem, *Flaggen, Wappen, Hymnen* (Battenberg, Munich, 1987)

Wilson, Tim, *Flags at Sea*, (HMSO, 1986)

Wise, Terence, *Military Flags of the World, 1618-1900*, (Blandford Press, Dorset, 1977)

INDEX